Welfare Rights

PHILOSOPHY AND SOCIETY
General Editor: Marshall Cohen

Also in this series:

Welfare Rights

CARL WELLMAN

ROWMAN AND LITTLEFIELD
Totowa, New Jersey

First published in the United States 1982 by
Rowman and Littlefield, 81 Adams Drive, Totowa, New Jersey 07512.

Library of Congress Cataloging in Publication Data

Wellman, Carl
  Welfare rights.

  (Philosophy and society)
  1. Social justice. 2. Civil rights. 3. Public
welfare—United States. I. Title. II. Series.
JC578.W43   1982   320′.01′1   82-3728
ISBN 0-8476-6759-6   AACR2

Printed in the United States of America

Contents

Introduction

Newspapers write editorials about the "welfare crisis," local officials cry that their treasuries are being squeezed dry, politicians take to the platform to denounce the shiftless who don't want to work, and lawmakers struggle with efforts to alter the law in the midst of philosophical differences so immense that they produce a stalemate.

Lucy Komisar

The primary purpose of this book is to settle the most important of these "philosophical differences" in order to help break the political stalemate. More specifically, formulating and defending a theory of welfare rights will provide practical guidance for the reform of our public welfare programs. No question makes more difference to theory or practice than this: Does the needy individual have a right to public welfare benefits?

If what is at issue is a legal right to welfare, it seems clear that no such right existed in the United States until the last few decades. At least until the passage of the Social Security Act in 1935, welfare legislation in this country followed the general principles of the Elizabethan Poor Law and recognized no right to welfare. *Goldberg* v. *Kelly* (397 U.S. 254(1970)) held that eligible individuals do have a legal right to Aid to Families with Dependent Children (AFDC) payments at least, although it is not clear that this can be generalized to cover all forms of public welfare, such as the general assistance provided by the states without federal funding.

Moreover, it is clear that this legal right is a conditional one. *If* some state participates in the federally financed AFDC program, then eligible residents of that state have a legal right to receive AFDC payments. But no state is under any legal obligation to so participate, and if some state should decide to withdraw from the program entirely, then no resident of that state would continue to have any legal right to AFDC payments. But would such a withdrawal by some

1

state violate some more fundamental welfare right of its residents? Does the needy individual have some moral right as a human being or as a citizen to be provided with specific welfare benefits? This is where the philosophical differences are most sharp and why these differences undercut any attempt to establish what our welfare law ought to be.

Who cares? What difference does it make whether or not the needy individual has a right, moral or legal, to welfare benefits? A needy individual may be decently provided for by a benevolent society without regard to any right to welfare, and an individual may possess welfare rights that are flagrantly ignored and violated by some unprincipled and ruthless government. Why all this fuss about welfare rights? Let us explore this question, first on the legal level and then on the level of moral rights.

Put in legal terms, the issue is whether welfare benefits are a privilege or a right of the eligible individual. Goldberg, Commissioner of Social Services of the City of New York, maintained that welfare is a legal privilege. Any public welfare benefit, such as AFDC payments, is a gift or gratuity made freely by a state that is not required to provide any such benefits at all. The eligibility conditions specified in welfare law serve only to exclude those ineligible to receive aid; within these legally defined boundaries, the welfare agency has complete discretion to decide which applicants shall or shall not receive benefits. The aggrieved individual has no appeal from an adverse decision by the welfare administrator, for his or her discretion is not subject to higher review. Most importantly, the individual whose welfare benefits have been reduced, or even terminated, has no cause for legal action no matter how arbitrary the decision of the welfare agency may have been. Since the state is not legally required to provide welfare benefits to any identifiable individual and can terminate such benefits at will, it follows that the state can make the receipt of welfare subject to any conditions it may choose, such as refraining from immoral conduct or spending the aid in a manner approved by the welfare worker. Welfare law permits the unequal treatment of applicants and recipients of welfare. In fact, the welfare authorities may have a responsibility to distinguish between the deserving poor and the undeserving poor in its distribution of limited welfare funds.

Kelly, and other recipients of welfare, argued that public welfare benefits are a right. They are not a free gift from the state, but payments due to the eligible recipient, much as the payment of a debt is due to the creditor. Legal rules of eligibility determine which individuals must be provided with welfare benefits by the state; within these boundaries each and every claimant must receive AFDC payments. This leaves no discretion to the welfare agency. On the contrary, the eligible individual has the discretion as to whether to apply for such benefits and whether to insist upon receipt of them. He or she can appeal any adverse welfare decision, and all such decisions are subject to review with due-process guarantees. In the event that administrative review is not forthcoming or not satisfactory to the individual claimant, he or she can sue in the courts to force the welfare agency to provide any benefits for which he or she is eligible by law. The state cannot attach any conditions to the continued receipt of welfare benefits other than the original eligibility conditions for the welfare program involved. Welfare law requires the equitable treatment of all individuals; it does not permit any discrimination between or among eligible claimants.

The practical importance of these legal theses explains why *Goldberg* v. *Kelly* was such a momentous decision. A welfare administrator would hold that public welfare is a legal privilege in order to preserve the welfare agency's freedom of action and to enable welfare workers to use limited welfare funds more efficiently by determining individual need and worthiness on a case-by-case basis. Eligible individuals will argue that they have a legal right to welfare benefits in order to secure the receipt of such benefits in the face of unpredictable and arbitrary decisions by welfare adminstrators who may reduce or terminate payments in the hope, or on the pretence, of providing more aid to the more deserving. Any society that hopes to reduce, or at least limit, the financial burden of providing welfare will insist that public welfare benefits are only a legal privilege. A society that wishes to ensure the equitable treatment of individuals and some minimal provision for the needs of every individual will establish a legal right to public welfare.

Actual societies differ greatly on their public policies and their welfare law. What stand ought any society to take on these legal issues? At this point, two fundamentally opposed moral philosophies of public welfare come into play. One philosophy insists that public welfare is charity. The state may give or withhold welfare as it pleases. Any state action of providing public welfare is either the performance of an imperfect duty—a kind of act that society ought to engage in with reasonable frequency, but one that is not morally required on any particular occasion—or an action over and beyond the call of duty. If the state denies welfare benefits to some needy individual, it is not treating the individual unjustly. Such a denial may be wrong, if the individual is in dire need, but it is not a wrong to that individual. To make charitable giving compulsory would be to destroy the virtue of loving kindness. It would be wrong for any individual, no matter how destitute, to demand welfare benefits; the individual may only petition or beg the benevolent welfare authorities for aid in his or her distress. And in the event that welfare aid is forthcoming, the appropriate response by the fortunate recipient is gratitude. Those who conceive of public welfare as a form of charity often, although not always, presuppose that the needy individual is responsible for his or her own plight. Society should pity such miserable individuals and treat them charitably, but they deserve no more from the benevolent society or industrious taxpayer than this.

Opposed to this conception of welfare as charity is the philosophy that needy individuals have a moral right to public welfare benefits. Providing welfare is a perfect duty of society; that is, the state has a moral obligation to provide welfare benefits to each and every needy individual in the society. Since the individual has a moral claim to appropriate welfare benefits, to withhold such benefits is both morally wrong and a wrong to the individual denied his or her rights. The appropriate motive for a public welfare program is neither love nor pity, although these are admirable motives, but a respect for individual rights. In the event that welfare benefits are not provided by the state, the needy individual can demand them as an entitlement. And when welfare benefits are provided, the appropriate response is not gratitude as much as that self-respect felt by one whose moral rights are recognized and respected by others. Those who affirm the existence of a moral right to public welfare often presuppose that the needy individual is not responsible for his or her plight. They recognize that in modern society prolonged childhood dependence, unemployment, disability and illness, and poverty in old age arise from social forces beyond the control of the individual. Hence, society has a moral obligation to provide adequate welfare benefits for its most unfortunate members, and each needy individual has a right to public welfare.

Although each of these welfare philosophies has manifold moral implications, they divide most crucially on three issues. First, if public welfare is charity, then it is up to each society how generous it wishes to make its public welfare programs; if public welfare is a right, then every society has a moral obligation to provide adequate welfare programs no matter how great the required sacrifice may be. Second, if welfare is charity, then each state has moral discretion to decide in any way it wishes who shall receive benefits and in what amounts; if welfare is a right, then the needy individual has the ethical power to claim adequate welfare benefits if and when he or she chooses. Third, if welfare is charity, then the needy individual can only beg for compassion and must accept gratefully as much or as little as the affluent are willing to share from their abundance; if welfare is a right, the needy individual is the moral equal of the more fortunate member of society and can claim what is rightfully his or hers without any loss of self-respect. It is no wonder that philosophical differences so momentous are hotly debated. It is only to be expected that moral disagreements so radical should produce a political stalemate.

Probably the concept of a stalemate is too static to capture the political realities. Public welfare programs in this country have been traditionally shaped by the philosophy that welfare is and ought to be charity. In 1965, Charles A. Reich wrote:

We need a radically new approach to the field of social welfare. Today the nation's poor stand as far from the enjoyment of basic rights as did the Negro at the beginning of the Civil Rights movement. ("Individual Rights and Social Welfare," p. 1245)

Since Reich called for this new approach, the Civil Rights movement has given birth to a Welfare Rights movement that has established and defended many legal welfare rights of needy individuals in the United States and proclaimed the view that public welfare is not charity but a moral right. Today, however, the rising number of welfare claimants and the escalating costs of funding welfare programs have called forth a reaction that has put the welfare rights advocates on the defensive. If the welfare rights movement is to regain its momentum, it needs a philosophy of public welfare solid enough to unite its supporters and persuasive enough to convert some of its opponents, at least some of the undecided. The goal of this book is to formulate and defend a philosophy of welfare rights sound in theory and at the same time specific enough to give practical guidance to welfare lawyers, politicians, and voting citizens. To this end, general principles and abstract arguments, hand in hand with detailed applications to our Aid to Families with Dependent Children program, will be developed.

As one might expect of an analytic philosopher, I begin with the conception of a welfare right. The recent legal and philosophical literature provides many insights, especially those of Hohfeld and Hart, that can increase our understanding of the language of rights. After explaining how I conceive of legal and moral rights, I define what distinguishes welfare rights from other sorts of rights. Before proceeding, it is necessary to refute the most important arguments of those who maintain that all talk of rights to welfare benefits, especially allegations of moral rights to welfare, is self-contradictory or unintelligible.

Since I use legal rights as models for moral rights, the second chapter shows how I would conceive of two sample legal welfare rights—the right to receive Aid to Familes with Dependent Children and the right to a welfare hearing. These examples serve to illustrate my general conception of a right and, at the same time, show how my philosophical theory of rights can spell out their content in a manner detailed and specific enough to be useful to practicing lawyers and judges.

It is one thing to discover what specific welfare rights exist in our legal system; it is quite another to determine which legal welfare rights ought to exist. The third chapter discusses critically three sorts of justifications for enacting and maintaining—or for repealing or not enacting in the first place—any specified legal welfare right. These arguments appeal respectively to utility, justice, and ethical rights.

The next order of business is to see what sorts of ethical welfare rights might exist. I define with some care three sample rights: the human right to social security, the civic right to fair share, and the moral right to equitable welfare treatment. The first two are examples of primary welfare rights—rights to some welfare benefits; the third is a secondary welfare right—a right concerning—but not to—welfare benefits. These examples reveal the parallels between legal and moral rights as well as the way in which my conception of a right clarifies the practical import of alleged rights.

Clearly, the human right to social security and the civil right to a fair share have important implications for the reform of our welfare programs *if* they exist. But are there really any such rights? Chapter 5 explores the most likely grounds of ethical rights to welfare and examines critically various arguments for the existence of such rights. Although I can find no firm foundation for the human right to social security, I argue that the civic right to a fair share can be grounded on wrongful harm.

Finally, in the last chapter, I show how ethical rights, especially the civic right to a fair share and the moral right to equitable welfare treatment, can generate specific conclusions concerning the reform of our present Aid to Families with Dependent Children program. Thus, what beings as an abstract analytic discussion of the concept of a right becomes, in the end, a practical program for welfare legislation in the coming decade. With this goal in view, let us move on to the serious business of working out a philosophy of welfare rights.

1

The Conception of a Welfare Right

Although the appeal to rights is increasingly common in political debate and ethical theory, there is no common understanding of the concept of a right. Controversies about whether human fetuses or nonhuman animals can intelligibly be said to possess rights stem in part from confusion about precisely what it might mean to ascribe a right to such entities. Again, there has been heated debate about whether the so-called social and economic rights asserted in the United Nations *Declaration of Human Rights* are really rights in any literal sense or should more properly be said to be ideals or goals of aspiration. Closer to home is the contention that there is a fundamental conceptual confusion in the expression "a welfare right" because welfare, in contrast to free speech or due process, is simply not the sort of thing to which one could have a right. Clearly, one cannot progress very far in one's thinking about welfare rights until one has achieved greater clarity about the conception of a right in general.

The Concept of a Right

The place to begin this enterprise of conceptual analysis, I suggest, is with the analysis of legal rights. Although all talk about rights is open to various interpretations, talk about legal rights seems less problematic than other sorts of rights discourse, for two reasons. Jurisprudence has developed alternative theories about the nature of legal rights that are clearer and considerably more precise than comparable theories of natural or moral rights to be found in the literature of ethics. More important, it is relatively easy to find clear cases of legal rights by which to test the accuracy of any analysis of legal rights. It is much harder to find generally accepted instances of moral rights or human rights by which to judge a proposed analysis of nonlegal rights. I propose, therefore, to begin by constructing a model of a legal right and then to go on to generalize my model so that it will apply to the other species of rights.

7

When it comes to understanding legal rights, the beginning of wisdom lies in Wesley Hohfeld's *Fundamental Legal Conceptions*. Through a careful examination of many passages in the legal literature, he showed that the expression "a right" is ordinarily used to refer indiscriminately to any kind of legal advantage. In order to resolve this ambiguity, he distinguished between four very different legal conceptions—a claim, a liberty, a power, and an immunity:

1) One party x has a *legal claim* against some second party y that y do some action A if and only if y has a legal duty to x to do A. Thus, a creditor has a legal claim against the person who borrowed money from him that the debtor repay the debt on or before the due date, and a patient has a legal claim against his or her physician that the physician not treat the patient without his or her free informed consent.

2) One party x has a *legal liberty* in face of some second party y to do some action A if and only if x has no legal duty to y to refrain from doing A. Thus, I have a legal liberty in face of my neighbor to walk by his house on the public sidewalk that cuts across the front of his property, but I do not have a legal liberty in face of my neighbor to take a shortcut across his lawn or through his garden.

3) One party x has a *legal power* over some second party y to bring about some specific legal consequence C for y if and only if some voluntary action of x would be legally recognized as having this consequence for y. Thus, my neighbor has the legal power over me of conferring on me a legal liberty of walking across his property without trespass simply by giving me permission to do so, and I have the legal power over my neighbor's son to impose upon him a legal obligation to mow my lawn by accepting his offer to do so and paying him the contracted sum in advance.

4) One party x has a *legal immunity* against some second party y from some specified legal consequence C if and only if y lacks the legal power to do any action whatsoever that would be recognized by the law as having the consequence C for x. Thus, I am legally immune from my neighbor's depriving me of title to my house because there is nothing my neighbor could do that would be recognized by the law as terminating my property rights to my home, but I am not immune in face of my neighbor from losing my legal liberty of picking flowers in his garden because I would lose this legal liberty were he to withdraw his permission for me to do so.

Hohfeld is surely correct in distinguishing four very different legal advantages and a failure to distinguish them can lead only to confusion. Since Washington University is situated on private property, if I park my car near my office without permission, I am trespassing and my car may be towed away. I can obtain a permit to park in the lot near my office by paying the specified yearly fee. Having paid the fee, I now have a legal right to park near my office. But suppose that I arrive late one morning, seconds before my class is scheduled to meet, and find all the parking spaces taken. Has my legal right been violated? If I have purchased a legal claim-right that imposes a corresponding duty upon Washington University to make available to me a parking space near my office, then my right has been violated; but if I have purchased only a liberty-right so that in return Washington University has merely extinguished my legal duty to refrain from trespassing on its property but has not incurred any duty to provide a parking space for me, then my right has not been infringed in any way.

Just as important as the distinction between a liberty-right and a claim-right is the distinction between a liberty-right and a power-right. Imagine that I have been appointed treasurer of our philosophy department. With this office goes the right to draw checks on our departmental bank account. Do I now have a legal right to spend departmental funds on wine, women and song? I do have a legal power-right to do so. If I take my mistress to an expensive night club and pay the bill with a check drawn on our departmental bank account, my act of payment will be legally recognized as transferring the specified amount of money from the departmental account to the account of the night club. But I certainly do not have any legal liberty-right to do so. My act would be an abuse of my legal powers as treasurer and, presumably, I could be sued for recovery of the misappropriated funds.

It is obvious that any adequate conception of a right must clearly distinguish between fundamentally distinct legal advantages: between legal claims, liberties, powers and immunities. Hohfeld went too far, however, when he concluded that the expression "a right" is ambiguous between these four very different legal advantages. Indeed, in classifying them together as advantages, he recognized something in common to every application of the expression "a right" in the law. Since he imagined that he was identifying fundamental or ultimate legal conceptions, he presumed that they shared no "common denominators." Unfortunately, he never did explain what he meant by a legal advantage. The most popular interpretation seems to be that a legal advantage is a legal position that is advantageous, beneficial, and in one's interests to possess. If this really is what he had in mind, then I suggest that he is mistaken. I certainly have a legal liberty to smoke or drink so heavily that I ruin my health and die a miserable death, and I probably have the legal power of giving away all my wealth and rendering myself penniless and destitute. But neither of these legal advantages is beneficial to me or really in my interests.

A less obvious, but more profound, interpretation is that a legal advantage is a legally favored position: a position in which the law favors one's will in any confrontation with some opposed will. What

Hohfeld has recognized is that the language of rights is always and necessarily used in the contest of some conflict between one party who has or alleges to have some right and some second party or parties who stand in opposition to and conflict with that party. It is no accident that the full title of Hohfeld's essays is *Fundamental Legal Conceptions as Applied in Judicial Reasoning*. As an American Legal Realist, he interprets the language of the law in terms of its significance for a court case in which two adversaries confront one another before a judge. In court, a legal advantage is any legal position that will enable one to win one's case; whether winning one's case is beneficial to one or in one's best interests is another matter. What Hohfeld recognized to be true of rights in the civil law is, I believe, true of all rights. A right is always possessed by one party in face of some second party or parties in some actual or possible conflict or confrontation of wills. This is no accident. It is essential to the very concept of a right that a right is necessarily an advantage of one party vis-à-vis some second party.

A third important insight of Hohfeld is that the concept of a right belongs to our practical discourse. Of course, Hohfeld was not the first to say this by any means. Who would think of denying that the right to life has practical implications? But does my right to life consist in or imply my legal liberty of doing whatever I think necessary to preserve my life, or my legal claim against others that they not kill me, or my legal claim against the state that it protect my life, or my legal claim against someone to provide me with the means of livelihood, or what? Almost everyone has assumed that somehow "a right" is typically a normative expression with primarily practical significance. But Hohfeld has explained much more clearly than others just how this is so and has shown us how to translate rights language into clearly practical terms.

Fourth, Hohfeld provides a way of analyzing complex legal phenomena into simpler elements. The complexity of legal rights is typically obscured by our language. What could be simpler, or more correct, than to say that I own this typewriter upon which I am writing? But my property right in this typewriter consists at least in my legal liberty of using it when and as I wish, my legal claim against others that they not use it without my permission, my legal power of giving others permission to use my typewriter, my legal claim against others that they not dispossess me of it, my legal power of giving or selling it to some second party, etc. The names we usually give to rights are little more than labels, like the tags on Christmas presents, that give very little idea of the contents of each right. To have any clear and precise conception of the content of any right, one must characterize it in terms of something like Hohfeld's fundamental conceptions. Although I do not propose that he has identified the ultimate and indefinable legal conceptions, I do agree that the elements out of which rights are constituted include such elements as claims, liberties, powers and immunities.

I choose to begin with Hohfeld's analysis of our language of legal rights because I am convinced that his insights are essential to an understanding of the concept of a right. Although the expression "a right" need not be ambiguous, the distinctions between claims, liberties, powers and immunities are real and important. Every significant use of the expression "a right" presupposes some actual or possible adversary relation in which the will of the possessor of the right stands opposed to that of one or more second parties. Since the language of rights belongs to our practical discourse, its significance can be understood only when the specific actions to which it implicitly refers are made explicit. And the complexities hidden or obscured by our rights labels are best revealed by the analysis of any right into the Hohfeldian elements—the claims, liberties, powers, and immunities—that constitute it.

Although I began with Hohfeld's analysis of the language of rights, I refuse to end with his conception of a right. He insists that in the strictest sense, the expression "a right" refers to a single claim, a conclusion he reaches by a double argument. Since rights and duties are logically correlative, it is more logical to identify a right with a claim, which is the correlative of a corresponding duty, than with a liberty, power, or immunity. Since each element in any rights-complex is logically distinct and legally separable from all the others, the only real unity is the simple element itself.

To my mind, Hohfeld's argumentation is doubly dubious. His first assumption is that rights and duties are logically correlative. Although popular at one time, this presupposition has often been severely qualified or completely rejected in the recent literature. At the very least, it cannot be taken for granted and used as the starting place for reasoning about the conception of a right. Nor is there any reason to believe that claim-rights are rights in any stricter sense of the expression "a right" than, for example, liberty-rights. When Raphael distinguishes between rights of action and rights of recipience on the basis of his reflections upon our ethical and political language, he is neither misusing nor stretching ordinary English. Thus, I can see no compelling reason to restrict the language of rights, even when used most carefully and strictly, to claims.

His second argument begins with the premise that each Hohfeldian element is logically distinguishable and legally separable from every other such claim, liberty, power, or immunity. I readily grant this premise. It does not follow, however, that there cannot be complex structures made up of such elements or that complexes so constructed lack real unity. I shall later try to show that there are such structures and that it is to these that the expression "a right" quite properly and usefully refers.

A philosopher who has used Hohfeld's fundamental legal conceptions materially to advance our understanding of the concept of a
right is H. L. A. Hart. Although he is careful to distinguish between
liberties, claims, powers, and immunities, he is equally careful not to
reduce a right to any one such Hohfeldian element. He explicitly
suggests that there is no important legal or philosophical purpose
served by identifying a right with a "naked" liberty. Only when
protected with one or more duties, which limit permissible interference with the exercise of that liberty, can one usefully speak of a
right. Thus, Hart recognizes explicitly the complexity of legal rights,
and by implication moral rights also. His reason for insisting upon the
complexity of rights is that only a complex of Hohfeldian elements
could capture what is distinctive in the concept of a right and thus
avoid making the language of rights redundant upon the language of
duties. I agree, but I must postpone explaining why I agree until I am
in a position to explain what is distinctive in the concept of a right.

What need not and should not be postponed is the challenge that to
introduce complexity into a right is necessarily to destroy its unity.
Hart has shown us how to meet this Hohfeldian challenge. A right is
no mere aggregate of Hohfeldian elements; it has a unifying structure. We can glimpse this structure in the picture of a right suggested
by the language Hart uses in his "Bentham on Legal Rights": a plot of
ground surrounded by a fence—a field of action within which the
possessor of the right is free to act as he wishes, surrounded by a
barrier to keep away all those who would interfere by preventing or
restraining the activity covered by the right. Note Hart's expressions
"protective perimeter," "perimeter of obligations," and the example
of a man's "right to look at his neighbor over the garden fence" (p.
176). This picture can easily and revealingly be translated into an
analytical model of a right. The paradigm case of a liberty right
consists of a bilateral liberty protected by one or more duties restrict-
ing permissible interference with the exercise of this bilateral liberty.
For example, a man's right to look at his neighbor over the garden
fence consists in the man's liberty of looking at his neighbor, paired
with his liberty of refraining from looking at his neighbor, together
with the neighbor's duties not to interfere with the activity of looking
by shooting the man or punching him in the eye and the duties not to
interfere with the activity (if this is the right word) of *not* looking by
ordering him to look over the fence at gunpoint. Although this right
is a complex of liberties and duties, it is a structured whole with a
unity that Hart sums up with the expression "a choice respected by
law" (p. 197).

I do not believe that Hart's analytical model can deal with the full
range of rights. In fact, Hart himself rejects his model as a general
theory of rights in the very essay in which he introduces it. But let us
not discard his model without learning from it. Hart has shown us

how a complex of Hohfeldian elements can be a structured unity. His picture of a central field with a surrounding fence is also revealing. My suggestion is that we generalize his model and conceive of a right as a central core together with associated elements. I shall try to show that my own analytical model preserves the insight of Hart while freeing our vision from a perspective in which choice is the only focal point.

There is more to be learned from Hart. From first to last, one of his themes has been that there is something distinctive about the concept of a right, something that is lost if rights are reduced to duties or if rights-conferring norms are interpreted as a special case of duty-imposing norms. In "Are There Any Natural Rights?" he suggests that "we must distinguish from the rest of morality those principles regulating the proper distribution of human freedom" (p. 178). That the concept of a right belongs to this special part of morality is evidenced by the fact that one typically uses the expression "I have a right to . . ." either to claim some special justification for interfering with the freedom of another or to resist as unjustified another's interference with one's own freedom of action (p. 183). Recognizing the essential connection between rights and "the distribution of freedom of choice" also renders intelligible how it is that special rights, such as the promisee's right that the promisor perform the promised act, can arise from voluntary transactions, such as the act of promising, between the possessor of the right and the duty-bearer (p. 184). Although somewhat unclear, Hart's insight here is profound. There is an essential conceptual connection between rights and freedom. It is no accident that the great proclamations of rights have been documents of human freedom. Moreover, rights essentially concern the *distribution of* freedom. Hart has recognized that rights concern the freedom of the possessor in face of one or more second parties who might threaten that freedom. His characterization of the circumstances in which one typically uses the expression "I have a right to . . ." implicitly confirms Hohfeld's recognition that the language of rights is always used against the background of some adversarial relation, some conflict of wills.

It is Hart's recognition of the necessary connection between rights and freedom that has led him to place a bilateral liberty in the center of his analytical model of a right. But this poses a problem. What corresponds to a liberty in Hohfeld's fundamental legal conceptions is the absence of a contrary duty; one person's liberty never implies any corresponding duty of any second party. But many rights do seem to imply correlative obligations; for example, the creditor's right to be repaid implies the debtor's duty of payment. How can Hart explain this correlation of rights and duties within his liberty-right model of rights? In "Bentham on Legal Rights" he does this by proposing that the possessor of a claim-right has been given by the law a bilateral liberty of exercising certain powers over the duty-bearer, such as the power of waiving the duty, of suing for enforcement of the duty or for compensation in the event of nonperformance, or of waiving the obligation to pay compensation arising from any breach of the duty (p. 192). Thus, the link between the creditor's right to repayment and the debtor's duty to repay is the control over the debtor's duty given by the law to the creditor. It is because Hart recognizes the essential place of control in the concept of a right that he rejects any interest or beneficiary theory of rights and develops his version of the will theory. What is distinctive about the right is the way it gives the will of its possessor some special standing in the law, a standing to be understood in terms of legal control. What is distinctive about the concept of a right must, if Hart is on the right track, be explained in terms of control as well as freedom. Freedom and control are both essential to any right, but Hart was never able to achieve a conception of a right that integrated these two notions. This was probably because his preoccupation with freedom led him to place a bilateral liberty central to his model of a right. This, in turn, caused him to overemphasize the centrality of choice to the language of rights. A new analytical model is needed, more complex and more balanced than the one he offers.

Accordingly, I propose that we conceive of a legal right as a system of Hohfeldian advantages that, if respected, confers autonomy concerning some specified action or actions on its possessor in face of one or more second parties. In this model, the elements of a legal right are the claims, liberties, powers, immunities, duties, etc. identified by Hohfeld in his *Fundamental Legal Conceptions*. Each of these is a legal advantage to its possessor vis-à-vis some actual or potential second party in the sense that it favors his will in any actual or potential conflict with the will of the second party. The possessor of a legal advantage will not in fact always have his way in any confrontation with some second party but, if respected, the legal advantage will be on his side in any conflict of wills. To my mind no single legal advantage could constitute a legal right, because no single advantage could possibly be decisive in any confrontation. Thus, the creditor's claim to repayment would be unavailing against a reluctant debtor unless the creditor also has an immunity against the debt's being cancelled simply by repudiation of the debtor. Every legal right is a complex of legal elements of the sort identified by Hohfeld.

A legal right is more than a mere aggregate of Hohfeldian elements; it is a system. It is this systematic unity that makes the complex of Hohfeldian elements into *a* right. At the center of each right stands a defining core. This may be a single element, such as the creditor's claim to repayment, or more than one element, such as a speaker's liberty of speaking out on controversial issues together with his liberty of remaining silent on such issues. But if the core of a right is complex, the elements that make it up must be conceptually tied together or the total structure ceases to be a single right. This defining core specifies the essential content of the right. Although other elements in a legal right can be added or subtracted to a given right, to change the core of a right is to extinguish one legal right and create another in its place. The core also determines the modality of the right as a whole. Thus, the creditor's right to repayment is a claim-right because its core is a legal claim, and the right to free speech is a liberty-right because its core is a bilateral liberty. The core also identifies the possessor of any legal right. The right "belongs" to the party for whom its core is a legal advantage. Finally, the core unifies the complex right because any additional elements are constitutents in the right by virtue of their relation to its central core.

Around the central core of any legal right is arranged a number of associated elements. Each associated element necessarily contributes, if respected, some sort of freedom or control concerning the exercise or enjoyment of the core to its possessor in face of one or more second parties. Let me try to explain this relation between associated element and core.

1) As Hart observed, legal rights allocate or distribute freedom and control. Thus, what makes any Hohfeldian element a part of or constituent in a right is that it contributes some measure of freedom or control to the total structure or system that is the right. For example, the creditor's liberty of accepting repayment gives him some degree of freedom with respect to the enjoyment of his claim to be repaid, and his power to waive repayment gives him some control over his enjoyment of this same claim.

2) At this point a qualification is necessary. The associated element contributes freedom or control only if it is respected by second parties or by the courts. Liberties, claims, powers, immunities, duties, and all the other Hohfeldian elements are normative; freedom and control, on the other hand, are factual. The possession of a legal liberty may not confer freedom to exercise it, for it may not be respected by those who illegally prevent its exercise. Similarly, a legal power does not automatically give its possessor actual control, for it may not be recognized by a corrupt or mistaken judge.

3) Not every Hohfeldian element that contributes freedom or control is relevant to or an ingredient in any specified right. The creditor's power of suing for divorce or his liberty of dressing as he pleases within the bounds of decency have nothing to do with his right to repayment. The relevant freedom or control concerns the exercise or enjoyment of the core of the specified right. In this way, every associated element is essentially related to the core of the right, and the core unifies a complex right consisting of several Hohfeldian elements. This means that any complete specification of any associated element in a right must mention the core or at least be

formulated in language derived from the specification of that core. If it did not, then it would not, even if respected, contribute freedom or control concerning the exercise or enjoyment *of that core.*

4) This is doubly true when one recognizes that any associated element must *necessarily* contribute freedom or control concerning the core. Other Hohfeldian elements might, but need not, confer such freedom or control. Consider a politician's legal right of free speech. Its core is a legal liberty of speaking out, even on controversial issues. My liberty of contributing to his campaign fund might, but need not, contribute to his freedom of exercising that core liberty for I might, but need not, so contribute even while respecting my liberty and his. But my duty not to prevent him from speaking out necessarily contributes to his freedom of exercising his legal liberty of speaking out unless I fail to respect, and thus perform, my legal duty.

5) Each associated element contributes freedom or control to the possessor of the core of the right and in face of one or more second parties. In this way, each associated element concerns the allocation or distribution of freedom or control. Moreover, its contribution of freedom or control to one party *rather than* to some second party means that its place in the right is to be understood in terms of an actual or potential confrontation or conflict of wills between the possessor of the right and one or more second parties. This is just what one would expect, given the adversarial conception of a right I have been articulating.

Since each associated element in a right confers freedom or control upon the possessor, the right as a whole confers freedom and control upon its possessor. One must recognize that freedom and control are inseparable aspects of a single practical reality. I am free to speak out on controversial issues only if my opponent has no control over my activity of speaking; I may exercise my liberty of speaking only if my political opponent has no legal power to take away my legal liberty of free speech. Conversely, I cannot effectively exercise legal control, perhaps by taking legal action in the courts, if I am not free to bring suit at my own initiative. What a respected right confers, then, is not freedom and control, but a single freedom-control. The essential unity of freedom-control can appropriately be called "autonomy." I do not use this word in the Kantian sense of legislating for oneself nor in the more popular sense in which autonomy is an independence of the self that amounts almost to a self-sufficiency that atomizes inter-personal relationships. What I have in mind is autonomy in the sense of self-determination: a legal right, if respected, confers upon its possessor the ability to determine by his or her own will whether he or she will exercise or enjoy the right in question.

The conception of a legal right I am articulating clearly falls within the tradition of will theories, rather than interest or beneficiary theories, of rights. But my theory is not simply another version of

Hart's legally respected choice theory, for I do not place choice at the center of my model of a legal right. Hart suggests that the core of a right is typically a bilateral liberty surrounded by a perimeter of protective duties. I hold that any sort of legal advantage—a liberty, claim, power or immunity—can stand at the center of a right, and that this core may be protected and facilitated with immunities, powers, claims, and even liberties, as well as duties. A right does confer upon the will of its possessor some special legal standing, but this status does not consist simply or primarily in the possession of a respected choice. The core of every right is a legal advantage, some Hohfeldian element that, if respected, supports the will of its possessor in face of one or more conflicting wills. To this are added the various freedoms and controls related to that core conferred by the several associated elements making up the total right. Thus, the essence of a legal right is not a legally respected choice but legally respected autonomy.

To be respected in the law is one thing; to be effective in practice is another. Although the two tend to go together, they do not always or necessarily coincide. Someone may possess a legal liberty but not be free to exercise it, either because he lacks the necessary resources or abilities or because the legal authorities wrongly prevent him from engaging in the relevant activity. Similarly, even when a creditor has a legal claim to repayment, he may not be in a position to exercise his legal power to sue in the event of nonpayment or if the debtor lacks the funds to comply with a court order to repay the debt. Accordingly, only when respected does a legal right confer autonomy (i.e., freedom and control) on its possessor. To be effective in practice the legal right must be respected by the legal officials, recognized and enjoined by the courts, and enforced or allowed by those who enforce the law. Even more important is the degree to which the legal right is respected by the private citizens and honored in action without need of court action or police intervention. Thus, a legal right, if respected, confers autonomy upon its possessor.

The autonomy conferred by any legal right is of course limited, and different legal rights confer different spheres of autonomy. The core of any given right defines the limits of the autonomy it seeks to confer. Each associated element in a right confers some sort of freedom or control relating to the core of the right. Hence, the autonomy conferred by the right as a whole is autonomy concerning the exercise or enjoyment of its core. We normally speak of exercising a right. Since one does exercise a liberty or a power by engaging in the action specified in or by the content of the liberty or power, one can accurately speak of exercising liberty- or power-rights. But one does not in any direct or literal fashion exercise a claim- or immunity-right. The creditor's claim-right calls for repayment by the debtor. But one can hardly speak of the debtor's act of repaying as the creditor's exercise of his claim-right; nor should the creditor's act of accepting repayment be equated with his exercise of his right to be repaid. The creditor enjoys repayment when the debtor repays him. He may, of course, exercise his power to sue for repayment should the debtor refuse to repay him on the due date. But this act of suing is not exercising his claim-right to repayment; it is at best exercising his power-right to sue for repayment. Similarly, I do not do anything that constitutes exercising my claim-right not to be attacked by others; I enjoy my claim-right whenever and wherever others refrain from attacking me. To repeat: any legal right, if respected, confers freedom and control concerning the exercise or enjoyment of its core, which defines the limits of the autonomy conferred by each specific right.

Every right is someone's right. It is part of the very concept of a right that a right is possessed by some party, whether a natural person, a group of natural persons, or an artificial person such as a corporation. In this way legal rights distribute or allocate autonomy among the persons subject to the legal system. What is less often recognized and is of equal significance is that each right confers autonomy to its possessor *in face of* one or more second parties. To give a public speaker autonomy concerning the exercise of his liberty-right of free speech is to deny such freedom and control to those who would silence the speaker if only they could. Again, to give the creditor autonomy concerning his enjoyment of his claim-right to be repaid is incompatible with giving the debtor autonomy concerning the same enjoyment. Each legal right, if respected, confers autonomy concerning some core to its possessor vis-à-vis any second parties with whose wills the will of the possessor might clash concerning the exercise or enjoyment of his right. For this reason, rights are especially and peculiarly relevant to situations in which there is a confrontation between first parties and second parties, the possessors of the right and those who stand opposed to their desires, choices, and actions.

In sum, I propose that we conceive of a legal right as a system of Hohfeldian advantages that, if respected, confers autonomy concerning the exercise or enjoyment of a specific core upon its possessor in face of one or more second parties. To illustrate this conception, let me again use the examples in the previous pages. The core of the legal right to free speech is bilateral, the legal liberty of speaking out or remaining silent on any subject, no matter how controversial, within the limits of libel, slander, and the clear and present danger to the public. Associated with this core element are at least the following Hohfeldian elements: (a) Legal claims against interfering with one's public speaking by attacks or threats of force upon one's person or by destroying one's property or in other ways that violate one's relevant civil rights; (b) the legal power to seek remedy in the courts against those who threaten to or have wrongfully interfered with the exercise of one's liberty of speech; and (c) a constitutional immunity against any legislation that would purport to limit or extinguish one's legal liberty of speaking out on any issue or subject. These, and probably additional, associated elements confer upon the possessor of the core liberty of speaking out various sorts of freedom and control concerning the exercise of that core. In this way, the various elements constitute an integrated system of Hohfeldian elements.

Another paradigm case of a legal right is the creditor's right to repayment. In my conception, the core of this legal right is the creditor's legal claim against the debtor that he repay the amount due on the due date. Around this defining core claim are at least these associated elements:

1) the creditor's bilateral liberty of exercising or refraining from exercising the power to sue in the event that the debtor threatens or actually fails to repay the debt;

2) the power to waive the debt and cancel the debt;

3) the legal power of accepting payment and thereby completing the transfer of the ownership in the payment from the debtor to the creditor;

4) the legal liberty of exercising one's legal power of accepting payment tendered;

5) a legal immunity against the cancellation of the debt by mere notification by the debtor.

No doubt the law covering the creditor-debtor relation is complex enough to contain additional Hohfeldian elements implicit within this legal right. But the sample is probably rich enough as it stands to illustrate the conception of a system of Hohfeldian elements that, if respected, confers autonomy concerning the enjoyment of the core upon the creditor in face of the debtor.

Since the language of rights is most common in and around the law, my suggestion is that we use legal rights as our model of rights in general. My conception of a legal right is articulated in terms of Hohfeld's fundamental legal conceptions. In order to generalize this conception, therefore, it will be necessary to identify and define analogous fundamental conceptions in all those other areas in which one can meaningfully speak of rights.

Legal rights are only one species of institutional rights—those created, defined, and maintained by a legal system. But other sorts of institutions also have their rules and regulations that function much like the law of the land. It is a short step from legal liberties, claims, powers, and immunities to other sorts of organizational liberties, claims, powers, and immunities. For example, under the rules and regulations of Washington University I have a liberty of using Olin Library, a claim against my students to completion of all assignments, a power of assigning grades to students enrolled in my courses, and an immunity against losing my appointment as full professor without due cause, as specified in the tenure document. In terms of such organization analogues of Hohfeld's fundamental legal conceptions, one could easily develop a conception of other organizational rights strictly analogous to my conception of legal rights.

Not all institutional norms are rules and regulations issued and applied by those who hold office in some organization; other social norms are conventions, such as the mores of a society. Surely, our moral code imposes duties upon the members of our society, by virtue of which the conception of a morality liberty may be defined. Since our moral code recognizes promises, it must also involve such morality powers as the power of making a promise and of releasing the promisor from a duty to perform as promised. In terms of these conceptions of a morality duty and a morality power, it will be easy enough to define the conceptions of a morality claim and a morality immunity. Along these lines a conception of morality rights can be developed that is parallel to my conception of a legal right. In this way, legal rights can presumably be used as models for other sorts of conventional rights, such as rights created and defined by the norms of etiquette in any given society.

Legal, other organizational, and conventional rights are all institutional. It is a considerably longer step, some would say a leap, to ethical rights, such as human rights or other sorts of moral rights. I suggest, however, that we take this leap and see where we land. I maintain that the notion of an ethical duty is no more problematic than any of the other fundamental conceptions of ethics. I propose to define fundamental ethical advantages analogous to the fundamental legal advantages identified by Wesley Hohfeld.

1) One party x has an ethical liberty to perform some action A if and only if x does not have an ethical duty not to do A. For example, I have an ethical liberty to dress as I please within the bounds of decency and an ethical liberty of buying my wife flowers whenever I can afford them.

2) One party x has an ethical claim against some second party y that y perform some action A if and only if y has some ethical duty to x to do A. Thus, a promisee has an ethical claim against the promisor that he or she perform as per their agreement, and any human being has an ethical claim against other persons that they not attack him or her without due cause.

3) One party x has the ethical power to bring about some ethical consequence C if and only if x possesses the competence required for performing some act with this ethical consequence. For example, I have the ethical power of making a promise, an act that brings into existence an obligation to do what I have promised to do, but a young child, who does not understand the commitment involved, or a mentally incompetent adult lack any such ethical power of promising because no utterance of theirs of the form "I promise to . . ." would constitute an ethically binding promise.

4) One party x is ethically immune from some specified ethical consequence C if and only if there is no second party y such that y is competent to perform some action with this ethical consequence C. Thus I am ethically immune from any moral obligation to perform promises made "on my behalf" by anyone I have not authorized to bind me morally in this way, because no act by any unauthorized person saying "I promise that Carl Wellman will . . ." creates any moral obligation binding upon me. Any adequate analysis of such fundamental ethical conceptions would require extended discussion and multiple illustration, not to mention a consideration of obvious objections to this approach to ethical rights. But the nature of my project should at least be clear, and I have begun a more systematic treatment in "A New Conception of Human Rights."

Once fundamental organizational, conventional, and ethical conceptions analogous to Hohfeld's fundamental legal conceptions have been identified and defined, my conception of a legal right can be generalized to provide a conception applicable to every species of right. A right is a system of normative elements that, if respected, confers autonomy concerning the exercise or enjoyment of some specified core upon its possessor in face of one or more second parties whose wills are or might be opposed. This general definition of a right contains the same essential features as my conception of a legal right. The constituents of any right are normative elements, such as liberties, claims, powers, immunities, and duties. Every right has a structure made up of a central defining core, together with associated normative elements that confer freedom or control relating to that core. Together, freedom and control may be called autonomy, and the total system of normative advantages confers autonomy upon one party vis-à-vis one or more second parties in some actual or possible confrontation of wills. Hence the distinctive feature of rights language, its application to the problem of whose will is to be decisive or effective when there is a conflict of wills in any social situation or situation in which a number of moral agents is involved.

Welfare Rights

One familiar class of such confrontations concerns public welfare. A resident may apply for Old Age Assistance or Aid to Families with Dependent Children and be denied aid by the state welfare agency. When a welfare recipient obtains part-time employment, the welfare agency may terminate further benefits immediately, and the recipient may demand a fair hearing before the termination of his or her welfare payments. On a different political level, a welfare agency may request appropriations sufficient to enable it to meet the basic expenses of all eligible applicants, but a legislative committee, intent upon holding down taxes in an election year, may recommend reduced funding for welfare. In contexts such as these, the appeal to welfare rights is linguistically appropriate and often legally or politically effective.

What are welfare rights? I am not asking what sorts of welfare rights, whether legal or moral, we actually have, but what we mean by the expression "a welfare right." Having explained my conception of a right in general, what remains is to identify the specific features of welfare rights. The obvious place to begin is with proposed definitions, or at least characterizations, of welfare rights in the literature.

The conception of a welfare right most often cited in the philosophical literature is probably that suggested by Martin Golding. ("Towards a Theory of Human Rights," pp. 540–48). In his view, a welfare right is a claim to one of the goods of life. Plausible examples might be the rights to an elementary school education, decent housing, and adequate health care, yet even this definition of a welfare right is not adequate for Golding's purposes. He introduces his conception of a welfare right to mark off a class of rights in contrast to what he calls option rights. Thus, a fuller and more accurate definition of his conception would include the proviso that the realization of the good is independent of the option of the possessor (p. 547). Surely the use of my car is one of the (somewhat modest) goods of life; I would hardly value possession of my car without the use of it. Yet the right to the use of my car is hardly a welfare right. (In fact, Golding himself gives it as an example of an option right.) Let us formulate his conception of a welfare right, therefore, as a right to one of the goods of life such that the realization of that good is independent of the option of the possessor of the right.

Even this definition is too broad for our purposes. Golding cites the right to be protected from unauthorized intrusion into one's home and the right to compensation for damage inflicted by others as paradigm cases of welfare rights. Yet police protection of one's life and property is not ordinarily regarded as public welfare. Nor is this a mere idiomatic pecularity of our language or a cultural quirk of our society; police protection is a very different sort of benefit from Aid to Families with Dependent Children or Medicaid. An even clearer counterexample is the right to compensation for damage inflicted by others. No doubt such compensation is as much one of the goods of life as money received from a welfare agency, but is can hardly be classified as a welfare payment. This is not to suggest that Golding has misunderstood or misinterpreted the word "welfare," for his use of the word falls within the range of meanings in our language. It is to insist, rather, that his conception does not capture what is distinctive of the subject of this book, public and private welfare.

A somewhat different, but often cited, conception has been put forward by H. J. McCloskey in his paper entitled "Rights." He characterizes the welfare concept of a right as "an entitlement to the efforts of others . . . to aid and promote our seeking after or enjoyment of some good" (p. 120). This does seem like a promising definition of a welfare right, for Medicaid, Old Age Assistance, Aid to Families with Dependent Children, etc. are all forms of aid that promote the enjoyment of one or more human goods. But as McCloskey himself recognizes, this characterization is excessively broad. I have a right to be paid by Washington University at the end of each month. My right to payment by my employer is an entitlement to the efforts of Washington University to promote my enjoyment of an adequate income. But this is hardly a welfare right. Thus, McCloskey distinguishes welfare rights from special rights, such as the right of a creditor to repayment of his loan, and presumably, the right of an employee to payment of his salary. Let us make this distinction explicit and define his concept of a welfare right as a general entitlement to the efforts of others to aid and promote the right-holder's seeking after or enjoyment of some good.

This definition of a welfare right may well be both too narrow and too broad. It may be too narrow precisely because it excludes all special rights. Even though many special rights, such as my right to my salary and the creditor's right to repayment, are not welfare rights in any strict sense, some other special rights are welfare rights in the strictest sense. Most public welfare in the United States comes within the social security system, and this is a categorical system of welfare aid. Welfare is provided, not to every citizen or even to any needy resident, but only to certain specified categories of persons. Thus, it is *as* a member of a family with dependent children, or *as* someone over the age of retirement, or *as* someone totally and permanently disabled that one has a legal right to welfare in most cases. Such legal rights certainly seem to be special rights and surely must count as welfare rights. Accordingly, it may be a mistake to exclude all special rights from the class of welfare rights.

On the other hand, McCloskey's concept of a welfare right is far too broad because it does not specify which kinds of goods are to count as welfare. A citizen has no need of special standing to be entitled to the efforts of the state to protect him from criminal attacks or murder, or from invasion and devastation from some foreign power. But since police protection and national defense are very different from welfare, these rights should not be included within welfare rights. Again, I need no special standing to be entitled to the services of a public library or librarian, but my right to library services is not really a welfare right. Once more, a concept of a welfare right that may be useful for some purposes hardly serves to define a right to welfare benefits in the usual sense.

Although Rodney Peffer does not discuss public or private welfare as such, his characterization of rights to well-being is a plausible candidate for a definition of a welfare right. In fact, he does what Golding and McCloskey fail to do; he specifies the limited range of goods that might fall within the province of welfare rights as those necessary to the fulfillment of our basic needs as human beings. His conception might well be formulated in this way: a welfare right is a right to some type of good or service that we require if we are to survive and to have any sort of worthwhile life ("A Defense to Rights to Well-Being," pp. 65 and 80). Examples might be rights to food, clothing, and housing, or to the minimum income required to purchase such necessities. Since many have suggested that welfare rights are ultimately grounded in our basic human needs, this definition of a welfare right would presumably be attractive to many.

It may be that welfare rights are "conceptually connected to our basic needs as human organisms" in some way, but surely Peffer has not explicated that connection correctly. After paying the checkout person for the groceries in my shopping basket, I have a right to that food. I also have a basic human need for food to survive. But my right to that food is not a welfare right in the same sense that the right of an unemployed mother to food stamps is a right to welfare; my right is a contractual right to receive delivery of goods in return for consideration tendered. Similarly, my right to have Blue Cross pay my medical bill pursuant to my contract with this private insurance company is not a welfare right, although the right of someone unable to afford Blue Cross coverage to have his or her hospital bill paid by Medicaid is a paradigm case of a welfare right. The difference is not that the welfare recipient has a basic human need for food and medical care that I lack, but is in the disparity between the grounds of our respective rights. My rights to food and to the payment for medical care arise from my contractual arrangements, together with the fact that I have fulfilled my part of the contract by the appropriate monetary payments. That the goods or services to which I have a right do in fact satisfy my basic human needs does not transform my rights into welfare rights. At best it might be maintained that a welfare right is a right to some type of good or service which is grounded in the basic human need of the possessor for that type of good or service. This would exclude my rights because they have different grounds.

I doubt, however, that any such move would save the definition. The reformulated definition remains at once too broad and too narrow. Human beings have a basic need for protection from criminal attacks on their property, life, and limb; they also have a basic need for protection from external invasion and the devastations of warfare. But police protection and national defense are not properly classified as public welfare programs. Hence, our rights to such goods or services are not, strictly speaking, welfare rights. Conversely, imagine that our society becomes more affluent, or humane, or frivolous, and incorporates into its Aid to Families with Dependent Children the distribution of free symphony tickets or tickets to sports events. I see no reason to deny that these would, in such an expanded welfare program, be genuine welfare benefits. The fact that there may be no basic human need to hear symphony concerts or to attend professional athletic contests, although it may be an excellent reason for eliminating this fringe benefit from the welfare budget, is no reason to deny that they are one more form of welfare. Since those eligible for this new form of welfare would presumably have a right to receive it, this right clearly not grounded in any basic human need would still be a welfare right.

It may seem unkind, even unjust, of me to ascribe to Peffer a definition of a welfare right when he speaks instead of rights to well-being, and then to refute the definition on the grounds that it fails to match our conception of welfare. I do this for two reasons. First, I believe that he clearly articulates a popular but unexplained conception of welfare rights current in the literature. Second, it seems to me that he does advance our understanding of welfare rights by suggesting that they are conceptually connected with human needs. Although the precise connection remains to be discovered, Peffer has given us a valuable clue to guide our search.

To generalize, all three conceptions of a welfare right discussed in this chapter, and these are the most plausible ones I have found in the literature, have a common failing. None captures the meaning of "welfare" in the sense of the various social security programs which exemplify public welfare, or the work of private orphanages or the Salvation Army, which illustrate private welfare. This is not to criticize Golding, McCloskey, and Peffer, who had very different problems in mind and introduced their respective conceptions to serve different, although not entirely unrelated, purposes. My point is simply that we cannot profitably use their conceptions, at least without major modification, in any discussion of the legal and moral rights that bear on public and private welfare. For the special purposes of this book, some other and more relevant conception of a welfare right is necessary.

An essential preliminary to defining any right to welfare is some clear conception of what is, and what is not, included in welfare. Let us begin by reminding ourselves of the public welfare programs that constitute the paradigm instances of welfare in our society. These include Aid to Families with Dependent Children (AFDC), Supplemental Security Income (which replaced Old Age Assistance, Aid to the Blind, and Aid to the Permanently and Totally Disabled), Medicaid, Medicare, and unemployment insurance, all of which provide welfare benefits in the form of money. There are also other sorts of benefits. Public housing and Food Stamps, purchased by the recipient, constitute a form of benefit because they are subsidized by the government. Other benefits take the form of welfare services, such as legal services provided by the Office of Economic Opportunity, family services provided through the Aid to Families with Dependent Children, and vocational services provided by the Work Incentive Program. All are forms of assistance made available to individual recipients to provide an acceptable level of individual welfare or well-being. Accordingly, I propose to define a welfare benefit as some form of assistance provided to an individual in need. The word "welfare," in the special sense relevant to this book, is simply a collective name for any and all welfare benefits.

My proposed rough definition will serve to delimit for practical and even most theoretical purposes an identifiable and important area of individual, social, legal, and moral concern. Additional description might characterize the recipient of welfare benefits as financially needy, below the poverty level, one of the poor. In practice this is usually the case, but I do not wish to build this into my definition for two reasons. First, some welfare benefits are actually provided for individuals who are in fact above the poverty level. For example, someone temporarily out of work is eligible to receive unemployment insurance without having exhausted his financial reserves, and the aged may be eligible for Medicare without being impoverished. Second, the concept of need is both somewhat elastic and partly independent of income. As a society becomes more affluent, its conception of what the individual needs in order to achieve an acceptable level of personal well-being changes. And I would not wish to rule out by definition the notion that a society might decide that middle-class individuals, clearly above the poverty level, need assistance of certain sorts, such as financial aid in financing higher education or in meeting certain categories of medical expenses, both of which are so expensive that they might disrupt individual and family life even for those who are not properly classified as poor. Therefore, I define welfare benefits in terms of an individual "in need" in the sense that the individual needs, or is judged to need, assistance in order to achieve an acceptable level of well-being. Thus, Peffer was on the right track when he introduced the notion of need into his definition of rights to well-being. But for our purposes, the relevant sense of need is not that of needing the good or service to satisfy a basic need, but that of being in need of assistance.

My definition of a welfare benefit as some form of assistance provided to an individual in need not only covers paradigm examples of welfare in the United States today; it also draws the line between what is and what is not welfare. For example, Medicaid payments are a form of welfare but payments on a Blue Cross or Blue Shield policy are not, because the former are assistance necessary to achieve an acceptable level of personal well-being, while the latter are payments rendered under the terms of a paid-up contract, independent of the need of the individual covered by the contract. Similarly, Old Age Assistance, or the newer Supplemental Security Income for the elderly, is a welfare benefit paid to the aged person, who is presumed to need assistance in maintaining an acceptable level of personal well-being; but the retirement benefits received by someone under an industry program or a company-subsidized retirement program are contractual rather than welfare benefits. Some of the social security benefits were, I think, originally intended to be similar contractual benefits under a public compulsory insurance system. If they were in fact nothing more than payments made in return for premiums paid, then their governmental source would not in and of itself convert them into welfare benefits in the relevant sense. But in point of fact, premiums paid into the social security insurance programs were supplemented out of the general treasury, and coverage was extended to persons who had paid few, if any, premiums into the insurance pool. Therefore, they have become a form of assistance to the needy rather than merely a public form of insurance.

Again, an AFDC payment is a form of assistance to an individual, usually a mother, who needs such assistance to maintain an acceptable level of personal welfare for herself and her dependent child or children; but an NSF or NEH grant or fellowship to support scientific research or humanistic scholarship is not welfare, because it is provided to assist in the pursuit of research. Finally, food stamps are, but postage stamps are not, welfare, even though both sorts of stamps are federally subsidized. Once more, this is because the former are, but the latter are not, a form of assistance to the individual in need.

Having established, or at least rendered plausible, my definition of a welfare benefit by showing that it fits clear cases, let us apply it to more controversial borderline cases. Is public education, especially on the elementary and secondary level, a form of public welfare? All residents of the United States are eligible for public education at the appropriate age and often in continuing education programs. Nevertheless, many families who elect to send their children could afford private education, so, public education is the United States today is not, strictly speaking, a form of public welfare. Yet one can imagine a society in which it would be: the affluent would be expected to pay for the education of their children, but education would be provided for those children whose families could not afford private education—either in free public schools, for which only the needy were eligible, or through monetary grants to enable needy families to send their children to private schools.

Government programs relating to medical care take many forms, and it is not always clear which forms should be considered welfare programs. Medicaid is a paradigm case of public welfare, for only those judged to lack the financial resources to purchase private medical care are eligible for its benefits. Medicare is a less clear case, because retired persons or their spouses are eligible even when they could, if necessary, sell their homes or deplete their savings to obtain medical care. Still, it seems clear that the purpose of the legislation creating the Medicare program is to assist the elderly, who are generally presumed to have increasing needs for expensive medical care that they cannot provide for themselves on their limited fixed incomes, which become increasingly inadequate as inflation advances. Thus, even though Medicare is provided for all the elderly in our society, this is because the elderly are judged to be in need of such assistance.

Suppose medical payments were made available to all citizens of every age and financial situation by a universal, compulsory system of government medical insurance. Would this be a form of welfare? If the system were self-supporting through income derived from the payment of insurance premiums by the individuals covered by the system, and if the medical benefits were simply a return to which recipients were entitled on a contractual basis, it would not be public welfare any more than the Blue Cross and Blue Shield programs are a form of welfare. But if the income from premiums were supplemented by the general treasury and if individuals were eligible for medical benefits even though they had been unemployed or were unable to pay the usual premiums, then it would become a form of welfare. In its essential features it would be similar to other social security insurance programs that are a mixture between compulsory insurance schemes and outright welfare programs.

What would be the status of a universal national health service that would provide medical care for all citizens without cost or for a nominal charge? If the system were self-supporting and each eligible individual were required to pay his or her share of the total cost of the system, its governmental character would not be sufficient to make it into a welfare program; it would be comparable to a private group medical plan in which the recipients pay for all services rendered and in which eligibility is derived from payments made to the group medical care plan. But if the national medical service were made available to the citizens because they were incapable of providing adequate medical care for themselves in the private market, then it would become a form of assistance for those who need such assistance and would be a form of public welfare.

This suggests that the word "welfare" when it occurs in the expression "a welfare state" has a somewhat different meaning from the same word when it occurs in the expression "a welfare benefit" or "he is on welfare." I suppose any state that provides public programs of assistance to the needy could be considered a welfare state, but the ideal of the welfare state goes beyond this. The welfare state may well have a wide range of programs that contribute to the welfare of its citizens, perhaps national subsidies to the arts or support for higher education or nationalized transportation, that are not forms of governmental assistance to maintain personal well-being in those incapable of providing it for themselves. The welfare state may provide many services which its citizens could well provide for themselves but which, it is thought, could be better provided by the government for one reason or another.

Not all welfare is public welfare; there is also much private welfare in most countries, provided by private organizations rather than the federal, state, or local governments. Thus, quite distinct from the legal services program of the Office of Economic Opportunity are the many private Legal Aid Societies around the country. Many churches and church-sponsored organizations provide assistance to the needy in the form of monetary payments, donations of food, various counseling services, etc. Indeed, the churches were in the welfare business before the governments, at least in the recent history of our society. The Salvation Army operates many welfare programs. The Red Cross relief to disaster victims is another important form of private welfare. The Hunger Task Forces that provide food to the needy in our country today are another form of private welfare. All of these and may other private organizations supply assistance to those in need.

Although it is usual to speak of private welfare organizations and many such organizations have the word "welfare" in their names, it is not common to speak of individual welfare. Yet I think that it is a natural extension of the term to do so. Thus, the doctor who provides medical care free of charge or at very lost cost to a patient unable to afford the going rate may properly be said to be supplying a welfare benefit. This doctor is giving the patient a form of assistance to the needy in exactly the same sense that Medicaid does. The individual who gives food or money to someone who is destitute should also be seen as giving welfare. No doubt, most individuals contribute to welfare primarily through their tax dollars and their contributions to charitable organizations. Still, some welfare benefits are provided by individuals in our society.

Many more welfare benefits are provided by the family. There is an irony in the name of the best known public welfare program in the United States today, Aid to Families with Dependent Children. *All* families have dependent children, for every child is born completely dependent and remains so for years. Yet most families are ineligible for AFDC because they are not judged to be in need of public assistance. While most families can provide for the needs of their children without aid from the government, this should not blind us to the equally important fact that the children in even the most affluent families *do* need assistance. They obtain it, of course, from their parents or from other members of the family. The food, clothing, housing, and various forms of care from their families are welfare in the sense of assistance provided to those who need it. Nor are these the only sorts of welfare benefits provided by the family. Usually the family, rather than Medicaid or Medicare, pays for a family member's needed medical care, feeds, clothes, and houses a high school graduate unable to find employment, and cares for the needs of the elderly, the blind, or the permanently and totally disabled. In short, every major public welfare program is a supplement to similar forms of welfare benefits normally provided by the family. I suggest that it would be entirely proper and quite illuminating to consider the assistance provided by the family to its needy members as welfare, for then we would recognize that the most important welfare institution in our society is the family.

We have finally arrived at an accurate definition of welfare, a collective noun used to refer to any and all forms of welfare benefits. A welfare benefit is any form of assistance—monetary payment, good, or service—provided to an individual because of his or her need. We can now define a primary welfare right as a right to some welfare benefit or benefits. Examples of welfare rights would be the legal right of a mother with one or more dependent children to AFDC payments, or the right of an elderly person entitled to social security payments to Medicare as well.

Such examples could be multiplied indefinitely, but even an extended list of primary welfare rights as we have defined them would not include most of the rights listed by the National Welfare Rights Organization in its "Bill of Welfare Rights." These include "the right to appeal a denial of aid and to be given a fair hearing" and "the right to be treated in a way which does not invade your privacy." The latter hardly seems a welfare right at all; as formulated, it is simply the right to privacy, a right that extends to many areas having nothing to do with any sort of welfare benefit. Still, one can understand its inclusion in a list of welfare rights. Welfare applicants' privacy is often violated when the welfare department investigates their personal affairs to determine their eligibility for aid, and the notorious midnight searches to find a man in the house have violated the right to privacy of many recipients of AFDC.

Again, the right to a fair hearing, although it is one aspect of the much more general right to due process, does have a meaning specific to our public welfare programs. It is defined especially in the *Code of Federal Regulations* section 205.10. Accordingly, I define a secondary welfare right as a right concerning, but not to, some welfare benefit. All of the rights listed in the NWRO "Bill of Welfare Rights" are either primary or secondary welfare rights, and I can think of no obvious examples of welfare rights that do not fall into one or the other category. I suggest, therefore, that we accept as our working definition of the concept of a welfare right a right to or concerning some welfare benefit or benefits.

Precisely what specific welfare rights exist is a matter to be deter-

mined only by detailed and prolonged investigation, but this conception of a welfare right allows for the possibility that a wide range of
welfare rights exists. Surely there are many legal welfare rights, and
there are probably a variety of ethical welfare rights as well. The
human rights to social security and to an adequate standard of living
are probably welfare rights—rights to assistance, in achieving these
necessary conditions of an acceptable level of individual well-being.
The child's moral right to special protection by its parents seems also
to be a welfare right. Although one may wish to prevent the multipli-
cation of welfare rights beyond necessity, one does not wish to rule
any contender out of court arbitrarily and merely by definition.

Alleged Conceptual Incoherence

I have proposed that we conceive of a right as a system of normative
elements that, if respected, confers autonomy concerning the exercise
or enjoyment of some specified core upon its possessor in face of one
or more second parties. I then suggested that the content of a primary
welfare right is some welfare benefit, some form of assistance to be
provided to an individual in need. But it has been alleged that there is
a conceptual incoherence in the notion of a right to welfare. This is a
radical challenge indeed. The suggestion is not simply that in fact
there are no rights. This deficiency, if such it is, could easily be solved
by legislation to create such rights. Rather the contention is that there
could be no right to welfare, as opposed to a right to free speech or
due process, because there is some sort of hidden logical inconsistency in combining the expressions "a right to" with "welfare." In
exploring this allegation, it will be helpful to keep the distinction
between legal rights and moral rights in mind, for their logics are
rather different.

In a frequently cited article, "Towards a Theory of Human Rights,"
Martin Golding distinguishes between option rights and welfare
rights. He believes that some such distinction is necessary because
the possessor of a right to decent housing or adequate medical care
does not enjoy such a welfare right at his or her option. Although
Golding does not himself reject the conceptual possibility of welfare
rights, his line of argument could be extended to do so. Along the
same lines, it could be alleged that there is a conceptual incoherence
in combining an autonomy conception of rights, such as mine, with
the conception of a core claim to a welfare benefit just because the
possessor of any claim to a welfare benefit could not have autonomy
with respect to its enjoyment.

This allegation seems plainly mistaken with respect to legal rights
to welfare benefits. For example, the possessor of the legal right to be
provided with Aid to Families with Dependent Children has a consid-

erable amount of autonomy over the enjoyment of its core claim. The legal duty of the state to pay AFDC benefits is contingent upon the application of the eligible individual, and the individual can withdraw her or his application at any time. Accordingly, the possessor of the right to receive AFDC can create or extinguish the duty to provide aid. If aid is denied, the eligible individual can take legal action against the welfare agents of the state and, if she or he wins the case, compel satisfaction of the core claim. Short of legal action, the applicant has the legal power to challenge any adverse decision of the welfare agency and to demand a fair hearing to consider, and perhaps enforce, her or his core claim. Moreover, the possessor of the right to receive Aid to Families with Dependent Children has the bilateral legal liberties of exercising or not exercising each of these forms of legal control as he or she wishes. It is hard to see how there can be the slightest conceptual incoherence in speaking of the right to receive this welfare benefit as a system of normative elements that confer autonomy over the enjoyment of its core claim to welfare upon its possessor in face of any resistent welfare agency.

The situation is not quite so clear when one turns from legal rights to moral welfare rights. Consider the moral right of the individual unemployed through no fault of his or her own to a minimal livelihood from the state or the right of an elderly person without adequate financial means to be cared for by his or her family or provided for by the state. For present purposes it does not matter whether there actually are any such moral rights to welfare; the issue is whether it makes sense to speak of them at all. If they exist, they are moral claim-rights against the family or the state or both. Unlike the legal right to Aid to Families with Dependent Children, it does not appear that the moral obligation to provide such welfare benefits is always, or perhaps ever, contingent upon the application of the individual in need. Still, it is very likely, and surely not inconceivable, that the ethical claim to such benefits can be waived by the possessor of the welfare right. Thus, if my elderly mother declines my aid, my moral obligation to provide it seems at least temporarily extinguished. And although ethical claims cannot be taken to court, there is something like taking legal action even here. Thus, if my impoverished mother demands that I provide for her basic needs in her last years, her act of claiming this welfare benefit increases my moral obligation to satisfy her ethical claim against me, and if she claims some remedy for my past nonperformance of my duty to care for her, her act of claiming itself creates some extra obligation to make up for my past neglect of my duty to her. I must admit that needy individuals have considerably less autonomy with regard to their ethical claims to welfare benefits than they typically have with regard to legal claims to welfare. But as long as they have some autonomy with regard to such welfare claims, it makes sense to speak of moral rights to welfare. It may be, of course, that with regard to some ethical claims to welfare benefits such autonomy is virtually nonexistent. But this is not fatal to my theory. In such cases, I would hold that the claim to welfare is genuine but that it is not the core of any moral right.

In any event, this first challenge to the intelligibility of the conception of a right to welfare can be dismissed. There is no logical inconsistency or category mistake in combining an autonomy conception of a right with the conception of a legal or ethical claim to a welfare benefit. The possessor of a legal right to a welfare benefit typically has considerable freedom and control over her or his enjoyment of that core claim, and the possessor of a moral right to a welfare benefit sometimes has some such freedom and control. Even if the degree of actual autonomy was considerably less in regard to welfare benefits, there is no more conceptual incongruity in the notion of autonomy with regard to a claim to welfare than with regard to a claim to anything else. Therefore, unless one is prepared to reject the very conception of a claim-right, one must accept the concept of a welfare right, at least until some more awkward difficulty is uncovered.

A second alleged conceptual incoherence in the notion of a welfare right is the incongruity between the definiteness essential to any genuine claim and the ineradicable indefiniteness of the content of any welfare benefit. Every legal or ethical claim must have some definite content. This is because every claim of x against y implies a duty of y to x. Unless the claim has a definite content, it is impossible in principle to determine what must be done to satisfy it. Accordingly, any purported legal claim that lacks defined content is not justiciable and, hence, not a genuine legal claim-right; any purported ethical claim that lacks defined content implies no definite correlative duty and, hence, has no practical or ethical significance. But, the argument continues, purported claims to welfare benefits cannot have any clearly defined content because the very concept of a welfare benefit has no clearly defined limits. A welfare benefit is some form of assistance to be provided to those in need, that is those who need the benefit to maintain an adequate level of well-being and who need it provided for them because they are unable to provide it for themselves. But the notion of need is a very flexible one and one that seems to vary from society to society and even from individual to individual. Thus, there is no way to define what really is needed and, therefore, no way to give any definite content to any ostensible claim to welfare. Since any genuine legal or ethical claim must have a definite content and since there is no way to define the content of any welfare benefit, the very notion of a claim to welfare is incoherent.

This argument is often illustrated by citing the language of various purported welfare claim-rights. Consider Article 25 of the *Universal Declaration of Human Rights*. "Everyone has the right to a standard of living adequate for the health and well-being of himself and of his family . . . and the right to security in the event of unemployment, sickness, disability, widowhood, old age or other lack of livelihood in circumstances beyond his control." Precisely what standard of living is adequate and below what level is one's livelihood inadequate? It is hard to imagine any definite measure of adequacy and, were one proposed, it is harder still to imagine any way to decide whether it is the correct measure. And exactly what duties are imposed upon the family or the state in order to provide security in the event of unemployment, sickness, or old age? Similarly, one looks in vain for language in the United States Constitution to define any constitutional welfare rights. The obvious candidate is the expression "the equal protection of the laws," but there seems no way to translate this into legal claims to specifiable welfare benefits that would be justiciable. But a purported claim to "something or other" is no genuine claim at all. Therefore, there are and can be no claims to welfare.

Even if everything asserted in this argument were granted, it would not establish the conceptual incoherence of the notion of a claim-right to welfare. This is because the previous argument does not touch statutory welfare rights. Thus, the legal right to receive Aid to Families with Dependent Children or the legal right to receive Medicaid does have a very definite content, a content specified in dollars and cents, because of the legislation together with welfare regulations that have set the level of benefits for which anyone is eligible. For this reason, claims to such welfare benefits can be taken to court and the court has no difficulty in determining when the legal claim-right of the plaintiff has or has not been fulfilled. Clearly, then, there is no incompatibility between the definiteness of a genuine claim and any inevitable indefiniteness of a welfare benefit.

At the most, this charge might show that there could be no constitutional or moral rights to welfare. But clearly there is no impossibility in principle of amending the Constitution to add language definite enough to ground constitutional claim-rights to welfare benefits. In fact, the same result might be achieved through the more gradual process of judicial interpretation of the existing language. More serious is the question of whether any purported ethical right to welfare can be given a defined content. I see no reason why this could not be done. Notice, first, that absolute precision is not required. An ethical claim to welfare would be definite enough for all practical purposes if it identified some clear cases of fulfillment and some clear cases where the claim is not satisifed; the existence of additional borderline cases would not render the ethical claim entirely pointless or empty. Thus, it might be easy to carve out a clearly defined content for some welfare right within the clear cases and know that there is an ethical claim-right to at least this welfare benefit. In this way, minimum standards for moral welfare rights could in principle be specified definitely, even if it proved impossible to set any definite upper limit to justified ethical claims to welfare. Thus, although one might not be able to draw any clear line between an adequate and an inadequate standard of living, one might be able to show that someone living in dire poverty was definitely below the indefinite borderline. My conclusion is that there is probably no conceptual incoherence between the required definiteness of an ethical claim and the inherent indefiniteness of a welfare benefit and that there is certainly no such incoherence in the notion of a legal claim-right to welfare.

A third alleged conceptual incoherence in the very notion of a right to welfare is a confusion between a claim to and a claim against. A welfare benefit is some form of assistance to be provided to an individual because of his or her need. Thus, any claim to welfare must be grounded in the need of the individual for that form of welfare benefit. Now the need of some dependent child or unemployed person may well be a ground of a claim to some sort of assistance; the fact that the individual needs special protection or a substitute income may well be a valid reason for his or her claim to it. But the core of any claim-right to welfare must be a claim against someone, not simply a claim to some benefit. This is because a claim-right by its very nature implies a corresponding relative duty. The conceptual problem is that the need of x, although it may ground a claim to some welfare benefit, does not identify any second party y who has the corresponding duty to provide that benefit to x. And if there is no identifiable second party with an obligation to provide the welfare benefit in question, then it is a conceptual confusion to say that x has a right to that benefit, for every right is a right in face of one or more second parties.

This challenge does point to a real difficulty with asserted ethical rights to welfare. It is entirely true that the need of the individual does not, in and of itself, identify any second party against whom that individual has an ethical claim to be provided with the needed welfare benefit. But why assume that the ethical right to welfare is grounded in the need *in and of itself*? Any valid ground for a genuine claim to a welfare benefit must be grounded in the need of the claimant together with his or her special relation to some second party against whom the claim holds. Thus, not every hungry child has an ethical claim against me to be provided with adequate nutrition; my child does because of his or her need for food together with the fact that he or she is related to me as my child. And an orphan might well have an ethical claim against his or her state to be provided with food because of his or her relation as citizen of or subject of that state. Since the special relationship between some needy individual and some second party may well impose upon that second party some special moral responsibility for the welfare of that individual, there is no reason to conclude that the need of the individual can ground only a claim to and never a claim against some second party. Accordingly, there can be moral claim-rights to welfare benefits, at least in principle.

That a claim to a welfare benefit can intelligibly be said to be a claim against some identifiable second party is much more obvious in the case of legal welfare rights. The possessor of a legal claim is the party who has the legal power to sue for performance or remedy in the event of threatened or actual nonperformance of the corresponding duty, and the party against whom the legal claim holds is the party against whom the plaintiff has the power to take legal action. When it comes to legal welfare rights there is no difficulty at all in identifying the party against whom action can be taken. In recent landmark welfare cases decided by the Supreme Court of the United States, Smith sued King, Commissioner, Department of Pensions and Security of Alabama; Thompson sued Shapiro, Commissioner of Welfare of Connecticut; and Rosado sued Wyman, Commissioner of Social Services of New York. Although each defendant tried to prove that he had not acted improperly or illegally, none contended that he had been incorrectly identified as the second party of a claim to welfare in his state. Obviously, then, there is no conceptual incongruity in interpreting legal claims to welfare benefits as claims against second parties. Thus, there is no reason to believe that there is always a confusion between a claim to and a claim against when one speaks of a right to welfare.

A fourth alleged conceptual incoherence in all talk of rights to welfare is the category mistake of confusing rights with mere ideals. No doubt it would be highly desirable for every human being to have an adequate standard of living and for each unemployed citizen to have the appropriate form of social security, but it does not make sense to assert that needy individuals have a right to such welfare benefits. This is because any genuine right to welfare would have to be a claim-right, and every claim-right logically implies a correlative duty to fulfil the content of the core claim. There cannot, however, be any duty to do the impossible. And given the limited resources available to individuals, private organizations, and governments it is often impossible to provide needed welfare assistance. Since under such circumstances there can be no duty to provide welfare, it does not make sense to claim any corresponding universal right to welfare. And since any genuine human, moral or civil right must be possessed by all those with the necessary standing, no individual can be said to possess any such right.

Maurice Cranston has charged that "the effect of a Universal Declaration which is overloaded with affirmations of so-called human rights which are not human rights at all is to push *all* talk of human rights out of the clear realm of the morally compelling into the twilight world of utopian aspirations." ("Human Rights, Real and Supposed" p.52) Thus, it makes no sense to affirm that "everyone has the right to a standard of living adequate for the health and well-being of himself and his family" when many societies in our world lack the resources to overcome famine, disease, ignorance, and premature death. It is similarly utopian for the *Declaration of the Rights of the Child* to say "the child shall have the right to adequate nutrition, housing, recreation and medical resources" when many families even in affluent societies do not have the resources to perform what would be, were it not impossible to fulfill, the corresponding duty. The lack of resources undermines the concept of a legal right to welfare in a related manner. The notion of a legal claim-right is logically tied to that of a remedy obtainable by the claimant by taking legal action, but a court is not in a position to order programs of delivering welfare benefits, such as medical care or adequate housing, because these require the establishment of administrative programs with adequate resources that can come only from legislative action. Since welfare rights would involve claims upon resources that are often not available, to speak of rights to welfare benefits is to confuse mere ideals, desirable as they no doubt are, with genuine rights that necessarily entail correlative duties.

It must be admitted that courts typically lack the resources to provide welfare benefits. But it does not follow that taking legal action in the courts is not an effective way to enforce one's legal claim-right to a welfare benefit. Notice first that the problem of resources is not limited to welfare rights. A creditor has a legal claim-right to repayment against a debtor. Now in order to provide a remedy for nonpayment of the debt, it is not necessary for the court to repay the creditor out of its own limited operating budget. Typically it orders the debtor to pay the creditor and threatens punishment in the event that the debtor is found to be in contempt of court. Again, the court typically lacks the resources to impose any threatened or ordered punishment; for this it relies upon police and correctional officers funded by legislative appropriations. The moral is that courts can provide legal remedies required to make any claim-right genuine only because their decisions are respected and enforced by other branches of government. And if this is so, then there is no reason in principle why a court could not order some governmental agency to provide welfare benefits. In fact, recent court cases in the United States have ordered large-scale busing programs to further racial integration of the schools, as well as the payment of Aid to Families with Dependent Children and other forms of public welfare. Clearly, then, the fact that any legal claim to a welfare benefit imposes a legal duty that can be satisifed only with adequate resources poses no conceptual obstacle to meaningful talk about and judicial enforcement of legal rights to welfare.

Purported human rights to welfare benefits raise more difficult questions. A human right is supposed to be a right that all human beings possess simply by the virtue of being human. But how can all human beings have a right to some welfare benefit, such as an adequate standard of living, social security, or necessary medical care, when clearly in many societies there is no individual and no public agency that has the resources to provide any such benefit? Well, it may be that there are some basic human needs that cannot be met. If so, there can be no human claim-right to forms of assistance that would meet such needs. For example, there probably can be no human right to health because many individuals simply cannot be restored to good health with available medical technology. There might, however, be a human right to medical care because it is always possible to provide some medical care appropriate to every medical need. But how much medical care, for different societies have very different amounts of medical resources? Again, can there be any human right to adequate nutrition when many societies have insufficient food supplies? If one sets the standard so low that every society can meet it, then one will be asking far too little of the affluent societies. If one sets the standard at a level appropriate to a society with abundant resources, then the entailed duties will be impossible to fulfill, and hence not genuine duties, in most other societies. I suggest that one can solve the problem of varying levels of resources only by inserting a proviso into the definition of every asserted human right to welfare. The individual human being should be said to have a right to some welfare benefit adequate to meet his or her basic need to the extent of the second party's available resources. Thus more affluent societies will have an obligation to provide fuller welfare benefits, but poorer societies will still have a genuine duty to do what they can to meet the human needs of the individual.

A similar proviso should be considered to be implicit in each moral right to a welfare benefit possessed, not by every human as human, but by other classes of persons. Thus, each child has a moral claim-right against its parents to adequate nutrition, clothing, and housing to the extent of that parent's resources. But some parents may be completely lacking in resources. How can one then meaningfully assert that every child has a moral right to this welfare benefit when some children's ethical claim is undermined by the impossibility of doing anything to feed, clothe, or house the child? This question makes explicit the fact that the lack of resources of some second parties poses a threat to the very concept of a welfare right only because of the universalizability of every ethical principle. Given the requirement of universalizability, it would appear that if some children can have no moral claim against their parents, then no child can have such a claim. But the requirement of universalizability is that a purported moral principle must hold good for all instances that are similar in relevant respects. Now the lack of available resources needed to fulfill a purported ethical claim is clearly a morally relevant difference between an impoverished parent and more affluent parents. Therefore, this does not rule out the required universality of any moral claim-right to welfare.

This is fortunate, for if it did, it would rule out all claim-rights, not simply rights to welfare. The paradigm case of a claim-right is the right of a creditor to repayment or the right of a promisee to performance of the promise. But some debtors find themselves completely without available funds or liquid assets when the repayment date arrives. Similarly, I may have promised to use my station wagon to help a friend move only to have my wagon demolished the day before I promised my assistance. In such cases, there can be no moral duty to repay the debt or drive my station wagon, simply because it is impossible for the second party to do any such thing. But suppose that the debtor does have some money left, only not enough to repay the debt fully. It will hardly do for him to plead that he has no duty to make any payment to the creditor on the grounds that his duty is to repay the debt fully and that act is impossible for him. Again, presumably I would have a duty to drive my Volkswagen to help my friend move even if I am unable to drive my larger and more helpful station wagon. These examples illustrate two points. First, the problem of the lack of resources is not peculiar to welfare rights. Hence, if we can admit the concept of a claim-right at all, we have no special reason to deny its coherence when speaking of a claim-right to a welfare benefit. Second, even in apparently simpler and less problematic rights, there is implicit in the content of such rights a proviso to the effect that if one cannot fully perform the obligation correlative with the moral claim, then one ought to come as close as one can to the extent of one's available resources. Thus, my proposed solution to the difficulty about asserting universal human rights in a world containing impoverished countries is not ad hoc; it is simply a special case of a solution we already accept in the case of less problematic and more traditional rights. I conclude that the frequent lack of resources to provide welfare benefits does not show that there is any conceptual incoherence in all talk of rights to welfare. At most, it reveals the fact that some asserted welfare rights are not genuine rights but merely ideals. This leaves open the possibility that other asserted rights to welfare benefits are fully real.

A fifth alleged conceptual incoherence in the very notion of a right to welfare is revealed by the observation that the denial of a welfare benefit is not, as such, an injustice. Of course, to deny a black a welfare benefit because he or she is black is an injustice, but this is because this is an act of racial discrimination and not because it is a denial of assistance to the needy. "A human right is something of which no one may be denied without a grave affront to justice"

(Cranston, "Human Rights, Real and Supposed," p. 52). More generally, it is often held that, by the very concept of a right, every violation of a genuine right is an injustice. But the denial of a welfare benefit to a needy individual is never, as such, unjust. It may be harmful, even wrongful, but it is at worst uncharitable rather than an injustice to the needy individual. Therefore, the needy individual cannot properly be said to have a right to welfare.

Three replies can be made to this challenge to the very concept of a primary welfare right. 1) It is not clear that rights and justice are conceptually tied in the way presupposed by this allegation. That is, it is doubtful that the violation of every genuine right is an unjust act. Presumably every person has a right to personal security. Now if I harrass blacks by attacking or threatening to attack their persons, this probably is treating members of this minority race unjustly; but if I beat up weaker persons because I am a bully in need of ego-reenforcement, this does not seem to be at all the same sort of discriminatory, and therefore unjust, treatment. Again, if I typically insult and abuse women in my lectures, this violation of their right to equal respect does seem unjust; but if I fail to prepare my lectures carefully so that the right of all my students to my best teaching is denied, there seems nothing particularly unjust in my action. To spy on someone is surely to violate his or her right to privacy, and to kill someone is presumably to violate his or her right to life. But is is hard to see any injustice, any unfairness, in such denials of the rights of individuals. But if the denial of a right need not be unjust, then the fact (if it were a fact) that the denial of a welfare benefit is never as such an injustice, would not show that there is no right to welfare.

2) One might, I suppose, maintain that there is some sort of injustice in each of the counterexamples I have given. Or one might define injustice as the violation of one or more rights. Either way, one insists on a tight conceptual connection between the denial of a right and injustice. But in that case, the argument seems to beg the question at issue. For if there were a right to welfare, then the denial of a welfare benefit to an eligible individual would, on this view of injustice, be an injustice. To claim that the denial of welfare is not unjust is to presuppose that there is no right to welfare and, thus, to beg the question.

3)Moreover, there is some independent reason to think that the denial of welfare benefits often *is* an injustice. In a society where there are gross disparities in wealth, it does seem unfair for the affluent to live in luxury while failing to do anything to meet the fundamental human needs of those in dire poverty. Imagine further that many of the affluent have not earned their wealth (perhaps they have inherited it) and that many of the poor are deprived through no fault of their own (perhaps they are orphans or disabled). It seems even more unjust for the privileged to fail to provide welfare benefits to the needy. Finally, imagine a prosperous society that maintains its standard of living by an economic system in which there are always large numbers unemployed. Is it not grossly unjust for this society to deny welfare benefits to those unemployed by the very nature of the economic system? Thus, even if there can be no genuine right the denial of which is not an injustice, there might well be rights to welfare in such a society. Accordingly, there is no conceptual incoherence in the very notion of a primary welfare right.

The case is even clearer when one turns from human or moral rights to legal rights to welfare. Any legal claim-right to a welfare benefit must be grounded in certain rules or principles of the legal system. If the purported right is not so grounded in the law, then it is not a genuine legal right at all. But if there is some legal rule or principle according to which the individual has a valid claim to a welfare benefit, then to deny the individual this benefit is to treat him or her unjustly. This is because it is to treat this individual differently from the other individuals covered by the grounding law. But suppose that every individual covered by this welfare law were denied the welfare benefit so that all were treated equally? Well, in that case, the individuals covered by this law would be denied the equal protection of the law, since those covered by other legal rules and principles would be treated as called for in the law. Thus, the very nature of a legal system assures us that any denial of a legal claim to a welfare benefit must be an injustice. This fifth and last alleged conceptual incoherence, like the others, turns out not to be tenable.

Conclusion

It is possible to define the conception of a welfare right in a way that applies a philosophical theory of rights to that area of political and moral concern to which we refer when we speak of public or private welfare. A right is a system of normative elements that if respected, confers autonomy (freedom and control) concerning the exercise or enjoyment of some specified core upon its possessor in face of one or more second parties whose wills are or might be opposed. A primary welfare right is a right to some welfare benefit—to some form of assistance provided to an individual in need. A secondary welfare right is a right concerning, but not to, some welfare benefit. The expression "a welfare right" can best be interpreted as referring to either a primary or a secondary welfare right.

2

Legal Welfare Rights

There is no conceptual incoherence in the very notion of a right to welfare. Accordingly, talk about welfare rights does make sense, a sense I have explicated in the first chapter. What welfare rights there actually are, of course, is another matter. Here I shall examine two legal welfare rights in some detail—the primary welfare right to receive Aid to Families with Dependent Children (AFDC) payments and the secondary welfare right to a fair welfare hearing. These examples will serve to illustrate the nature of such rights and, at the same time, to test my general conception of a right by seeing how much light it can throw on this species of rights.

The Right to Receive AFDC Payments

The first example of a welfare right is the legal right to receive Aid to Families with Dependent Children payments created by a maze of statutes, court decisions, and regulations pursuant to Title IV of the Social Security Act. This Title provides for the federal participation in and regulation of the AFDC programs of the several states. Through these programs, the largest amount of public welfare assistance has been expended from the federal treasury. Thus, the economic and human significance of AFDC can hardly be in doubt. Nor can the existence of a legal right to receive AFDC payments be seriously questioned. What can be, and is, debated is the nature of this primary welfare right.

On my conception of a right, the essential content of any right is defined by its core. Just what is the core of the legal right to receive AFDC payments? It is on precisely this issue that debate has been most intense. Is the Hohfeldian element at the center of this welfare right a legal liberty to receive aid or a legal claim to receive aid? On the former interpretation, eligible individuals do not have any legal duty to refrain from accepting AFDC payments if and when provided by a state welfare agency. On the latter interpretation, a state welfare agency has a legal duty to the eligible individual to provide AFDC payments, and the eligible individual has the legal power to sue in the courts in the event of threatened or actual nonperformance of this core duty. Well, which interpretation best fits the law of our land?

Before I go on to answer this question, I wish to make two observations of some significance. First, the right to receive aid is not reduced to triviality if it turns out to be a liberty-right. To be sure, welfare lawyers and organizations have been fighting to create, sustain, and enlarge a legal claim to aid; and welfare recipients are much more secure if they in fact have a legally enforceable claim to their welfare payments. Still, there is some significant legal point and purpose to the legal liberty of accepting welfare payments even if such payments may be made entirely at the discretion of the state agency. To say that eligible individuals have a legal liberty to receive AFDC payments is to say that they have no legal duty to refrain from accepting such payments. If it were illegal to accept welfare checks from the state agency, then the recipients would be liable for the recovery of any amounts they had accepted and might be subject to legal penalties for accepting and cashing the checks. Welfare recipients are now legally liable for the recovery of overpayments under the law; and if they had no legal liberty to receive aid, every payment might be construed to be an overpayment. Again, welfare recipients are now subject to legal penalties for receiving welfare payments in illegal ways, as through fraud. A legal liberty to receive welfare aid would, then, assure the needy individual that he or she could accept the payment offered by the state agency and would not later suffer legally for this act.

Second, although my present concern is to identify the core of the right to receive AFDC payments, the way in which this core is defined affects much more than the core itself. A legal right consists of a defining core together with a system of associated Hohfeldian elements that serve to confer autonomy, freedom and control, concerning the exercise or enjoyment of this core upon the possessor of the right. Now the nature of these various associated elements will obviously depend upon the core with which they are associated. If the core is a legal liberty, the associated elements will include such elements as an immunity against a suit for the recovery of aid accepted, an immunity against prosecution for the act of accepting welfare aid, and even a legal claim against interference with one's acceptance of aid. If the core is a legal claim, the associated elements are more likely to include a legal power of applying for welfare aid, a bilateral legal liberty of suing or not suing in the event of threatened or actual nonprovision of aid, and perhaps legal claims against various forms of interference with one's efforts to obtain aid. Although the core is only one part of the legal right, the definition of the core determines the associated elements that complete and structure the right as a complex whole.

Now on to the debate. Whether the legal right to receive AFDC payments is a liberty-right or a claim-right is a matter of great practical importance. This is why welfare lawyers have been battling in the courts to obtain decisions affirming a legal right to receive aid and welfare rights organizations have been trying to convince the public that the right to welfare is, or at least ought to be, a claim-right. Underlying these legal and political struggles are two very different conceptions of public welfare. The traditional conception is that welfare is charity freely given by the state in response to the need of the recipients. Welfare payments are given at the discretion of the state agency within the limits of eligibility set by federal and state law. The specified conditions of eligibility set the outer limits for aid; the agency must not give aid to a single ineligible individual. But within these limits, the agency may give or withhold aid as it sees fit and on any additional conditions it wishes to impose, provided only that it does not discriminate arbitrarily or unreasonably between individuals or groups. The newer conception of public welfare is that welfare payments are something to which the recipients are legally entitled. It is not up to the state agency to decide to whom it wishes to give aid and under what conditions. Rather, it has a legal duty to give aid to all individuals who are eligible for it. The conditions of eligibility do not set outer limits within which the agency may exercise its discretion; they identify the individuals to whom the agency must give aid whether it wishes to do so or not. According to the traditional conception, the right to receive aid is a liberty-right; according to the newer conception, it is a claim-right. Leaving aside for the moment the moral issue whether the needy individual ought to have a legal claim, or merely a legal liberty to receive aid, let us try to determine the actual content of the legal right to receive AFDC payments under Title IV.

After prolonged debate in the courts, it is fairly clear today that the core of the legal right to receive Aid to Families with Dependent Children payments is a legal claim, that the welfare agency has a legal duty to provide aid to each eligible individual, and that each eligible individual has the legal power to sue for performance or remedy in the event of threatened or actual nonperformance of this duty. In 1970, the Supreme Court declared unambiguously that welfare "benefits are a matter of statutory entitlement for persons qualified to receive them" (*Goldberg* v. *Kelly* 397 US 262). The statutory basis for their decision was the requirement in Title IV of the Social Security Act that state programs shall provide "that all individuals wishing to make application for aid to families with dependent children shall have opportunity to do so, and that aid to families with dependent children shall be furnished with reasonable promptness to all eligible individuals" (42 USCS section 602 (a)(10)). This decision was foreshaddowed by an earlier decision in which "substitute father" requirements were declared a violation of Title IV on the ground that such requirements violate the federal requirement that aid be furnished to *all* eligible individuals (*King* v. *Smith* 392 US 317). Accordingly, individual welfare recipients have legal standing to bring action to enforce their claim to receive aid (*Dandridge* v. *Williams* 397 US 489).

Eligible individuals have a legal claim to receive AFDC payments, but this claim is a doubly conditional one. The state welfare agency has a legal duty to provide public assistance *if* and as long as the state participates in the federally funded Aid to Families with Dependent Children program under Title IV. The stated purpose of this program is to *enable* each state to furnish aid as far as practicable under the conditions in that state. But if a state should at any time decide that it could not afford to participate in the AFDC program or that it wished to use its limited resources for other purposes, it could withdraw from the program. In such an event, it would no longer be legally bound by the provisions of Title IV and the residents of the state would lose their legal claim to receive payments under the AFDC program. But *if* a state chooses to remain in the program, then each eligible resident is legally entitled to receive aid.

Provided, that is, the eligible individual applies for such aid. The legal claim to receive AFDC payments is in this respect like the legal claim to repayment of the creditor who holds a note payable on demand. The debtor has a duty to repay the creditor if, but only if and when, the creditor demands payment on the note. Similarly, the state welfare agency has a legal duty to provide AFDC payments to the eligible individual *if*, but only if, that individual applies under the provisions of the Aid to Families with Dependent Children program. The state has no legal duty to provide aid to eligible individuals who do not apply for it, much less any duty to seek out eligible individuals and proffer checks to them. Thus, each eligible individual has a legal claim to AFDC payments *if* his or her state participates in the program and *if* she or he has applied for such aid.

How much aid is one entitled to receive? The legal claim to aid would not be of much practical value if the state could discharge its legal duty by paying, say, one dollar each month. Since the AFDC program is a cooperative federal-state venture, Title IV alone does not set the amount of aid that must be paid to eligible individuals. The purpose of this Title is that of "enabling each State to furnish financial assistance . . . as far as practicable under the conditions in each State" (42 USCS section 601). Accordingly, the courts have always recognized that the states have a great deal of discretion, both in establishing a "standard of need" and in deciding what "level of benefits" will be paid. The Supreme Court has even declared that the state may reduce the percentage of benefits paid as much as it deems necessary or desirable (*Rosado* v. *Wyman* 397 US 413). Fortunately, this does not completely destroy the practical import of the individual's claim to aid. Although the state may pay only a percentage of the standard of need it sets, it must calculate this standard of need in accordance with federal regulations (*Rosado* v. *Wyman* 397 US 413). More important, it cannot deny aid to one individual, or even reduce the amount of aid provided, without regard to the aid given to other comparable individuals. Aid to Families with Dependent Children must be given on an equitable basis. "The groups selected for inclusion in the plan and the eligibility conditions imposed must not exclude individuals or groups on an arbitrary or unreasonable basis, and must not result in inequitable treatment of individuals or groups in the light of the provisions and purposes of the public assistance titles of the Social Security Act" (45 CFR 233.10(a)(1)). Thus, each individual has a legal claim to receive aid equal in amount to that given to all other individuals in the same class, where the classification is nondiscriminatory and reasonable in the light of the purposes of the federally funded welfare program.

Such, then, is the core of the legal right to receive AFDC payments in the United States today. It is a legal claim against the state welfare agency to be provided with AFDC payments equal in amount to that provided for other comparable residents of the state *if* the state participates in the federally funded program and *if* the eligible individual has applied for such aid. Around this core claim cluster many associated Hohfeldian elements that fill out the right and make it into a system of autonomy. Since AFDC is a cooperative federal-state program, the legal right to receive aid under this program is created, defined, and maintained by a combination of federal and state law. To simplify my exposition, however, I shall cite only the relevant federal legislation, regulation, and court decisions on the assumption that for the most part the intermeshing state law conforms to and pretty much matches the federal.

Although I make no pretense of completeness in my analysis, I will mention a few of the associated elements that confer freedom or control concerning the claim to receive AFDC payments upon the eligible individual. 1) The legal power of any resident of a state to apply for Aid for Families with Dependent Children. Title IV of the Social Security Act requires that every state plan must provide some procedure whereby any individual residing in the state who wishes to do so can perform an action that constitutes applying for aid (42 USCS section 602 (a)(10)). This legal power of the eligible individual gives that individual control over the state's duty to provide aid, for the state *must* provide AFDC payments to *all* eligible individuals if, but only if, they have applied for it.

2) The legal claim of any resident of a state to an opportunity to apply for aid. Not only must there be some action that legally constitutes applying for aid; every resident must be put in a position where he or she can perform this act-in-the-law if she or he wishes to do so (42 USCS section 602 (a)(10)). This Hohfeldian element ensures the control of the eligible individual by imposing upon the state a duty, not only to refrain from making the exercise of the legal power to apply for aid difficult for the individual, but even to facilitate the exercise of this legal power.

3) The legal claim of the individual against the welfare agency that it permit assistance in applying. Federal regulations specify that each applicant may, if she or he so desires, be assisted by an individual of his or her own choice, who may but need not be a lawyer (45 CFR 206.10 (a)(1)). This associated element protects the control of the individual by ensuring, or helping to ensure, that any attempted exercise of the legal power of applying for AFDC will be legally efficācious.

4) The legal claim of each applicant to a prompt decision by the welfare agency. Except in unusual circumstances, the agency must make a decision on an application for AFDC aid within 45 days (45 CFR 206.10 (a)(3)(i)). Without this regulation, the agency could in effect deny aid to any individual simply by delaying action on her or his application indefinitely. Since this legal element deprives the welfare agency of this sort of control, it is one of the associated elements that confer overall control to the individual rather than the agency in any potential confrontation.

5) The legal power of the applicant to withdraw his or her application at any time (45 CFR 206.10 (a)(8)(i)). Thus, the possessor of the claim to AFDC payments is legally able to waive his or her claim to receive aid by notifying the welfare agency that such aid is no longer desired. Since the duty to provide aid is extinguished when the claim to aid is waived, this element confers control over the state's legal duty to provide aid to the eligible individual.

6) The legal claim of each recipient of AFDC that the state welfare agency not terminate or reduce the aid before a fair hearing if the individual requests one. In *Goldberg* v. *Kelly* (397 US 254) the Supreme Court decided that since the right to receive aid is a statutory entitlement of the most vital (literally) kind, no recipient may be deprived of welfare aid without due process of law, including a fair hearing *before* payments are terminated. Later cases have extended this principle to the reduction of welfare benefits. Since this Hohfeldian element denies to the welfare agency one sort of control over the enjoyment of the core claim to receive AFDC payments, it helps to tip the balance of control toward the individual in any confrontation between the individual recipient and the welfare agency.

7) The legal power of each recipient to challenge the validity of a

state plan on federal statutory grounds (*Rosado* v. *Wyman* 397 US 397) and on constitutional grounds as well (*Shapiro* v. *Thompson* 394 US 622-627). The legal standing of a recipient to seek and obtain judicial review is an important part of her or his legal control over the enjoyment of the core claim to receive AFDC payments, for it enables the individual to initiate enforcement of that legal claim against the welfare agency.

8) The legal immunity of the individual applicant or recipient from state statutes or regulations inconsistent with the Constitution or the Social Security Act. Such welfare legislation or regulation is often used to deprive classes of individuals of welfare payments by making them ineligible. But the individual is immune from such eligibility conditions when they will be declared "invalid" by a court on the grounds that they are inconsistent with the Constitution or federal statutes. (see *Shapiro* v. *Thompson* 394 US 642 and *King* v. *Smith* 392 US 333). By depriving the state of this sort of legal control over the core claim to receive aid, this associated element helps to allocate overall control to the individual vis-à-vis the state agency.

9) many bilateral liberties of the individual. Examples are the legal liberty of any resident of a state to apply or refrain from applying for AFDC aid, the legal liberty of any applicant to withdraw or refrain from withdrawing her or his application, and the legal liberty of any recipient notified of the impending termination or reduction of aid to request or refrain from requesting a hearing. It would be tedious to specify all the legal liberties involved in the complete right to receive AFDC payments. The important point is that it is such legal liberties, together with the various legal powers, claims, and immunities previously listed, that together confer autonomy, or freedom and control, concerning the enjoyment of the core claim upon the individual who possesses the legal right to receive aid. It should now be apparent that a primary welfare right can be an autonomy right. Hence, there is no incoherence in my conception of a welfare right and no need to supplement autonomy rights with welfare rights as Golding and the many who cite him imagine.

The Possessor of the Right to Aid

Precisely who is it that has this legal right to receive Aid to Families with Dependent Children payments? The three prime candidates are the parent, the child, and the family. The difficulties in deciding between these three candidates arise from two sources, legal ambiguity and conceptual confusion. The law itself, both as formulated in the relevant statutes and as declared in court decisions, seems to be ambivalent on this question. Some aspects of legal language and practice suggest one candidate, and other aspects another. This legal ambiguity can have very practical import. The case of *Dandridge* v. *Williams* concerned a Maryland regulation setting a maximum AFDC grant such that, after a certain family size, the amount of the AFDC payment did not increase with each additional child in the family. Assuming that each dependent child has a right to AFDC payments, the appellees argued that this regulation denied the welfare rights of the youngest children in large families. But the Supreme Court upheld the Maryland regulation on the grounds that the AFDC payment is a family grant and that no family is denied aid by this regulation (397 US 477). Identifying the possessor of the legal right to receive AFDC payments is also made difficult by unclarity in the very conception of what it is to have a right. Interest theories of rights tend to identify the possessor with the beneficiary or presumed beneficiary; will theories of rights usually identify the possessor with the claimant. It will be illuminating to resolve the legal ambiguities and then to provide a sound philosophical interpretation of the legal facts.

The first candidate for possessor of the right to receive AFDC payments under Title IV of the Social Security Act is the parent. Usually this parent is the mother of one or more dependent children, but sometimes it is the unemployed father and occasionally a parent-substitute, such as another relative, a foster parent, or a child care institution. Using the word "parent" in this broad sense, there are four pieces of evidence to show that it is the parent who possesses this legal right to aid. 1) Title IV of the Social Security Act of 1935 arose out of the mother's pension movement. The problem of caring for needy children had been recognized for years. The obvious solution was to put the child into a child care institution, either public or private, and care for it there. But this solution was criticized on two grounds: first, it costs more to care for a child in an institution than to supplement the income of the parent so that the child can remain in its own home, and second, taking the child out of its home deprives it of the emotional support and educational environment provided by its family, particularly its mother. Hence, many states enacted mother's pension laws that provided public assistance to mothers so that they could continue to care for their children deprived of the fathers' support. Congressional debates indicate that Title IV was enacted with the purpose of financing the continuation and extension of such aid by the states. 2) It would seem to be the parent who exercises the legal right to receive AFDC payments. Typically, it is the parent who applies for such aid or who chooses not to apply for it. Again, the parent can terminate such aid at any time by notifying the welfare agency that she or he no longer desires such aid. 3) It is the parent who enjoys the right to receive AFDC payments. The payee on an AFDC check is the parent, usually the mother. Thus it is the parent who actually receives the AFDC payment, and presumably the welfare agency provides the aid to the party with the legal right to receive it. 4) The parent has legal standing to take action in the courts against a state welfare agency that wrongly withholds or reduces Aid to Families with Dependent Children payments. For example, all of the appellees in *Shapiro* v. *Thompson* (394 US 622-626) were mothers who had been denied aid because they failed to satisfy a durational residency requirement. At first glance, it is the parent who has the legal right to receive AFDC payments.

On second glance, it appears to be the child who possesses this right. This conclusion can be supported with at least six kinds of legal evidence. 1) The original Title IV of the Social Security Act of 1935 was entitled and constantly referred to as "Aid to Dependent Children," and this label became the generally accepted name for the welfare program administered under this law. If the aid is *to* the dependent child, it would seem that it is the child who has the legal right to receive such aid. 2) The purpose of Title IV, as formulated in the original statute, was "to enable each state to furnish financial assistance . . . to needy dependent children." That the legislative intent was indeed to aid the child is substantiated by an examination of legislative debate and committee reports prior to the enactment of the Social Security Act of 1935. 3) One of the fundamental features of the Social Security Act of 1935 is that it provides a categorical welfare program. That is, public assistance under this act is not extended to the general public simply on the basis of need; certain categories of individuals are specified who alone are eligible for aid under the program. The category defined by Title IV seems clearly to be the dependent child, not the parent of such a child. The language throughout this title refers again and again to "the dependent child," or "the needy child," or even "the needy dependent child." 4) The right that concerns us here is the right to receive AFDC payments. Until 1950, this aid was defined as "payments with respect to a dependent child or dependent children." If the aid is defined in terms of the child, then one would assume that it is the child who has the right to such aid. 5) That it is the child rather than the parent who has the right to AFDC payments is indicated by the fact that welfare assistance may take the form of payments to some individual, agency, or institution other than the natural parent when a court decides that continuation in the home would be contrary to the welfare of the child. Although this could be interpreted as a change in the parent, as legally defined, with the aid being transferred from the old to the new parent, it seems more naturally to be explained as a continuation in a new way of payments to satisfy the continuing right of the child to receive AFDC assistance. 6) The evidence introduced in this paragraph has referred mostly to portions of Title IV that have since been amended in various ways. However, the language of several more recent decisions of the Supreme Court indicates that such amendments have not transferred the possession of the right to receive AFDC payments from the child to some other party. *King* v. *Smith* (392 US 313) affirms clearly that the category singled out for welfare assistance under Title IV is the "dependent child." In his dissent from *Dandridge* v. *Williams* (397 US 510), Justice Marshall supports this same conclusion with a quotation from a report of the Senate Committee on Finance asserting that the objective of Aid to Families with Dependent Children is "to provide cash assistance for needy children in *their own homes*." The clearest and most unambiguous assertion is by Justice Douglas in his dissent from the same case. "The aid provided through the AFDC program has always been intended for the individual dependent children, not for those who apply for the aid on their behalf" (397 US 494). There is substantial evidence, then, that it is the child who has the legal right to receive AFDC payments.

Recently, however, a third candidate for possessor of the legal right to receive AFDC payments has entered the picture, the family. 1) In 1970, the Supreme Court denied that AFDC programs that set a maximum grant for a single family irrespective of size deny the welfare rights of the youngest children in large families; rather such maximums diminish the financial assistance to the entire family. "In fact, it is the *family* grant that is affected" (*Dandridge* v. *Williams* 397 US 477-478, [court's italics]). The court supported its conclusion by noting that Title IV refers often to the family and makes it clear that it wishes to help children through the family structure. Although the court did not expressly assert that it is the family that possesses the right to aid under the AFDC program, its decision would at least support this inference and may have affirmed it implicitly. 2) There is considerable evidence that, whatever the original meaning of Title IV, today it is the family that has the right to aid. The title of the program has been changed from "Aid to Dependent Children" to "Aid to Families with Dependent Children." Presumably this indicates a change in legislative intent. 3) The amended purpose of the statute is in part to enable "each State to furnish financial assistance . . . to needy dependent children and the parents or relatives with whom they are living" (42 USCS section 601). 4) Accordingly, Aid for Families with Dependent Children is currently available, not only for "needy children," but also for "the parent or other caretaker relative of a dependent child and, in certain situations, the parent's spouse" (45 CFR 233.10 (b)(2)(ii)(b)). Since AFDC financial assistance is now provided for all or most members of the family containing a dependent child, this suggests that it is the entire family that has the right to receive AFDC payments.

The Supreme Court has spoken, but is has not spoken unequivocally, and it has not spoken with one voice. There is a logical ambiguity in the reasoning of the Supreme Court in the *Dandridge* decision. Is "the family" meant to be taken collectively or distributively? That is, does the expression "the family" in that decision refer to the family as a single unit or to the various and sundry members of the family individually? The logic of the majority reasoning seems to require that it is the family as a unit that has the right to receive aid. The reason given against holding that family maximums deny aid to the youngest children in a large family is that the grant is a family grant rather than a grant to the children individually. On the other hand, Justice Black *concurring* explicitly assumes, and takes the majority to be assuming, that individual welfare recipients can bring an action against state welfare authorities. Until the court clarifies its meaning, we must be wary of taking this decision as incontestible proof that it is the family that has the right to receive AFDC payments. Moreover, two justices dissented from the majority opinion, in large measure precisely on this point. Justice Douglas objected to the view that the family maximum merely reduces the family grant. His view is that although *in fact* some of the grant may be used to benefit other members of the family, it is given *by the State* only to the dependent children. "The aid provided through the AFDC program has always been intended for the individual independent children, not for those who apply for the aid on their behalf" (*Dandridge* v. *Williams* 397 US 494). The dissent of Justice Marshall also hinges on the premise that it is the dependent child who has the right to aid. He argues that family maximums violate Title IV because they deny aid to the youngest children in large families even though such children are eligible individuals under the provisions of the AFDC program and that they are inconsistent with the Equal Protection Clause because they provide less aid to a child in a large family than to a child in a small family (*Dandridge* v. *Williams* 397 US 509, 518).

Well, who does possess the legal right to receive AFDC payments? For the moment, I am not seeking any philosophically profound or theoretically illuminating answer, but only the answer that reflects present law on the matter. My guess, and I leave more firm opinions to practicing lawyers and presiding judges, is that it is the eligible individual members of families with needy dependent children. Since the Supreme Court has refrained from affirming any Constitutional right to welfare assistance, the legal right to receive AFDC payments remains a statutory right. The controlling language of Title IV currently requires that state programs shall provide "that all individuals wishing to make application for aid to families with dependent children shall have opportunity to do so, and that aid to families with dependent children shall be furnished with reasonable promptness to all eligible individuals" (42 USCS section 602 (a)(10)). Thus, it is individuals who possess the right to aid although their eligibility is defined in terms of their membership in a family with one or more needy dependent children. It is no longer possible to hold that the only family members who possess the right to aid are the dependent children themselves, for currently Aid to Families with Dependent Children is available also for "the parent or other caretaker relative of a dependent child and, in certain situations, the parent's spouse" (45 CFR 233.10 (b)(2)(ii)(b)). How, then, is one to read the *Dandridge* decision? Its legal meaning must be that each family with dependent children is entitled to receive a single AFDC payment, a *family* grant, sufficient to satisfy the legal rights to receive AFDC payments of all the eligible *individuals* in that family. That is, the amount of the payment may legally be calculated on a family basis without violating the welfare rights of the individual members of the family. This would seem to be the correct legal doctrine concerning the Aid to Families with Dependent Children program today.

But what philosophical interpretation are we to put upon this legal doctrine? Granted that a lawyer or judge may quite properly accept it at face value, what meaning are we to give to this legal doctrine in our theory of rights? A statement can be impeccable English and entirely true and still not wear its meaning on its sleeve. No one would think of taking "Jones is up to his ears in debts" literally, although it may be a grammatically correct and financially true description of Jones. Nearer to home, "A corporation is a person" is a true and profoundly important legal doctrine, but precisely what it means stands in need of elucidation. One might begin by suggesting that it means something like "Corporations have the same legal status as persons; that is, they possess legal rights and duties, can sue and be sued in the courts." But what does it really mean to say that a corporation takes legal action? Presumably that some person or persons acting as agents of the corporation perform certain actions that are taken in the law to constitute a legal action of the corporation. There is nothing very mysterious in all this, provided one does not imagine that corporations are literally persons and attempt to apply psychological principles of personality to them. On the other hand, only when one spells out in terms of legal realities what is involved in legal personality does one fully and clearly understand what it means to assert, truly and idiomatically, "A corporation is a person." I suggest that, on a deeper philosophical level, this statement about an artificial person should be interpreted to refer to natural persons acting as agents of or in their capacity as officers of the corporate organization.

Similarly, I suggest that the true statement "eligible individual members of families with dependent children possess the legal right to receive AFDC payments," although true enough as a description of the law, is misleading. Recall that the right to receive AFDC payments is a legal claim-right. Now the possessor of a legal claim is the party who possesses the power to take legal action to obtain performance or remedy in the event of threatened or actual nonperformance of the correlative legal duty. According to current United States law, it is the parent, usually the mother, who has the power to sue in the courts. Again, a legal right is a system of legal elements that confer autonomy, freedom and control, with respect to the exercise or enjoyment of the core upon some party. It is the parent, not other members of the family, who can apply for AFDC payments, waive the claim to such payments, and receive the payments him- or herself. Thus, looking at the legal realities in terms of my conception of a right shows that it is the parent who actually possesses the legal right to receive AFDC payments. It is the parent who possesses the core legal claim and upon whom the associated elements in the right confer freedom and control concerning the exercise and enjoyment of that legal claim.

I do not present my philosophical interpretation of the legal facts as showing that the legal doctrine—"the possessors of the legal right to receive AFDC payments are the eligible individual members of the families with dependent children"—is false. Quite to the contrary, this formulation seems best to fit the current legislation and court precedents. Rather, I am suggesting that this true legal doctrine, if taken at face value, is misleading and that it may be more revealingly interpreted in terms of my philosophical conception of a right to be saying that "the parent, *as* the parent in a family with dependent children, possesses the legal right to receive AFDC payments." This "as"-clause is crucial. Justice Douglas, dissenting from the majority decision in *Dandridge* v. *Williams,* wrote: "A further indication that the phrase 'all eligible individuals' as used in § 402(a) (10) refers to the individual beneficiaries of aid, and not to those who apply for and receive the payments, lies in the provisions of the Act that concern the computation of federal payments to the States" (397 US 499). The language of this sentence reminds us of the philosophical debate between those, like Bentham and MacCormick, who identify the possessor of a claim-right with the beneficiary, and others, like Hart and myself, who identify the possessor with the claimant. I do not intend to rehearse the complicated debate here. Let me merely observe that legal practitioners seem to identify the possessor of a legal claim with the party with the power to take legal action pursuant to that claim *and* that anyone who accepts my autonomy conception of a right will wish to identify the possessor of a right, not with the beneficiary of that right, but with the party upon whom the right confers autonomy. This is not at all to deny the importance of the observation made by Justice Douglas, but merely to reassess its precise import. He rightly observes that the legal right to receive AFDC payments is defined in terms of those individuals who are intended to benefit from Title IV of the Social Security Act. But this does not serve to identify the possessor of the legal right to receive AFDC payments; rather it serves to define the content of that right, to define the amount of the payment to which the parent has a legal right.

The main reason I have for insisting that it is the parent, and not the dependent child or other "eligible individual" in the family who possesses the legal right to receive AFDC payments, is that it is the parent, and not the child, who applies for such aid, receives the aid, and can sue in the event that the aid is denied. But legally speaking, the child does apply for and receive AFDC payments and can take legal action when such aid is denied. Notice the language of Justice Douglas once more: "The aid provided through the AFDC program has always been intended for the individual dependent children, not for those who apply for the aid on their behalf" (*Dandridge* v. *Williams* 397 US 494). That is, the parent's act of exercising and enjoying the legal right to receive AFDC payments is taken legally to be the act of the dependent child or of all of the eligible individuals in the family with dependent children. No doubt, it is correct legal doctrine to hold that the parent acts "on behalf of" the child. But precisely what does this mean? How shall we interpret this entirely true but somewhat enigmatic legal doctrine? Notice the ambiguity in the expression "on behalf of." One person can act on behalf of another either when the former acts in the interests of or when the former acts in place of the latter. I suggest the former sense is relevant here. Recall that Justice Douglas emphasized that the AFDC aid has "always been intended for the individual dependent children, "which surely suggests that they are the intended beneficiaries of that aid. But to say this is not to say that the legal acts of the parent constitute acts of the child. The law does not confer upon the child, who is legally a minor, the legal power to apply for AFDC payments, to receive such payments, or to take legal action to obtain them in its own name. Therefore, the child and the parent cannot stand in the same legal relation of principal and agent that I and my broker can assume when I authorize him or her to buy or sell stocks in my name. It is a legal fiction to say that the parent acts as agent of the other eligible individual members of the family, just as it is a legal fiction to say that a corporation takes legal action in the courts. The parent could not be literally said to act as agent of the child unless the child were legally capable of taking such action on its own behalf.

Why do I insist that perfectly correct legal doctrines should be interpreted philosophically as legal fictions? Two reasons. One is that the language of the legal doctrines obscures the legal realities. To be sure, practicing lawyers are seldom misled, for they are familiar with the relevant statutes, regulations, court decisions, and their bearing on concrete legal processes. Still, they are sometimes misled. Given the disagreement among the Justices of the Supreme Court as to who in fact possesses the legal right to receive AFDC payments, some of them must have been misinterpreting the law. And for politicians, philosophers, and citizens, the legal meaning of these doctrines is much more problematic because we usually lack the legal training to interpret them in terms of their import for actual cases. Therefore, it is more illuminating to consider the legal doctrine a fiction and to translate it into a formulation that is closer to the legal realities. Another reason for insisting upon a philosophical interpretation of such legal truths is to put the concept of a legal right in clearer focus. The function of a legal right is to confer a system of autonomy on one party vis-à-vis one or more second parties in some actual or possible confrontation. Now if this is the point of a right, the language of rights is more clear and more intelligible when interpreted in such a way that the possessor of a right is the possessor of the autonomy at issue. Just because the concept of a right is legally and morally so important, it is important to interpret the language of rights in a way that captures what is distinctive and significant about rights. To do this, a philosophical interpretation of some legal doctrine may be necessary. This is why I insist that, although legally speaking the possessor of the legal right to receive AFDC payments is the eligible individual(s) in the family, philosophically and more precisely speaking, it is the parent who possesses this legal right.

The Right to a Fair Welfare Hearing

My second example of a legal welfare right is the right to a fair welfare hearing—a right that has been much discussed in the recent literature and often central to much recent litigation. Since this is not a right to any welfare benefit, it is not a primary welfare right. In fact, it is a species of the generic right of due process. But since it concerns due process in the handling of claims to welfare benefits, it is a secondary welfare right.

As a first approximation, one can say that the core of this right is the legal claim of a welfare claimant against the welfare agency of his or her state to be provided with an opportunity for a hearing. Clearly, this secondary welfare right is a legal claim-right. But the core of this right stands in need of considerable elucidation. The possessor of this core claim is a welfare claimant. As defined by the Social Security Act and the relevant parts of the Code of Federal Regulations, this includes two distinct classes of individuals. First, there is "any applicant who requests a hearing because his or her claim for financial assistance . . . or medical assistance is denied, or is not acted upon with reasonable promptness"; second, there is "any recipient who is aggrieved by any agency action resulting in suspension, reduction, discontinuance, or termination of assistance" (45 CFR Part 205.10(a)(5)). Strictly speaking, therefore, the core of this welfare right is complex, consisting of two very similar legal claims. One is the claim of an aggrieved applicant for welfare benefits; the other is the claim of an aggrieved recipient of welfare benefits. These are distinct legal claims because the possessors are defined in different terms and their standing to take legal action pursuant to their respective claims depend upon different conditions. But since both are claims to an opportunity to a fair hearing and the rest of the relevant law is virtually identical, they are usually lumped together as a single legal claim of an aggrieved welfare claimant.

The second party against whom this legal claim, or pair of core claims, holds is the state welfare agency. The legal duty it imposes upon the welfare agency is not necessarily to provide a hearing to each aggrieved applicant or recipient, but to provide an opportunity for such a hearing. If the welfare claimant does not request a hearing, then no action is required of the agency. But if the claimant does request a hearing and does not withdraw her or his request, then the agency is legally required to arrange for a hearing, and if the claimant or her or his representative appears at the appointed time and place, then the agency is legally bound to proceed with the hearing. This hearing may be before the state agency or may be an evidentiary hearing at the local level with a right of appeal to a state agency hearing (45 CFR part 205.10 (a)(1)).

As I have defined the right to a welfare hearing, its core is a legal claim possessed by certain classes of applicants for or recipients of welfare benefits under the cooperative federal-state Social Security Program. Accordingly, the state welfare agencies are legally bound to provide an opportunity for a hearing concerning some Social Security benefit only as long as the state continues to participate in the program and to receive federal funding. Thus, the core claims in the legal right to a welfare hearing, *as I have defined it*, are conditional upon continued state participation. It is possible, of course, that some welfare claimant might have a right to a fair hearing that is not so conditioned. This remains unclear for two reasons. First, one can only speculate about the form that welfare benefits would take were a state to opt out of the Social Security System and attempt to provide anything like comparable coverage without federal funding. Second, the courts have been divided on the precise place of a legal right to a hearing in the general assistance programs of the several states. This is one reason why I have defined the right to a welfare hearing narrowly enough so that a relatively noncontroversial characterization of its content is possible.

To allege that my characterization of the core of the legal right to a fair welfare hearing is noncontroversial is not at all to imply or suggest that it is either complete or precise. Federal regulations and court decisions have distinguished in complex ways between situations in which this right exists and circumstances where there is no such right. Suppose, for example, that I were to apply for Aid to Families with Dependent Children, truly reporting the ages of my children and my annual salary on my application. No doubt my application would be summarily denied because I am ineligible for

AFDC payments on the face of it. Since the facts in my case are not in question, I supplied them myself, I would have no legal claim to be provided with an opportunity for a hearing no matter how aggrieved I might feel. Again, if some AFDC recipient's monthly check is discontinued due to state legislation modifying the conditions of eligibility or the level of need to be met, rather than any change in the recipient's situation, then the recipient would not have a right to a hearing regarding such a termination of welfare benefits. I shall leave such legal details to welfare lawyers. Important as they are for the practical purposes of needy welfare claimants, those of us interested in the nature of welfare rights can simply note the presence of such qualifications and then pass on to matters more central to the philosophical understanding of welfare rights.

Among these theoretically illuminating matters will be a specification of the more important Hohfeldian elements associated with this core claim to a fair welfare hearing to fill out the system of autonomy that constitutes the full right.

1) The legal power of the claimant to request a hearing (45 CFR part 205.10 (a) (5)(1)). The duty of the welfare agency is to provide an opportunity for an aggrieved welfare applicant or recipient; only if the claimant requests a welfare hearing does it have any legal duty to actually arrange for and carry out a hearing. Thus, the legal power of the claimant to request a hearing changes the legal duty of the welfare agency and confers upon the claimant an important measure of control over the enjoyment of her or his core claim to a hearing.

2) The legal claim of the claimant against the welfare agency and others not to limit or interfere in any way with the freedom to request a hearing (45 CFR part 205.10(a)(5)(ii)). This Hohfeldian element protects the control conferred by the legal power to request a hearing by ensuring, or seeking to ensure, that the welfare claimant's freedom of exercizing that control is not taken away by those who might prefer that he or she have no hearing.

3) The legal power of the welfare claimant to withdraw her or his request for a hearing (45 CFR part 205.10(a)(5)(v)). If the welfare claimant should withdraw her or his request for a hearing, then the legal duty of the welfare agency actually to provide such a hearing is extinguished. Here, then, is one more Hohfeldian element that confers control upon the possessor of the core claim to a hearing.

4) The welfare claimant's legal power to sue for judicial review of an adverse hearing decision that apparently denies him or her due process. The secondary claim-right to a hearing is a right to a *fair* hearing to decide whether some primary welfare right of the claimant has been infringed. To allow the welfare agency to satisfy this claim-right in a biased or merely *pro forma* way would be, in effect, to nullify the claimant's core claim to a hearing. Thus, the claimant's legal standing to take legal action in the courts to obtain judicial review of

the decision of the welfare hearing provided by the agency is an important measure of control over the genuine satisfaction of her or his core claim. The claimant's standing is established primarily by those portions of the United States Code that govern civil action for deprivation of rights (42 USCS section 1983) and civil rights and elective franchise (28 USCS section 1343).

5) Associated with the core claim to a welfare hearing are several bilateral liberties of exercising or not exercising the legal powers listed as associated elements (1), (3), and (4) above. Together, these confer upon the welfare claimant the freedom to choose whether or not to take advantage of the opportunity for a hearing to which he or she has a right and the freedom to do what is needed to obtain a hearing, if desired.

6) The legal immunity of the claimant from any decision of a welfare hearing that fails to meet the due process standards set forth in *Goldberg* v. *Kelly* (397 US 267-271). Although these standards are less stringent than those required in criminal cases, they still ensure the fairness of the welfare hearing to a considerable degree. They include timely and adequate notice of action taken that affects the claimant together with reasons for that action, an effective opportunity to confront any adverse witnesses, and presentation of his own arguments and evidence orally—an opportunity to appear personally, with or without counsel, before the welfare agency hearing body. Any adverse decision of a welfare hearing that fails to meet these and other standards of due process can be declared null and void by the courts. Thus, the welfare claimant is legally immune from any such purported adverse decision.

7) The legal immunity of the welfare claimant from having his or her core claim to an opportunity for a welfare hearing extinguished by state action, either statute or regulation, or by federal legislation or regulation. The former immunity is established by federal statute (42 USCS section 602(a) (4)) and the latter by the decision in the *Goldberg* case (397 US 254). Should the state or the federal government attempt to deprive the individual claimant of her or his core claim to a fair hearing, the attempt would be declared legally null and void by the federal courts. Thus, the claimant is immune from any action that would purport to have that legal effect. These legal immunities of the welfare claimant, by limiting the legal powers of those who might be second parties in any confrontation over welfare benefits, contribute to the balance of control in the hands of the possessor of the legal right to a welfare hearing vis-à-vis potential second parties. No doubt knowledgeable welfare lawyers could add to my list. But I have gone far enough to show how it is that the law confers upon the possessor of the legal claim to a hearing various forms of freedom and control concerning that core claim.

In sum, the secondary welfare right to a hearing has the structure typical of legal rights, that of a system of legal autonomy. At its core stand a pair of legal claims: 1) the claim of any welfare applicant for financial assistance or medical assistance under the Social Security Program whose application has been denied or not acted upon with reasonable promptness against the welfare agency that it provide an opportunity for a fair hearing provided it remains in the federally funded program; *and* 2) the claim of any recipient of welfare benefits under the Social Security Program whose benefits have been suspended, reduced, discontinued or terminated against the welfare agency that it provide an opportunity for a fair hearing provided it remains in the federally funded program. Clustered around this core claim are the legal powers of the claimant to request a hearing, withdraw a request for a hearing, and sue for judicial review of an adverse decision, the bilateral legal liberties of exercising or not exercising these associated powers, and the immunities from an unfair hearing and from any state or federal attempt to extinguish the core claim. Together this sytem of Hohfeldian legal elements confers autonomy concerning the enjoyment of this opportunity for a welfare hearing upon the possessor of this secondary welfare right.

Conclusions

I have described two examples of legal welfare rights: the right to receive AFDC payments and the right to a fair welfare hearing. What interesting conclusions, if any, can we draw from this very limited sample? First, legal welfare rights can accurately be conceived of as systems of legal autonomy. This is of some theoretical importance, for it demonstrates that my general conception of a right as a system of normative elements that confer autonomy concerning some core upon its possessor can be applied to the sphere of welfare rights. It also shows that there is no need to distinguish, as Martin Golding and many others do, between two fundamentally different kinds of rights—option or autonomy rights and welfare rights.

But this first conclusion is more than theoretically illuminating. It is also of considerable practical import. It shows that there is an essential connection between the possession of welfare rights and the autonomy, freedom and control, of the possessor. This helps to explain why those deeply concerned for the personal well-being of welfare claimants have fought so hard legally and politically to have welfare regarded as a right rather than as mere charity. Welfare claimants are almost always highly dependent persons and persons whose deprivations make them targets for the neglect and discrimination of others. Their condition has unfortunate, even frightening, implications for their self-respect, the quality of their lives, and hope for their futures. If welfare rights really are spheres of autonomy, then they speak directly to the predicament of those who need welfare and at the very least reduce their dependency, passiveness, and vulnerability.

A second conclusion we can draw is that legal welfare rights are very complex and specific. Although this is hardly news to any practicing welfare lawyer, it is usually not recognized by the general public or sufficiently appreciated by the social philosopher. The standard labels we use to name welfare rights and the short descriptions we generally give to their content fall far short of indicating the number and variety of Hohfeldian elements that go into making up such a right and the complications involved in specifying any one of these elements in a way that precisely fits the relevant provisions of the law. Even though my characterizations are admittedly incomplete and rough, they do hint at the complex structure and specific detail of any legal welfare right. In order to know what any legal welfare right actually contains and how it operates in legal practice, it is most helpful to spell it out in terms of Hohfeldian legal elements. Only thus can confusions and misunderstandings be avoided.

One conclusion should *not* be drawn from my limited sample. Both the legal right to receive AFDC payments and the legal right to a welfare hearing are claim-rights. That is, the core of both rights and the element that determines the legal modality of the right as a whole is a legal claim. It would be a mistake to infer, however, that all welfare rights are claim-rights. By definition, all primary welfare rights are claim rights, for a primary welfare right is a right to a welfare benefit. But some important secondary welfare rights do not belong in this category. Thus, the recipient of Aid to Families with Dependent Children has a liberty-right to spend his or her welfare payment as she or he sees fit. Any welfare claimant has, under specified conditions, a power-right to judicial review of adverse welfare agency action. This is a power-right, rather than a claim-right because its core consists of the legal power to sue in the federal courts in the event of such adverse welfare agency action. Again, any welfare applicant or recipient has a legal immunity-right not to be rendered ineligible for welfare benefits by any state eligibility requirements inconsistent with the Constitution. The state lacks the legal power to render the individual ineligible in this way because any state legislation or regulation attempting to accomplish this legal result would be declared null and void by the federal courts. Thus, not all legal welfare rights are claim-rights. All, however, are systems of legal autonomy, whatever their cores may be. It is this that constitutes their nature as rights.

3

Justifying Legal Rights

What rights there actually are in any given legal system is something to be determined by the lawyer, judge, or jurist. But what rights ought to exist in a legal system is a matter upon which the legal and moral philosopher might well have something to say. The sense of the word "ought" I have in mind is the broad practical "ought" rather than the more limited specifically moral "ought," for the most important question is surely whether, everything considered, some legal right ought or ought not to exist. To this question, every practically relevant consideration is pertinent, although presumably moral reasons will be included and will carry special force. To say that a specified legal right ought to exist in a given system is to say that those in a position to determine the rights in that system ought to create the right if it is not in force or to do what is necessary to keep it in force if it is. Thus, justifications or counterjustifications of a legal right are of importance, not only to the moral observer and critic of the given legal system, but even more to legislators, politicians, and citizens in the society in which the legal system is in force.

A legal right is a complex structure of Hohfeldian elements. Accordingly, any complete justification of a legal right would be very complicated indeed. It would have to contain arguments and present evidence to show that each and every legal liberty, claim, power and immunity included in the right ought to be in force in the given legal system. To formulate a complete justification of a sample legal right, such as the legal right to receive AFDC payments, would be a formidable undertaking; to formulate a range of such jusifications and to assess them critically would be a project far too lengthy to include in this book. In fact, complete justifications are seldom if ever given, unless one is willing to consider the entire legislative history of a legal right as such a justification. One reason this so seldom happens is that a statute enacting a new legal right seldom spells out the contents of that right in terms of Hohfeldian elements. Another is that legal rights have a way of growing gradually by amendment and judicial decision. One would have to examine the original legislative debates plus legislative discussion, both in committee and on the floor, of subsequent amendments together with a growing common law tradition of interpretation to find anything like a complete justification of the legal right.

Although a practicing lawyer is most likely aware of the complexity of a legal right, others tend to identify a right with its core. This is why what one finds most often in the literature is not a complete justification of the right but a core justification. A core justification is an argument to show that the core of a right, as, for example, the legal claim to receive AFDC payments from the state welfare agency, ought to exist in a given legal system. A core justification is all very well as far as it goes. If the argument is sound, then it does indeed justify the existence of the core of the legal right. But a right is more than its core. Not until one adds associated legal elements that confer freedom and control concerning that core does one have a genuine system of autonomy. Since a core justification ignores the autonomy that is distinctive of and essential to any right, it is not the proper subject of a chapter in a book on welfare rights.

What will repay our attention is a partial justification of a legal right. I use the expression "a partial justification" in a way precisely analogous to that in which Hempel speaks of a partial explanation. A partial justification is incomplete, of course, but it is incomplete in a very special way. It consists of reasoning to show that the core of the legal right ought to exist in the legal system together with arguments to show that the possessor of that core ought also to have some unspecified sort of autonomy concerning the exercise or enjoyment of that core. Thus, a partial justification of a legal right, although it does not show that precisely this right in all its particularity ought to exist, does show that some such legal right ought to exist. It is a partial justification because it does justify the conclusion that a right of its kind ought to exist, but it does not establish any conclusion as to which species of this genus is justified.

For the sake of concreteness and ready applicability, I shall focus my discussion upon the justification of a sample primary welfare right, the legal right to receive AFDC payments. The purpose of this chapter is not to justify the existence of this right in the legal system of the United States today, or even to show that some such right is actually justified, but to consider how in principle such a right might be justified. Several plausible arguments will be articulated and then critically examined. The goal will be to decide what kinds of arguments might be advanced as a justification or counterjustification and to determine, if possible, which kind is most compelling.

Utility

One sort of a justification of a legal right would appeal to the utility of that right, that is to the utility of the legislation creating and defining the right and the administrative acts sustaining that act in the legal system. Since the core of the legal right to receive AFDC payments is a legal claim, and a legal claim consists of a legal duty together with a legal power, a partial utilitarian justification of this right would include establishing the utility of the legal duty of the state welfare agency to pay Aid to Families with Dependent Children to eligible individuals together with the utility of the legal power of AFDC claimants to sue for performance or compensation in the event of threatened or actual nonperformance of that duty. But a legal right is more than its core; it is a system of autonomy. Accordingly, a partial justification of the right to receive AFDC payments must also include establishing the utility of the autonomy of the eligible individual concerning her or his legal claim to receive AFDC payments. If one could demonstrate the utility of all three—the legal duty, the legal power, and the autonomy—one would provide a very plausible partial justification of this legal welfare right. Let us examine each of these in turn.

First, one must establish the utility of the legal duty of the state welfare agency to pay Aid to Families with Dependent Children to eligible individuals. This amounts to showing that it would be more useful to have a law imposing such a duty in the given legal system than not having such a law in the system. But how does one estimate the utility of a duty-imposing law? Presumably the main point of having such a law is to cause those upon whom it imposes a legal duty to perform acts of the sort required by the law. Hence, most of the utility of having a legal duty lies in the utility of performances of that duty. In estimating this utility one must estimate the degree of compliance with the law as well as the utility of acts that do comply. Moreover, one cannot consider the utility of any such acts that would be performed in the absence of the legislation, if any, as part of the utility of the law itself. The utility of a duty-imposing law does not, however, reduce to the utility of the performances it brings into existence, for having a law in the legal system may have other consequences as well. Quite apart from any resulting acts of paying AFDC to eligible individuals, having such a duty-imposing law on the books might serve to project an image of concern for the needy and social justice that would reduce the alienation of the disadvantaged from society or serve as the formulation of a social goal to stimulate and guide political action in the direction of a more effective and beneficial welfare program. One must also consider the resulting cost of attempting to enforce the legal duty, unless one is prepared to leave compliance to the free choice of the duty-bearers.

Acts of paying Aid to Families with Dependent Children are obviously directly useful to the recipients of this welfare benefit. Eligible individuals almost always lack any alternative income adequate to meet their basic human needs. Being needy, they will use most of the aid paid to them by the welfare agency to provide food, shelter, clothes, and other necessities for themselves and their families. No elaborate argument is needed to show that it is much much better for these individuals to have nourishing food rather than nothing or very little to eat, decent housing rather than unheated and unsanitary shelter, if any, etc. The primary utilitarian case for making it a duty to pay AFDC is the tremendous good achieved for the recipients by the payments of the welfare agency. They may receive more subtle and less obvious benefits from these payments also. Their feelings of hopelessness and personal inferiority may be reduced and they may become better adjusted to our society and more prepared psychologically to cope with the challenges and opportunities it presents to them.

In addition to the direct benefits for the individual recipients, a program of acts paying AFDC probably indirectly benefits our society as a whole by helping to solve some of our most serious social problems.

a) Giving aid to dependent children will help solve the problem of underconsumption. Our society is prone to economic stagnation, recession, and even depression because the goods and services we produce are not purchased in sufficient quantities. Although dependent children desperately need many of these goods and services, their need cannot be translated into economic demand unless they have some source of income. Financial aid to dependent children is an efficient way of putting purchasing power where it will be used to stimulate our economy, maintain production, and reduce unemployment.

b) Undereducation is a problem of rapidly growing concern. It results in the personal misery of many who are unemployable, or employable at only the most rudimentary of jobs, and leaves these persons unfit to become responsible citizens or even self-supporting workers in our increasingly complex technological society. Without shoes or warm clothing, hungry and often ill, the unaided dependent child is unable to attend school regularly or, if attending, to learn what he or she will need to know as an adult. Aid to dependent children helps to solve this very real social problem.

c) Ill health is a serious problem in any society, for it causes personal suffering and impairs useful activity. In our society, the growing burden of providing medical care is felt by all. It is not just that those in need cannot afford the medical care they now require; they frequently suffer from malnutrition, unsanitary housing, and other conditions that lead to serious and often almost incurable medical problems in the future. Aid to Families with Dependent Children contributes to the reduction of illness in our society by eliminating many of its most potent sources. In the long run, it will enable us to allocate scarce resources away from medical care and into more productive, although not necessarily more urgent, uses.

d) Social alienation and maladjustment, ranging anywhere from mere passivity in all political processes to violent antisocial actions, is another problem of our society. Without aid, the dependent child has no real opportunity to function well in our society and is very likely to grow up a psychological alien in our land. Financial aid can be a means of transforming the home life of the child, so that he or she develops a more positive attitude and becomes capable of taking an active and useful part in society. In these ways and others, many acts of paying AFDC can be highly useful to society as a whole.

The direct benefits for the individual recipients and their families and the indirect benefits for society as a whole constitute the beginning of a utilitarian justification of the legal duty of the state welfare agency to make AFDC payments, but only a beginning. The state agency can perform its legal duty only if it has available funds to pay out to eligible individuals. Thus, one condition of any performance of this legal duty will be state acts of taxation to raise the required funds. Since these deprive the taxpayer of considerable portions of his income, they are presumably in and of themselves harmful. One might even imagine that the hardships imposed upon the taxpayers would just about balance out the benefits to the recipients of the total taxation-plus-welfare program. Fortunately, this is not so, for reasons explained by the theory of marginal utility. Those required to pay the taxes are relatively affluent, at least compared to the genuinely needy. They can spare the income taken from them without genuine hardship, although it would be naive to suggest that they do not suffer in any serious way. Since their basic needs are met by their remaining income, they would have spent the taxed amount on luxuries that would have contributed less to their welfare than will the necessities purchased with the same sums by the recipients of welfare, who will spend their aid on necessities for the most part. Thus, there is a utilitarian argument grounded in sound economic theory for the redistribution of income from those who pay the income taxes to those who receive these monies in the form of welfare benefits.

To be sure, eligible individuals do not receive all the money collected in taxation to finance the welfare program. It requires a very large and expensive government bureaucracy to levy and collect taxes and to administer a welfare program. Even assuming the existence of a revenue service that is capable of carrying the added load of increased taxation, financing a welfare agency capable of making AFDC payments is a major undertaking. Publicity must circulate, offices must be open, applications must be processed, payments must be made, appeals must be heard, etc. Obviously, all of this is very costly, and these costs must be taken into account when estimating the overall utility of the welfare program. At the same time, one cannot simply consider all monies spent on maintaining the welfare agency as a disutility. For the welfare workers will presumably be paid, and their incomes will be directly beneficial to them and indirectly beneficial to those from whom they purchase goods and services and even to society as a whole in various indirect ways. Still, some portion of the cost of operating the welfare agency must be counted as lost from more productive uses and hence its spending as a disutility of the welfare program.

So far we have been considering mainly the utilities and disutilities of the acts of performing the duty of the welfare agency to pay AFDC to eligible individuals. About all that we have shown clearly is that these acts, individually and collectively, have a variety of consequences and conditions and that any overall assessment of their utility is a highly complicated matter. But the existence of a legal duty will have additional consequences, some of which have been mentioned already, that might affect its utility. Let us glance at a few of these. A legal duty may increase or decrease respect for the law in the community, depending upon whether it is regarded as morally imperative and admirable or either morally objectionable or just plain silly. Again, by projecting the image of concern for human suffering and for social justice, the duty to make AFDC payments would probably reduce the alienation of the deprived segments of the society, even among individuals who are not themselves eligible for such payments. The existence of a legal duty will also tend to change expectations and thus modify human behavior in many ways. If the law merely gives to the welfare agency the legal liberty of providing benefits, many eligible individuals may not even bother to apply or to press their applications because they believe that the welfare officials will probably use their discretion to refuse them the benefits they need. But if the law imposes a legal duty upon the welfare agency, needy persons may be more likely to apply for AFDC payments. Since these payments would be used by the recipients for necessities that contribute in important ways to their welfare, it is highly useful to increase the proportion of eligible individuals who take the initiative to apply for AFDC payments. Against the utilities of having the legal duty to provide AFDC payments, one might weigh the cost of enforcing that duty. Still, it should be easier to enforce this duty than many other legal duties, especially the duties imposed by criminal law, for the officials of the welfare agency are presumably more law-abiding than most potential criminals are.

The utilitarian justification of the legal duty to provide AFDC payments is made even more complex and difficult because it must be comparative in nature. It is not enough to show that it would be useful, even highly useful, to have such a duty in the legal system of the given society. One must show that it would be more useful to have such a legal duty than not to have it. For one thing, one must demonstrate that it would be more useful for the state to use its limited resources to make AFDC payments than for any alternative use to which the same amount of money could be put. Given the number of alternative uses and the difficulty of accurately assessing the utility of each, this will be no easy task. Recall also that one use would be to leave the money untaxed in the hands of those from whom it was taken by taxation to be spent by them in whatever ways they individually deem most useful. Even if it is granted that needy dependent children should receive aid, one must show that it would be more useful to impose the duty to provide aid upon the state welfare agencies than upon any alternative party, such as private welfare or charitable organizations or the relatives of each needy individual. This part of the argument is easier to make, for it is highly likely that only the state has the resources to carry out such an ambitious program effectively.

But is it really desirable to have such an ambitious welfare program as Aid to Families with Dependent Children? There are many who would challenge the utilitarian justification put forth in the previous pages. They would contend that it ignores a host of disutilities— disutilities so great as to imply that the duty to provide AFDC payments is positively harmful. They offer what might be called a utilitarian counterjustification of this legal right. Let us remind ourselves of the disutilities they allege.

1) A welfare program, especially one that requires welfare officials to provide benefits whether or not they think them advisable, is counterproductive because it increases the dependency of its recipients. Many AFDC mothers become so economically dependent upon their welfare checks that they cannot, or believe they cannot afford to go back to work. Since the jobs for which they can compete are often low-paying, they are financially better off by remaining indefinitely on welfare. More insidiously, they become psychologically dependent upon welfare in something like the way one might become addicted to a mild drug. More and more they think of themselves as unable to care for their own needs, and any attempt to become self-sufficient is apt to bring on the "withdrawal syndrome" of great anxiety and disrupted activity. Clearly this dependency is very harmful to the recipients of AFDC payments.

2) Any adequate or nearly adequate AFDC payments will reduce the industry in the population. Obviously the recipient of welfare will be less motivated to get a job and engage in productive labor than he or she would be if driven by hunger or lack of shelter. More indirectly, those whose incomes are heavily taxed in order to finance the welfare program will have less incentive to increase production or

take on the added burdens of more responsible positions in the economy. Thus, the human resources of the society will be underutilized and the production of goods and services will be reduced. The welfare of the society will be accordingly lowered.

3) Welfare programs inevitably lead to serious inflation in the long run. The central purpose of making AFDC payments is to put buying power into the hands of those who do not have sufficient income because they are not economically productive members of society. This infusion of money into the economy, unbalanced by any comparable production of goods and services, necessarily boosts the economic demand with no balancing boost in the supply of available goods and services. The resulting inflation hurts everyone. It harms those who are productive members of society by reducing the satisfactions they can obtain with their hard-earned incomes. At the same time, it compounds the economic hardships of the needy by making the fulfillments of their basic needs more costly.

4) Welfare programs greatly reduce the savings available for capital investment. Since a welfare program like Aid to Families with Dependent Children is very expensive indeed, it can be financed only by progressive taxation in a society like ours. Heavy taxation of those in the upper-income brackets greatly reduces, if it does not destroy, the large fortunes of individual savers. But these large amounts of savings are economically necessary to encourage innovation and to finance any large new private enterprise. When large personal savings are lacking, economic control and the direction of our economy remain in the hands of established industries that are excessively conservative, unwilling to take risks, and too protective of their own capital investments to experiment with radically new products or methods of production. Thus, private enterprise loses its progressive force and tends to stagnate.

5) Public welfare programs undermine private charity, both that of individuals and that of private organizations. An AFDC program, for example, tends to displace the efforts of relatives of dependent children to care for their needs. An extreme example of this is the way in which fathers have sometimes abandoned their families in order to ensure their eligibility for AFDC. Other relatives may simply do nothing to help a mother with several dependent children on the grounds that their sacrifices are made unnecessary by the legal duty to pay AFDC to all eligible individuals. Traditionally, the needs of those individuals unable to provide for their own needs were set by the church or some other organization supported by private donations. As public welfare agencies gradually take on this function, private charity withers away. One might imagine that this would be beneficial, that a single public welfare agency would be more efficient than a complex of overlapping private welfare organizations. Many traditional economists argue, however, that this is not the case. The

single public welfare agency suffers from all the inefficiencies of any monopoly. It lacks the flexibility of the smaller organizations that can meet the needs of individuals much more effectively because they are more aware of local conditions and individual situations. Again, a single uniform welfare program does not allow the room for innovation and the experimentation with a variety of forms of welfare that contribute to more effective and economical welfare programs. And lacking the competition between a number of suppliers of welfare, each of which needs the support of the available donors, there is no incentive for welfare monopoly to remain efficient, much less increase efficiency.

6) Any large public welfare program creates an uncontrollable bureaucracy. Both from self-interest and from idealistic motives, this bureaucracy has a drive to expand—a drive not matched by any effective external control. No supervisory organization can be really effective because there is no objective standard of the needs of the recipients of welfare and because the complexity of a large welfare program is so great that only insiders really understand what is going on in the welfare agency. The result is an overextended welfare program that expends funds unnecessarily to meet imagined, or at least insignificant needs and that fails to allocate welfare benefits where they are most needed. The kinds of arguments I have been outlining here are frequently offered by those who believe in our traditional free enterprise system, but even those who reject more traditional capitalism may recognize a good deal of truth in them.

I do not propose to make any estimate, however tentative, of the overall utility of the duty of state welfare agencies to pay AFDC to all eligible individuals. I lack the knowledge of welfare economics, the grasp of human psychology, and the detailed information to do so. My purpose has been a very different one: to reveal the form that any adequate utilitarian justification or counterjustification of such a legal duty must take. It would center on the utilities and disutilities, both direct and indirect, for the individual recipients and for a society as a whole of anticipated acts of performing this duty. But it would also consider the conditions necessary for such performances of duty, such as taxation and the maintenance of the welfare agency that is to bear the duty. It would have to consider other consequences of having such a legal duty, such as the expectations it would engender and the costs of enforcement. And ultimately, the assessments of utility must be comparative so that the justification could show that having this legal duty would be more useful than not having it or than having some other legal duty in its place. Clearly, this is an exceedingly complicated and formidable undertaking.

It is also only one portion of even a partial justification of the legal right to receive AFDC payments. Since the right in question is a claim-right, its core consists of a legal duty of the welfare agency to the individual eligible for AFDC together with a legal power of the eligible individual to take legal action in the courts in the event of threatened or actual nonperformance of this duty. Accordingly, a second task of any utilitarian justification of this legal right will be to establish the utility of this legal power.

If it really is highly useful for the state agency to make AFDC payments to eligible individuals, for the reasons mentioned previously, then presumably it will also be useful to enforce performance of this legal duty, provided this can be done effectively and inexpensively. Suing in the courts is probably an effective method of enforcement because each eligible individual will know of any nonperformance of the welfare agency's legal duty to her or him and will be strongly motivated to remedy it. This method is also inexpensive because it does not require the creation of any large and expensive enforcement agency and each decided case will serve as a precedent for similar cases so that each will generate a generalized performance of the duty. Of course this entire argument is premised on the utility of the acts of paying AFDC to eligible individuals. If this utility is not granted, the argument collapses.

The logic of this argument is similar to the argument for the utility of a legal duty. Primarily, the utility of having a legal power in the system is derived from the utility of acts of exercising that power. But having the legal power of the eligible individual to sue for payment of AFDC benefits may have utilities in addition to this. Even when not exercised, the legal power imposes upon the welfare agency a liability to be sued for nonperformance of duty. This alone may be sufficient to encourage a high degree of compliance with the law imposing that duty. Again, knowing that they possess this legal power to take legal action, claimants might press their claims more strenuously before resorting to the courts and so render a great deal of expensive legal enforcement unnecessary.

In the end, any utilitarian justification of a legal power must show that it is more useful to enforce the law in this way than in some other way or in no way whatsoever. One could simply require state welfare agencies to make AFDC payments to all eligible individuals but provide for no enforcement machinery at all. This might in principle be sufficient, for the individuals who administer the welfare agency might well have sufficient concern for the welfare of their clients and sufficient respect for the law to perform their legal duty without the threat of sanction. But given the very limited resources available to most state welfare agencies and given the political pressures upon them to reduce the amounts spent on welfare together with the discriminatory attitudes of many welfare workers, it appears that this duty does stand in need of enforcement. An alternative method of enforcement would be to create within the welfare agency itself a branch to monitor the performance of this duty to make AFDC payments to all eligible individuals. This is not likely to prove a more useful mode of enforcement. Such a branch of the welfare agency is likely to be underfinanced so that it would be unable to perform its function effectively; what funds were made available to it would probably be diverted from other welfare funds and so reduce the amounts that could be more usefully expended in welfare benefits. It is hard to see how welfare administrators in this branch of the agency could have any very strong motivation to monitor the activities of administrators in another branch of the same agency, and they would probably be partial to the welfare administrator in any dispute with an external claimant. Another alternative would be to assign the enforcement of this duty to the public prosecutor, thus assimilating this portion of welfare law to criminal legislation. This method of enforcement is also not likely to be very useful. The office of the public prosecutor is already so overworked, that it would have little time and energy left to prosecute welfare workers. This task would doubtless be given a much lower priority than bringing "real" criminals to justice. One could set up a special branch of the prosecutor's office to conduct this business, but this would be expensive and it is not clear that its staff would know of most nonperformances of the duty to pay AFDC or that it would be in a position to know which cases might be more usefully expedited. The individual claimants are more likely, if given the power to sue in the courts, to take legal action when it is most useful. Those who could find some alternative source of income, and whose need for welfare benefits is accordingly less urgent, would probably not bother to sue. Those who rely entirely upon the welfare agency are the ones who will typically exercize their legal power. Therefore, this method of enforcement is more useful than other possible modes of enforcement or leaving the duty enforced.

A third component essential to any adequate partial utilitarian justification of the legal right to receive AFDC payments is a demonstration of the utility of conferring autonomy concerning the core claim to such payments upon the eligible individuals. A claim-right is more than its core claim; it is a system of autonomy centering on that claim. Hence, any justification of that right, even a partial justification, must justify the autonomy over the core possessed by the rightholder. For example, the law makes the duty of the welfare agency to pay Aid to Families with Dependent Children contingent upon the application of each eligible individual; the agency has no legal obligation to seek out needy individuals and to give them welfare benefits unasked. Again, the law confers upon any applicant the legal power to withdraw his or her application at any time, thus cancelling the duty of the welfare agency to continue to pay AFDC. Also the eligible individual has the bilateral legal liberty of exercising or refraining from exercising his or her legal power of taking legal action in the event of actual or threatened nonperformances of the state welfare agency duty to make AFDC payments.

Why might it be useful to confer some such autonomy, some such freedom and control, concerning the core claim upon the claimant? Such autonomy might go a long way toward eliminating, or at least reducing, unnecessary welfare expenditures. Eligible individuals who do not really need welfare assistance will tend not to apply for AFDC, and when a recipient ceases to need assistance, he or she will often withdraw his or her application. Since the utility of welfare payments declines as the need of the recipient decreases, these provisions will reduce low-utility performances of the legal duty to make AFDC payments. At the other extreme, those individuals most in need of welfare aid are most likely to press their claims insistently. Given their unusually urgent needs to be fulfilled by means of the income received from AFDC payments, the utility of these payments is higher than in the case of less needy recipients. Thus, conferring freedom and control upon the eligible individuals will tend to ensure the most useful of the performances of the duty to pay AFDC. More generally, since those for whom welfare aid is least useful will tend not to apply or withdraw their applications and those for whom such payments would be most useful will tend to use their freedom and control to ensure welfare payments, one can expect that the autonomy conferred will tend to be exercised to maximize the utility of the AFDC program.

Another reason why it might well be useful to confer autonomy over the enjoyment of the core claim upon the welfare claimants is that there is an intimate connection between autonomy and self-respect. To choose not to receive a welfare benefit may typically impose severe economic hardship upon the individual, but it does not convey any message of rejection and even condemnation in the way that being denied welfare aid willy-nilly does. Freedom and control conferred upon eligible individuals gives them some measure of control over their destinies and their lives. In this way, it reduces the dependency of these unfortunate individuals who have much less economic independence and psychological self-assurance than most of us. The psychological destructiveness and social alienation produced by dependence and rejection are established by ample evidence. The personal and social benefits of conferring some measure of autonomy, and hence of independence and self-respect, upon these individuals is commensurately large.

But is it more useful to confer autonomy concerning the core claim to AFDC payments upon the eligible individual than upon some alternative party? At this point, it would be well to remind ourselves of the context presupposed by significant talk of rights. This is a potential confrontation between the right-holder and some second party whose will conflicts with his. The most important and frequent confrontation presupposed by the claim-right to welfare benefits, as of any primary welfare right, is that between some individual who wishes to receive the welfare benefit at issue and the agent of the welfare agency that wishes to withhold that benefit. Now there would be some benefits to be derived from conferring autonomy over the core claim to the welfare agency. The welfare workers could then use their freedom and control to distinguish the most needy from the less needy and to expend their very limited resources in a way that would do the most good. In fact, for decades the welfare agency was given just such discretion. There is ample historical evidence that such discretion was abused, or at least misused. Many eligible individuals were denied opportunities to apply; applications were often not acted upon for long periods of time or were simply ignored indefinitely with no action ever taken; aid was often reduced far below subsistence levels; some groups were persistently discriminated against in awarding welfare aid; and payments were often terminated or denied arbitrarily. For these reasons, among others, welfare programs were not benefiting needy individuals anywhere near as much as they should have been doing, and they were failing to solve the urgent social problems they could at least have been alleviating to a considerable degree.

Now of course, autonomy conferred upon eligible individuals is also capable of abuse. Stories of welfare recipients driving Cadillacs are legion. One suspects, however, that if all those stories were true, the automobile industry would be much more prosperous than in fact it is. Given carefully formulated and reliably ascertainable eligibility requirements, it will not be easy for individual claimants to misuse the autonomy conferred upon them. Recall the disproportion between the economic resources and social power of the typical applicant for welfare and the welfare agency itself. It is much more likely that the welfare agency will be in a position to detect and prevent abuses of autonomy by the claimant than that the welfare claimant would be able to control any abuses of discretion allocated to the welfare agency. Thus, in addition to the reasons for believing that autonomy conferred upon the eligible individual will be employed usefully, there is the evidence that autonomy confered upon the second party in potential confrontations would be often misused. In this way, one can make a strong utilitarian case for conferring autonomy, freedom and control, concerning the enjoyment of the core claim upon the claimant in face of the welfare agency.

What, if anything, can we conclude from this cursory examination of a partial justification of the legal right to receive AFDC payments in terms of utility? At the very least, the complexity of any such justification has become apparent. To justify the creation or maintenance of a legal right to a welfare benefit, one must do much more than demonstrate the utility of a welfare program that makes such payments to needy individuals. The form or shape of an adequate justification is determined by the structure of the legal right it is to justify. In the example examined, even a partial utilitarian justification must show that (1) having a legal duty of the state welfare agency to pay AFDC to all eligible individuals, (2) conferring upon all claimants the legal power to take legal action in the event of threatened or actual nonperformance of that duty, and (3) conferring upon all eligible individuals some sort of legal autonomy concerning the enjoyment of the core claim all maximize utility. If one can do all this, then one will have given a partial utilitarian justification of the legal right to receive AFDC payments.

In practice, it will clearly be very difficult to provide anything like an adequate utilitarian justification of any specified legal right. The number of relevant utilities and disutilities is considerable, and they bear on the justifiability of the right in so many different ways that any overall utilitarian assessment will not be simple. Indeed, given the detailed factual information required and the controversial economic and psychological theory presupposed in estimating any single utility or disutility, controversy is liable to be persistent. Still, it should be possible in principle to give a very plausible approximation to all the relevant utilities. Is there any reason to consider such a utilitarian justification of a legal right inadequate in principle?

It is often alleged that a proper understanding of the nature of a right shows that rights cannot be grounded in mere utility. To ground a right in social utility is to undermine the very point or purpose of individual rights as such. While this argument has considerable force in the case of moral rights, I do not find it convincing even there. When one turns from moral to legal rights, however, the argument seems to lose its hold. It does seem possible to think of a legal right as nothing more than an institution or part of an institution to be judged as justified or unjustified purely in terms of its utility.

But what if this institutional right somehow violates justice or individual moral rights. It might seem that any purely utilitarian justification of a legal right must be inadequate because moral considerations necessarily take precedence over merely pragmatic ones. Hence, unless we know that there are no overriding moral considerations, no amount of utility can justify any legal right. There is a valid point here, but I would not concede that every utilitarian justification is inadequate. An adequate justification is one that meets every challenge actually made. The fact that additional challenges can always be made does nothing to prove the justification inadequate; it is merely tentative and subject to reexamination if and when an additional challenge must be met. Thus, IF there is no allegation of moral rights violated or other injustice, a purely utilitarian justification of a legal right could in principle be quite adequate. If such an allegation were to be made, then it is no response to point to the great utility of the legal right. One must meet a moral challenge in moral terms. Just how this will be done depends upon the challenge made and the available responses. What this shows is that a utilitarian justification may have to be supplemented with refutations of various challenges to remain adequate. But this does not show that before any such challenge was made that utility is an inadequate ground for the judgment that a specified legal right is justified.

Justice

A partial justification of a legal primary welfare right might demonstrate, not that the specified welfare right maximizes utility, but that it is demanded by justice. There are two very different ways in which one might appeal to justice in developing such an argument. First, one might appeal to some principle specifying the just distribution of burdens and benefits in a society. One might then conceive of the goal of a welfare program as the achievement of a just pattern of the distribution of goods and services. A legal right to some welfare benefit would then be shown to be a required means to this goal of distributive justice. Second, one might appeal to the moral requirement that the operations of a welfare program be just. It is unjust for a state welfare agency to discriminate arbitrarily between applicants for or recipients of welfare; justice demands that the welfare agency treat similar cases similarly and different cases differently. Society has a moral obligation not to engage in unfair treatment of individuals, and a legal welfare right is required in order to prevent injustice in the state action of giving and withholding welfare benefits. While the first sort of argument appeals to some pattern of just distribution of all sorts of goods and services, the second appeals to justice in the activity of distributing one very special sort of benefit: welfare aid. Also, while the first argument appeals to some just pattern of distribu*tion*, the second appeals to justice in the distribu*ting* of welfare. Finally, while the first sort of argument views distributive justice as a goal of the welfare program, the second sort views just treatment as a side-constraint upon the actions of the state welfare agency. Each of these appeals to justice deserves careful examination.

Let us begin with a somewhat tentative formulation of the first sort of justification of a legal right to AFDC payments grounded in distributive justice.

1. Any society in which the distribution of wealth is unjust ought to promote a more just distribution.
2. In our society the distribution of wealth is unjust.
3. In our society a legal right to AFDC payments would promote a more just distribution.

Therefore, our society ought to have a legal right to AFDC payments.

Offhand, I do not know how to establish the truth of the first premise. Presumably any complete theory of the grounds of obligation would explain just how justice imposes certain sorts of obligations upon society and any adequate analysis of distributive justice should surely make explicit what practical implications it has. In the absence of any fully adequate theory of either sort, one is reduced to sheer speculation or intuitive dogmatism. Still, it does seem plausible to assume that justice does somehow impose moral obligations and that at least some of these fall upon society as a whole when what is at stake is the distribution of all goods and services among the members of a society.

The second premise is also plausible, but here one has a clearer notion of how to argue for it. Presumably, one would appeal to some standard of distributive justice and show that the distribution of wealth in our society falls short of that standard. Many moralists seem to operate with a rough and ready standard to the effect that any gross disproportion of wealth is unjust, where a "gross disproportion" is any distribution that enables some individuals to live in great luxury while others lack even the barest essentials of life. John Rawls has offered us a much more precise standard in the form of his difference principle, his second principle of social justice. Better yet he has provided an elegant justification for his principles of justice. Although his principle is compatible with considerable economic inequality, it is hard to imagine any rational argument to show that the massive poverty in our society today is genuinely necessary for or contributes to the well-being of the least-advantaged segments of our society. In some such manner, then, provided some standard of distributive justice is accepted, one might well establish the premise asserting that in our society the existing distribution of wealth is unjust.

At first glance, it is even easier to argue for the third premise, that in our society a legal right to AFDC payments would promote a more just distribution of wealth. Obviously enacting and enforcing a legal right to AFDC payments, given the conditions of eligibility formulated in terms of need and the relatively heavy incidence of taxation upon those with above-average incomes, would serve to redistribute wealth from the more affluent segments of our society to those at or below the poverty level. Surely this is just what is demanded by Rawls' difference principle. On second glance, one begins to wonder whether the legal right to AFDC payments plays any essential role in this redistribution at all. After all, one could, as the United States in fact did, have an Aid to Families with Dependent Children Program that distributes AFDC payments to the needy without having any legal claim-right of eligible individuals holding against the state welfare agencies. It could even be argued that the addition of such a legal welfare right would actually hamper the promotion of distributive justice. Any such right would be open to abuse by welfare claimants who merely pretend to be in need. Recall the rumors of AFDC recipients driving to and from the welfare agency, and the bank, in Cadillacs, while we taxpayers are struggling to keep up the payments on our Fords and Chevrolets. Also, a legal claim-right to ADFC payments imposes a corresponding legal duty to pay upon the state welfare agency. This eliminates the discretion of the welfare worker to consider each case on its merits and to distribute welfare funds where they are most needed and will, therefore, do the most to reduce the unjust distribution of wealth in our society.

What we have uncovered here is a special case of a more general difficulty in the logic of this argument. There are many ways in which a society might choose to promote a more just distribution of wealth, only one of which is the creation of a legal right to AFDC payments. A society might adhere to the philosophy of free enterprise and gear its economic policies so that the private economy would sustain full employment and, since there is no large reservoir of unemployed workers to be exploited, pay each worker a just remuneration. In a more realistic but similar spirit, it might provide matching funds to private welfare agencies and generous tax deductions to private contributors to such agencies so that welfare benefits were entirely taken care of by private charity rather than public claim-right. At the opposite extreme, it might enact a universal welfare program covering every needy individual so that our present categorical welfare programs, such as AFDC, would become superfluous. Let us grant the moral obligation of a society to promote distributive justice. Given the variety of available means to this goal, how can one generate any argument for a moral obligation to use any single means, such as a legal right to AFDC payments?

Clearly the major premise of the argument must be reformulated, but how? The most obvious substitute, and one that would render the revised argument valid, is simply: (1a) Any society in which the distribution of wealth is unjust ought to promote a more just distribution using every available means. All that it would then be necessary to show is that a legal right to AFDC payments is in fact a means to this end of distributive justice. This revised premise solves the problem of choosing between alternative means to this end by mandating the choice of all available means. But surely this revised premise is implausible and even objectionable. The state cannot use each and every available means to achieve a more just distribution of goods because some means will be incompatible with others. For example, one means would be to encourage free enterprise and reduce governmental interference in the economy in an effort to reduce unemployment to the point where there would be few if any individuals left in dire need. But this approach conflicts with undertaking massive welfare programs within which there might be a legal right to welfare. Similarly, enacting a legal right to welfare that imposes an inflexible legal duty to give aid upon officials in some welfare agency is incompatible with designing a welfare system in which welfare officials have the maximum discretion to allocate their funds in a way that would be most beneficial to their welfare clients. Also, it might turn out that the goal of achieving distributive justice could be achieved by means of some subset of the available means. In such a situation, to insist that society has an obligation to use every available means is surely gratuitous; it might even be immoral, given the other imperative uses to which social resources ought to be put. Finally, some of the available means of pursuing the end of distributive justice are clearly impermissible. One way of reducing unjust inequalities of wealth in a society would be to decapitate the very rich and impose compulsory euthanasia upon the very poor. Although it would be linguistically inaccurate to call such decapitation "capital punishment," for the very rich have committed no crime (presumably) in accumulating their excessive wealth, one might pretend to justify decapitation on the grounds that they had not fully earned the amounts they now hold and that these large sums could be more usefully redistributed among the relatively poor. Not those who are poorest, of course. They have nothing but a miserable life in prospect and so ought to be put out of their misery as mercy dictates. Obviously, not every available means to the end of distributive justice ought to be chosen.

But perhaps it could be maintained that (1b) any society in which the distribution of wealth is unjust ought to promote a more just distribution using every necessary means. If society really ought to promote distributive justice, then surely it would be wrong not to use any means without which this end cannot be achieved. This presupposes, of course, that the end of achieving distributive justice, or at least a close approximation to it, is possible and that every necessary means is morally permissible. But these are not additional presuppositions, for they are built into premise (1) itself. If either of these is false, then society has no obligation to promote distributive justice at all. Since this premise is plausible enough, let us see whether it would rescue the original argument.

One could render the first sort of justification of the legal right to AFDC payments logically valid by replacing premise (1) with the premise (1b), provided one at the same time replaced premise (3) with the appropriately modified premise (3b): In our society a legal right to AFDC payments is a necessary means to promote a more just distribution. The question now is whether this premise might be shown to be true. Perhaps it could. One might try to show that efforts to provide for the fundamental needs of families with dependent children through private charity would, given certain facts about our society, inevitably prove inadequate to achieve full distributive justice. One might then go on to establish that it would not be sufficient to supplement private charity with a public Aid to Families with Dependent Children Program lacking any claim-right of eligible individuals against welfare officials because of political pressures in our society to deny adequate funds to any such agency and deep-seated prejudices of welfare workers that would deny needed welfare benefits to certain classes of eligible persons. I cannot here flesh out such an argument, much less establish its soundness convincingly. But the form such an argument might take is already clear and, in the absence of some important undetected flaw, it appears a possible way to develop a justification for a legal right to AFDC payments.

It is probably not, however, the only possible way to do this. And since it might turn out to be difficult to show that a legal right to AFDC payments is really necessary, given the number of alternative ways one might pursue the end of distributive justice, it is worth considering other reformulations of the first premise. When confronted with the problem of making a rational choice among alternative means to a given end, the most obvious move is to opt for the most effective of the available means. Accordingly, one might modify the argument by introducing the substitute premise (1c): In any society in which the distribution of wealth is unjust one ought to promote a more just distribution using the most effective of the available means. This sort of principle seems entirely reasonable in a situation where the most effective of the available means is also sufficient to achieve the desired end all by itself. But in the present case, this strikes me as highly unlikely. The factors determining the distribution of wealth in a society as complex as ours are manifold, and it is singularly implausible to imagine that any single measure the government might take would completely remedy any consequent distributive injustice. The problem, realistically speaking, is not to select one means of promoting justice from among many, but of selecting some sub-set or combination of means to promote this end.

Therefore, one might try to reformulate premise (1) more or less along the lines of premise (1d): Any society in which the distribution of wealth is unjust ought to promote a more just distribution using the most effective compossible set of available and permissible means. The central point brought out by this reformulation is that in justifying any legal welfare right, one is not justifying the choice of a single isolated means but one measure that, together with others, forms a coordinated method of pursuing some social objective, in this case distributive justice. In other words, the choice of this or that means of promoting distributive justice in any society must be looked at within the context in which other means have already been chosen and still others might be chosen. And whether or not it is rational to choose this means depends essentially upon how it fits together as a part of a set of means that together promote the end in view.

If a premise like (1d) is acceptable, then the argument can be made valid by replacing the original premise (3) with the substitute premise (3d): In our society a legal right to AFDC payments is one of the means in the most effective compossible set of available and permissible means to promote distributive justice. Can this be shown? I honestly do not know, but I can see no difficulty in principle with showing just this. One might give factual information about our society to show that the various means currently used to promote distributive justice will be less effective without this legal right than with it. One might give factual reasons to suppose that adding or retaining this legal right to AFDC payments would make the entire set of means more effective than adding some other means to the set or retaining the set minus this right. All of this is highly complex. Establishing premise (3d) is going to require much detailed information about the society and to presuppose many principles of social science and human psychology. Moreover the full argument must consider the comparative effectiveness of various combinations of means to achieve distributive justice. In practice, the necessary factual information and scientific theory may be lacking to complete the argument. But given some standard of distributive justice by which to define the desired end, I do not see why an argument along these lines could not be generated.

There is, however, one additional feature to any such argument that should be noted. A legal right to AFDC payments is a very special sort of means just because it consists of establishing and maintaining a legal right. Accordingly, to show that some such right is either a necessary means to, or one of the most effective compossible set of available and permissible means to, distributive justice, one must connect the necessity or efficacy of this means to the nature of a legal right. Since this is a legal claim right, one would have to show the necessity or efficacy of (a) imposing a legal duty of payment upon the state welfare agency and (b) giving the eligible individual the legal power of suing in the event of threatened or actual nonperformance of this legal duty and (c) conferring upon the eligible individual some sort of legal autonomy concerning the enjoyment of the core legal claim. I do not regard these as impossible to establish, but I do insist that any partial justification of a legal right to AFDC payments must include such sub-arguments.

The most obvious evidence to offer would come from the past history of our United States AFDC Program, before it contained any legal claim-right to AFDC payments. Many eligible individuals were denied aid or provided with less than full benefits under the program. Officials in the state welfare agencies and in the federal government were slow and often reluctant to correct failures to provide AFDC to individuals who remained in dire need. And our knowledge of human psychology and political power suggests that the individual most likely to ensure enjoyment of any legal claim is the claimant himself or herself. No doubt much more could and should be said, but my present point is simply that something along these lines is necessary to fill out this first sort of appeal to justice. It appears in principle that it would be possible to give a partial justification of a legal right to a primary welfare benefit by an argument showing that some such legal right is either a necessary means to or one of the most effective compossible set of available and permissible means to promote distributive justice. Although I cannot find any explicit and precise formulation of this sort of argument in the literature, there are approximations to it, and I have tried to show how these might be filled out to do the job.

Now let us turn to the second way in which one might develop a partial justification of a primary welfare right by appealing to justice. This second argument does not attempt to show that a legal right to welfare aid is demanded as a means to achieve the goal of distributive justice, but that it is demanded by the side-constraint of fair treatment upon the operations of the welfare program. A tentative sketch of the argument might go like this:

1. Every society ought to prevent the unjust treatment of individuals by its state agencies.
2. In this society, a legal right to AFDC payments is necessary to prevent the unjust treatment of eligible individuals by state agencies distributing AFDC benefits.

Therefore, this society ought to have a legal right to AFDC payments.

Although the rough outline of this argument is clear enough, it is far from obvious whether the argument is sound.

Premise (1) seems plausible enough. What could be fairer than to assume that every society ought to prevent the unjust treatment of individuals by its state agencies. But why? Let us grant that justice is a side-constraint upon the actions of every individual and organization. It obviously follows that it is morally impermissible for any state welfare agency to pursue its goals, such as relieving economic need or preserving its limited resources, by means of actions that treat individuals unjustly; the moral requirement of just treatment rules out any unfair or inequitable distribution of welfare benefits. But how does this negative moral duty of the state welfare agency to refrain from unjust distributing imply any positive moral duty of the society as a whole to prevent such wrongdoing by the welfare agency?

To suggest that the society as a whole ought to prevent its welfare agencies from acting unjustly seems at first glance analogous to suggesting that one person, perhaps a bystander, ought to intervene to prevent another person, such as a rapist, from mistreating some potential victim. Actually, it is more like the intervention of a policeman, who has a special duty to protect the public from some criminal's completing a crime. An even closer and more revealing analogy is the action of a master to prevent his or her servant from wrongdoing. The master-servant relationship is such that the master is morally responsible for the acts of the servant, at least to the degree that the servant is acting for and under the direction of the master. Similarly, the state welfare agency is distributing welfare benefits on behalf of and acting under the direction of the society, more precisely of the state or society *as* politically organized. This is why the society is morally responsible for the actions of its state agencies and why it has a moral duty to supervise and control the actions of its agencies to prevent any unjust treatment of any individuals. Precisely how the relationship between a society and its various state agencies can best be construed is a complicated problem in social philosophy. But it seems very likely that the relationship is morally analogous to that of master to servant and would, accordingly, somehow imply the responsibility of a society to prevent its agents from acting unjustly.

If premise (1) is acceptable, then attention shifts to premise (2). In this society, a legal right to AFDC payments is necessary to prevent the unjust treatment of eligible individuals by state agencies distributing AFDC benefits. To establish this premise, factual information must be collected to show that, without some such legal right to welfare benefits, the state agencies will refuse or fail to treat similar cases similarly and relevantly different individuals differently. It would not be hard to show that state AFDC agencies have tended to delay, reduce, and deny applications for welfare aid even when the welfare claimants were eligible. The record is there and undeniable. But precisely why such injustices could not be corrected or avoided without the creation and enforcement of a legal claim-right to AFDC payments would be harder to explain. One might point to the excessive case-loads of the welfare workers, which prevent them from investigating and considering each individual on her or his merits and exercising wide discretion in a fair manner. One might well show the presence of very strong fiscal and political pressures to cut down on the expense of full and fair payment of Aid to Families with Dependent Children to all those individuals who meet the conditions of eligibility. The danger of unjust treatment of eligible individuals could be even more strongly established if it could be shown that there was discrimination, either rooted in the beliefs and attitudes of the welfare workers or in the institutional structure of the welfare agency, that seriously disadvantaged certain categories of welfare claimants.

To fill out the argument I am merely sketching here, one would need to show just how these factual considerations bear on the nature of the legal right to welfare they are supposed to justify. More specifically, why do these facts show that it is necessary to have a legal duty of the state welfare agency to pay AFDC aid to all eligible individuals, to give each eligible individual the legal power to take legal action in the event of threatened or actual nonperformance of this duty, and to confer autonomy over this core claim upon the possessor of that claim. But if the facts establish a very strong tendency to treat eligible individuals unjustly and indicate the ability and will to stand up for their legal rights on the part of welfare claimants, then the argument might well go through.

Not, however, as it stands. Quite apart from the details of the factual evidence that must be marshalled to establish premise (2), it is clear that this premise is false. It is obviously not necessary to have a legal right to AFDC payments in order to prevent injustice in the distribution of AFDC benefits. A much simpler and more reliable way to prevent such unjust treatment would be to abolish the Aid to Families with Dependent Children program entirely. Abolishing the distributing of a welfare benefit absolutely prevents every instance of or act of distributing this benefit unjustly. What this means, of course, is that the argument tacitly presupposes the continuation of the AFDC program. All that is necessary, then, is to revise premise (2) accordingly to read: "In this society, if the AFDC program continues, then a legal right to AFDC payments is necessary to prevent the unjust treatment of eligible individuals by state agencies distributing AFDC benefits." This is not a trivial modification, for it reveals something important about this sort of partial justification for a legal right to welfare aid. The full argument must proceed in two stages. First, one needs to justify having a specific welfare program at all. Only then can one reasonably go on to justify giving such a program this rather than that shape or controlling it with this or that legal restriction. But let us not linger over the first stage of the argument. Has premise (2) of the second stage now been rendered acceptable?

Not yet. It is not enough to show a strong tendency toward the unjust distributing of welfare aid, for it might be quite possible to prevent this in other ways. One might make the abuse of discretion on the part of welfare workers a criminal offence and leave enforcement to the public prosecutor. Factual evidence would have to be advanced to show that this alternative would be ineffective. Perhaps the officials of the public prosecutor's office would be most reluctant to use their power to punish officials in another state agency. Perhaps they would be unlikely to learn of unjust actions taken by welfare agents. Public prosecutors might be overworked and more concerned about more serious crimes, or those more in the public eye. Another alternative would be to set up a monitoring division within the welfare agency to detect and correct unjust treatment of eligible individuals. But much the same sort of arguments could be used against this alternative. I do not intend to settle the issue. I merely hope to outline the sort of argument that would be needed to establish premise (2). The argument would use factual information and scientific theory to show that without a legal right to AFDC payments, such payments would often by distributed unjustly and to show that without some such legal right all other measures would be ineffective in preventing this unjust treatment of eligible individuals. Whether such an argument is sound for our society I leave to the judgment of others, but there seems no reason to deny the possibility of this sort of argument on principle.

Suppose, however, that the facts concerning our society are not sufficient to establish the necessity of a legal right to AFDC payments. One could weaken this premise somewhat to obtain a less powerful, but still forceful, partial justification. One could substitute (2a): "In this society, if the AFDC program continues, then a legal right to AFDC payments is the best available way to prevent the unjust treatment of eligible individuals by state agencies distributing AFDC benefits." It might be that this premise would be easier to establish. One need no longer prove that the primary legal welfare right is abolutely necessary to prevent injustice; one need only prove that it would be more effective and have fewer disadvantages than any of the alternative measures that could be taken by the society. Having noted this modified formulation of the argument, I return to the original stronger version.

Even with the substitution of modified formulations of the two premises, there remains a logical gap in this second sort of partial justification of a primary legal welfare rights. Just how do the obligation of the society to prevent injustice and the fact that a legal welfare right is necessary to do so logically imply that this society ought to have a legal right to AFDC payments? Implicit in the reasoning is a tacit premise *something* like (3): A society ought to do everything necessary to fulfill its moral obligations. The addition of some such premise would render the argument valid.

It remains to be seen precisely what this tacit assumption amounts to. One formulation would have it that (3a): A society ought to choose every necessary means to achieve any morally required end. On this interpretation, the moral obligation of a society to prevent the unjust distributing of welfare aid by its Aid to Families with Dependent Children agencies imposes upon the society the morally required end or goal of ensuring a distributing of AFDC payments free from unjust treatment of any eligible individual. But if this is the proper formulation of this tacit premise, then justice seems to enter into the second partial justification as a goal rather than a side-constraint and one alleged difference between the first and second partial justifications is illusory. Perhaps so. Nevertheless, even if this is a sort of means-end argument, it is of a very special sort. It is not simply a matter of choosing wisely between available means to achieve a desirable goal. The end is morally required, not simply desired or desirable. And since the means is necessary to achieve the mandated end, the means is also morally required. This, it serves as a constraint upon the action of the society in pursuing its other goals, such as relieving distress or avoiding administrative expenses.

I suspect, however, that the proper formulation of the tacit premise is more like (3b): A society ought to take every action that is a necessary part of any action that it ought to do. To be sure, the social act of enacting and enforcing a legal right to AFDC payments is causally related to the result of an AFDC program in which all distributing of welfare benefits is free from injustice. But recall that the obligation of the society asserted in premise (1) is to "prevent the unjust treatment of individuals by its state agencies." Now the concept of preventing is itself a causal concept; to prevent something is to act in a manner that causes it not to happen. Therefore, although the enacting and enforcing of the legal right is a cause of, and thus extrinsic to, the result of a just distributing by the welfare agency, the enacting and enforcing is part of and intrinsic to the act of preventing unjust distributing by the state agency.

This point can perhaps be brought out more clearly by noting an ambiguity in the language of means. We sometimes say that an act is "a means to" some end. For example, studying may be a means to a high grade or publishing may be a means to obtaining tenure at Washington University. It is this sort of means-end situation that stands opposed to the side-constraint situation. In contrast, we sometimes say that some act is "a means of" doing something. For example, one means of paying a debt is handing over the appropriate amount of cash; another means is giving the creditor a check in the amount due. Here the act of handing over the cash does not cause the paying of the debt; the action of handing over the cash is one way of performing the act of paying the debt. Now although one is not morally required to fulfill one's moral obligations in every way possible, one is never morally permitted to omit any action that is a necessary part of the morally required action. It is this premise that is tacitly assumed in the second sort of partial justification of the legal right to AFDC payments.

This sort of partial justification would appear to be quite promising. Provided one can justify having an Aid to Families with Dependent Children program in the first place, it seems reasonable to assume that the society ought to prevent the unjust treatment of individuals by its state agencies administering this program. Although the details of the reasoning are complex, there seems to be no reason on principle to doubt that it would be possible to marshal factual evidence to show that, in our society, a legal right to AFDC payments is necessary to prevent the unjust treatment of eligible individuals by state agencies distributing AFDC benefits. Then, since it is analytically true that a society ought to take every action that is a necessary part of any action it ought to perform, the conclusion follows logically that our society ought to have a legal right to AFDC payments. That such a partial justification is possible in principle does not, of course, show that it is sound, given the facts about the United States today. I leave the facts to be discovered by social scientists and used by politicians or political reformers. My task as a philosopher is to make clear the nature of the reasoning one could use to justify a legal primary welfare right.

Just as the friends of a legal right to some specific welfare benefit might appeal to justice, so might its enemies. There might well be one or more partial counterjustifications of a primary legal welfare right starting with premises about what is required or excluded by justice and concluding that no such legal right ought to exist. Currently the best known and most often debated counterjustification of compulsory welfare programs is that of Robert Nozick, who argues that all such programs are unjust because they violate the entitlements of those who are forced against their wills to pay taxes to support such programs. Since his entitlement theory of justice hinges upon his theory of rights, I shall postpone discussion of his argument until the next section of this chapter in which I deal with appeals to rights. There is, however, another counterjustification that deserves passing mention and brief examination. This is the argument that any legal right to a welfare benefit is unjust because it involves treating human beings in ways that do violence to their just deserts.

One way of formulating this counterjustification is as follows:

1. No society ought to require its state agencies to treat individuals unjustly.
2. In our society, a legal right to AFDC payments would require our state agencies to treat many individuals unjustly.

Therefore, our society ought not to have any legal right to AFDC payments.

Although I recognize that this is at best a rough formulation of the argument, I do not propose to worry about its invalidity as stated or to attempt any more precise formulation. Rather, I wish to understand the line of reasoning that lies behind its second premise.

One traditional conception of justice is "to each his own." One way of interpreting this conception is to hold that justice requires that each individual be treated as he or she deserves and that any form of action that fails to accord each individual his or her deserts is unjust. It is then suggested that any sort of legal right to AFDC payments will require state agencies to treat many individuals in ways they do not at all deserve. For one thing, it will require state welfare agencies to reward the idle and useless members of our society by giving them Aid to Families with Dependent Children payments. For another, it will require our state agencies of taxation to penalize the more able and industrious members of our society by forcing them to support such welfare aid out of their hard-earned incomes. Surely eligible individuals have done nothing to deserve the welfare benefits they receive, and the taxpayer does not deserve to be saddled with additional taxes just because he or she has managed to earn an honest income for productive labor. After all, these individual taxpayers are innocent parties; they are not responsible by virtue of anything they have done for the plight of those unfortunate enough to be eligible for welfare aid.

I am tempted to quibble with this popular counterjustification. Surely it is unfair to brand needy dependent children "idle and useless." They are no more idle and useless than their middle- or upper-class counterparts comfortably or luxuriously supported by their parents. At worst, it is the parent of the dependent child who is out of work and, consequently, not a productive worker in business or industry. But why should a mother caring for her dependent children with the help of very meager AFDC payments be considered any more idle and useless than a housewife in a more prosperous family who works hard and effectively in rearing the children, cooking the meals, and performing all the other essential tasks in the household economy? Conversely, it is not impossible that the taxpayer, hardworking and nonmalicious as he or she may be, is somehow responsible for the plight of those eligible for welfare aid. By their very acts of succeeding in a highly competitive economy and by their political actions of insisting upon a minimum wage that renders many who would wish to work unemployable, they may have contributed in very direct ways to the economic disadvantages of those below the poverty line in our society. I do not believe that these remarks are irrelevant or unimportant. It seems to me that the argument under examination derives some of its initial plausibility from our tendency to stereotype individuals as economic good guys and bad guys and that a deeper understanding of the economic realities would undermine our moral prejudices. But I do not insist upon any of this, for the theoretically interesting weaknesses in this counterjustification lie in the conception of justice it presupposes.

I am not sure that I wish to deny that justice demands that each individual be treated as he or she deserved, but I do wish to insist upon considerable clarification. The concept of one's just deserts, traditionally summed up in the slogan "to each his own," is far from clear. Just how do dependent children and their parents deserve to be treated and why? Conversely, just how do taxpayers deserve to be treated and why? Until the conception of desert or the criteria for determining just what an individual does deserve are spelled out, the theory remains so vague as to be virtually empty. This may not destroy its rhetorical utility, but it does undermine its guidance in dealing with complex specific moral issues. In attempting to clarify the conception of desert, it seems to me that any advocate is faced with a dilemma. Either one defines desert in terms of a narrow range of paradigm cases or one extends the concept of desert to cover all sorts of just and unjust treatment. If one does the former, one can achieve a moderately clear understanding of desert, but the concept becomes inapplicable to either welfare programs or state taxation; if one does the latter, one loses one's understanding of desert, and the concept implies no definite conclusions about anything.

The concept of desert is most at home in the context of reward and punishment. It surely is unjust to imprison the individual who has committed no crime or to sentence a person to life imprisonment for some trivial offense against the law. The parent who punishes a child fighting in self-defense or rewards a successful bully is not giving either child what is due to him or her. The runner who did not cross the finish line first or who did so only by tripping up some more able competitor does not deserve first prize. And the student who is penalized merely for disagreeing with the professor, no matter how articulately and reasonably, is unjustly treated. But welfare benefits are not in any literal sense rewards for good conduct or achievement, and taxes are not literally punishments for the "crime" of earning more than the maximum untaxed income. This is obscured by the rhetoric of those who say that welfare benefits "reward the idle and useless" and that taxes "penalize the able and industrious." If one limits the meaning of desert to its paradigm applications to rewards and punishments in the strict sense, then the concept becomes inapplicable to welfare rights and income taxes. On this interpretation, the theory of justice as desert is relatively intelligible, but it cannot serve in any counterjustification of the legal right to AFDC payments.

Others, of course, prefer a broader conception of desert, one that covers something like the entire range of just and unjust action. But then the concept becomes so vague that it is most unclear just what it does imply in this or that sort of situation. There are several criteria, each ably defended by this or that philosopher, competing for the position of defining the practical implications of the traditional formula "to each his own." It might be argued that one ought to distribute economic goods on the basis of economic contribution, so that the productive worker deserves to keep his or her earnings, but the unemployed noncontributor deserves nothing, at least from the economic standpoint. But others argue that economic need is equally relevant to the distribution of economic goods. Moreover, if the purpose of a welfare program is to meet the fundamental needs of certain members of society, then surely this defining purpose implies that need is the relevant criterion of just distribution. My point is simple. If one tries to stretch the concept of desert beyond its paradigm cases, then one simply does not know how to sort out true from false allegations of desert. Do we ever tax an individual because he or she "deserves" to be taxed? I have no idea how to answer this question. I suspect that the question should not be asked in the first place. If we are to make any sense out of the theory of justice as desert outside of the context of reward and punishment, then we must have some criterion for applying the concept of desert to this or that individual case. But one may not simply assert some criterion, such as moral virtue or economic value, without argument. In choosing between competing criteria, one must justify one's choice. I see no way to justify one of these criteria for any and all contexts. Most of these criteria seem context-dependent. This suggests that the concept of desert is equally context-dependent. If this impression is accurate, then this counterjustification of the legal right to AFDC payments falls to the ground.

To say that this particular argument is inadequate is not at all to assert or even imply that all arguments of this kind are unsound. Plausible justifications and counterjustifications of legal primary welfare rights are available. With imagination and care, these can surely be reformulated to ensure logical validity. The difficulties lie with the acceptability of the premises. One premise must consist in, or at least presuppose, some principle of justice. The problem here is that there are a number of very different conceptions of justice, some competitors and some very specific conceptions applying to quite different areas of practice. It is unclear which of these conceptions best fits legal welfare rights or precisely how the relevant principles of justice should be interpreted. On the factual side, the causal relation between the existence of a primary welfare right in the law and justice in the operations of a welfare program may be hard to establish. But there is nothing to suggest that such difficulties are necessarily insurmountable.

Each of the two sample partial justifications of the legal right to AFDC payments here examined has its strengths and its weaknesses. The argument that such a right is justified as a means to the promotion of distributive justice is based upon the most clearly articulated and cogently argued theory of justice we have, that of John Rawls. Moreover, it would be easy to find empirical evidence to support the contention that a legal right to AFDC payments would in fact result in a redistribution of wealth in our society more in line with Rawls' Difference Principle. The trouble is that there are many other means that might be used to promote the same end, and it will not be easy to show that this means is either necessary or included in the best set of compossible and permissible means to that end.

In some respects, the second sort of justification of the same primary welfare right is more satisfactory. The factual considerations required to prove that a legal right to AFDC payments is necessary to prevent unjust distributing by the state welfare agency are more limited in scope and more easy to establish than the facts supporting the choice of this legal right to promote distributive justice in the society as a whole. Also, the obligation of the government to prevent unjust treatment by its state agencies is less debatable intellectually and more stringent morally than the obligation to use the legal system to promote distributive justice in a society affected by many nonlegal and nongovernmental factors. On the other hand, this second argument is conditional upon the continuing existence of the Aid to Families with Dependent Children. Only if this welfare program can be independently justified does this second sort of partial justification of the legal right to AFDC payments go through. Whatever one may conclude about the relative merits of these two arguments, one should not dismiss either as unworthy of serious consideration.

Ethical Rights

A third category of partial justifications of some legal primary welfare right would appeal, not to utility or justice *per se,* but to some specified ethical right. The argument would be that some ethical right, assumed or proven to exist independently of the legal system of the society, implies somehow that the society ought to have the legal right to some specified welfare benefit. One class of rights to which such appeals are often made are human rights. A variety of alleged human rights appear relevant to welfare benefits. The most promising candidates for a partial justification of a legal welfare right are probably the human right to social security and the human right to an adequate standard of living, both affirmed in the *United Nations Declaration* of 1948. Those who reject such newfangled social and economic rights might appeal to the more traditional human right to life, interpreted to entail positive duties to preserve human life as well as the negative duty to refrain from killing human beings. Or a legal right to welfare aid might be derived from the very general human right to aid when in distress. No doubt others could be added to this list, especially the human right to equal opportunity, but one sample will suffice for present purposes. To illustrate the kind of argument required, I will discuss a partial justification based upon the human right to social security.

Although the various documents in which this human right is affirmed do very little to define its precise content, I propose to postpone any debate about its proper interpretation. I shall take its defining core to be an ethical claim of each individual human being against his or her society to be provided with the means sufficient to sustain human life in the event that he or she is deprived of a livelihood through circumstances now beyond his or her control. This is obviously a very general ethical claim, much broader than the claim to AFDC payments. It is also an ethical claim presumably possessed by all human beings, not merely those eligible for our AFDC program. Any partial justification that can bridge these gaps is likely to be a two-stage argument. The first stage would argue that the fundamental human right to social security implies a more specific derivative moral right of the eligible members of families with dependent children to welfare payments from the state. The second stage would argue that this moral right implies that there ought to be a corresponding legal right in that society.

The first stage of this sort of partial justification is, as philosophical arguments go, relatively unproblematic. We might formulate it something like this:

1. Every human being has a human claim-right against his or her state to be provided with the means sufficient to sustain life in the event that he or she is deprived of a livelihood through circumstances now beyond his or her control.
2. In our society every individual eligible for AFDC payments is deprived of a livelihood through circumstances now beyond his or her control.
3. AFDC payments in our society would constitute the means sufficient to sustain life.

Therefore, in our society every eligible individual has a moral right to AFDC payments.

As it stands, there are two minor defects in this formulation. Some of its premises are false, and it is logically invalid. The argument is not formulated in any standard logical form because it does not make explicit precisely how any general human right is logically related to the more specific moral rights that fall within its scope. But surely a more specific ethical right follows somehow from a more general ethical right under which it can clearly be subsumed as a special case. Thus, it is possible in principle to render this argument valid by making its logical structure more explicit.

The falsity of premises (2) and (3) is slightly more serious. These are universal factual generalizations, and no doubt there are exceptions to both. Although the vast majority of individuals in our society who are eligible for AFDC payments are deprived of a livelihood through circumstances now beyond their control, there are some eligible individuals who possess the means to sustain their lives without any state welfare aid. Likewise, the fit between the amount of the AFDC payment in our society and the amount needed to sustain life and no more is somewhat loose. Still, since these premises are rough approximations to the truth, let us pretend that they are acceptable. What interests us is the sort of partial justification that is being attempted. We can leave to others the task of formulating an impeccable version of this appeal to human rights.

The most serious and puzzling difficulties concern the second stage of this partial justification of the legal right to AFDC payments.

Granted that individuals eligible for Aid to Families with Dependent Children always, or at least usually, have a moral right to welfare aid from the state, how does this imply that there ought to be a legal right to AFDC payments? There is one analysis of moral rights that would make this inference true by definition. Although Jeremy Bentham rejected the rhetoric of natural rights, especially absolute natural rights, as nonsense, he did admit that there is one interpretation that could make sense of talk about moral rights ("Anarchical Fallacies"). Once it is recognized that all rights are essentially institutional, one understands that the assertion that some specified moral right exists really means that some corresponding legal right ought to exist. Thus, the only salvageable sense of assertions of natural rights is as assertions of what the law ought to be.

It is easy enough to formulate the second stage of the partial justification of the legal right to AFDC payments in terms of this analysis of moral rights. Its starting point is the conclusion of the first stage of the justification.

4. In our society every eligible individual has a moral right to AFDC payments.
5. To say that someone has a moral right to something means that that person ought to have a legal right to it.
Therefore, in our society every eligible individual ought to have a legal right to AFDC payments.

The logical validity of this argument is clear. What remains unclear is the truth or acceptability of premise (5), of Bentham's analysis of moral rights.

Two powerful lines of argument refute the view that to say that someone has a moral right to something means that that person ought to have a legal right to it. One of these points to instances of moral rights that ought not to be embodied in the law. There are several reasons why some moral rights ought not to be enacted into enforceable legal rights. Some moral rights are too trivial to be worth enforcing by the legal machinery of the state. Even a relatively unimportant promise confers upon the promisee a moral claim-right that the promisor do as he or she has promised, but the state would not be justified in giving the promisee the power to take legal action to enforce, say, my colleague's promise to meet me for lunch on Tuesday. Some moral rights might invite abuse if made into corresponding legal rights. Presumably a benefactor acquires some sort of moral right to reciprocation, if only to an expression of gratitude or to special consideration when acting in ways that might be detrimental to the benefactor. But a corresponding legal right to reciprocation would place in the hands of potential benefactors a dangerous power of imposing legal obligations upon others against their wills; witness the institution of the potlatch among the Northwest Indians.

In other cases, the legal enforcement of a moral right would inevitably invade the privacy of the rightholder in unjustifiable ways. I have a moral right that the members of my family not read my mail or listen in on my telephone calls, but it would be an even greater invasion of my privacy to have the police enforce my right to privacy by detecting and punishing those who violate it. Finally, since rights presuppose an actual or potential confrontation between the first and second parties, the legal enactment and enforcement of a moral right is often out of place when the two parties stand in a personal relationship that is, or ought to be, intimate and loving. Probably a husband has a moral right to the sexual fidelity of his wife, and a wife has a moral right that her husband undertake his fair share of the homemaking tasks. But whatever might be thought about the justice of the corresponding legal rights, their existence would do much to destroy all that is most precious in the marital relation. I may, of course, be mistaken in asserting the existence of one or more of these five moral rights, but this does not seriously undermine my line of argument. If my argument makes any sense at all, if it is intelligible, then the Benthamite analysis of moral rights must be mistaken. For on that analysis, it would be sheer nonsense to assert that there might be a moral right that ought not to be a legal right.

A second refutation of Bentham's conception of moral rights points to the way in which it mislocates and distorts the implications of statements about moral rights. Suppose saying that eligible individuals have a moral right to AFDC payments were saying that eligible individuals ought to have a legal right to such payments. Since this is a moral claim-right of the individual against the state, presumably it implies some corresponding moral duty of the state to the eligible individual. At first glance, the Benthamite analysis suggests that the correlative moral duty of the state is to enact and enforce a legal right to AFDC payments; this is precisely what makes that analysis useful in the partial justification under examination. But surely the logical correlative of the moral right to be provided with AFDC payments is the moral duty to provide such payments, not to enact this or that legislation.

On second glance, it is not clear that the proposed analysis suggests any corresponding moral duty at all. "The eligible individual has a moral right to AFDC payments" is taken to mean "there ought to be a legal right to AFDC payments." But how can one translate the language of what ought to be into some assertion about who ought to do which actions? Does this imply that the welfare agency ought to make AFDC payments even if they are not authorized to do so by law or that the several citizens in the society ought to work politically to elect representatives who will enact such legislation or what? If it makes sense to assert the moral claim-right of the individual to AFDC payments, then this assertion must imply some correlative moral duty to make such payments. Bentham was driven to his analysis of the language of moral rights by his scepticism of natural rights. I do not believe that this scepticism was either neccessary or justified. But if it was, then it would be much better to abandon all talk about moral rights than to pretend to translate it into talk about what the law ought to be. If there are any genuine moral rights, they impose moral duties upon identifiable second parties and do not merely project a moral ideal of a legal system.

Accordingly, the logical transition from the existence of a moral right to the obligation to enact and enforce a corresponding legal right cannot be justified by the mere linguistic analysis of the very concept of a moral right. If this sort of partial justification of a legal welfare right is to go through, we need to find some normative replacement for Bentham's definition. The obvious candidate seems to be (5a): The state ought not to violate the moral rights of the individual. The truth of this premise can hardly be doubted. Presumably the very concept of violating a moral right carries with it the moral obligation, at least a prima facie obligation, not to do so. What is less obvious is the relevance of this premise. It would hardly provide any bridge from every moral right to some corresponding legal right, for the state can hardly violate those moral rights that hold against private individuals or private organizations rather than against the state. But the moral right to AFDC payments derived from the human right to social security is a moral claim right of the individual against the state. Therefore, one might be able to generate the obligation to enact and enforce a corresponding legal right from the state's obligation to refrain from violating this moral right.

Let us explore this approach by reformulating the second stage of the partial justification of the legal right to AFDC payments grounded in the human right to social security.

4. In our society, every eligible individual has a moral right to AFDC payments.

5a. The state ought not to violate the moral rights of the individual.

6. If there is not a legal right to AFDC payments, then the state will violate the moral right to such payments of some eligible individuals.

Therefore, in our society every eligible individual ought to have a legal right to AFDC payments.

The parallel between this argument and the second way in which a partial justification of a primary legal welfare right might appeal to justice is readily apparent. In that argument, it was assumed that a legal right to AFDC payments is necessary to prevent the unjust treatment of eligible individuals; here it is assumed that a legal right to AFDC payments is necessary to prevent the violation of a moral right of eligible individuals.

Why? Part of the answer lies in the nature of a moral right. Hart and others have emphasized the distributive nature of rights. Rights are possessed or had or "owned" by individuals, either natural persons or corporate bodies. This is why the existence of a moral right to AFDC payments does more than impose upon the state the moral obligation of creating and funding an Aid to Families with Dependent Children program that will make welfare payments to many eligible individuals. Each eligible individual has his or her own moral right to AFDC payments, and each such right imposes a corresponding moral duty upon the state to provide AFDC payments to this individual and no other. No matter how widely the state may provide welfare benefits, if this individual is not provided with AFDC payments, then the state has violated the moral right of this individual. This suggests why a program of Aid to Families with Dependent Children that lacks a legal right to such payments for each and every eligible individual might not be sufficient to prevent the state from violating the moral rights of some of those eligible for welfare assistance.

The other part of the answer lies in factual information about our society—facts that show that, without the existence of a legal right to AFDC payments, the welfare agency will actually refuse or fail to make AFDC payments to some eligible individuals. We have rehearsed such facts already. If the law does not impose upon the welfare agencies a legal duty to make AFDC payments to each and every eligible individual, then the welfare workers will have discretion as to which applicants should receive welfare assistance. Even granted wise and dedicated welfare workers, they are bound to exercise their discretion mistakenly in some cases. In these cases, they will be violating the moral rights of eligible individuals denied aid. Moreover, there are strong political pressures operating in our society to reduce funding of very expensive welfare programs, such as the AFDC program. These pressures, unless resisted by a legally enforceable right, will virtually force welfare agencies to violate the moral right of some individuals to receive welfare aid. Finally, both individual prejudice and institutional discrimination against certain groups of welfare claimants, such as blacks or unmarried mothers, will inevitable result in the violation of the rights of such individuals unless each eligible individual has the legal power to take legal action to require the state welfare agency to provide AFDC payments.

Admittedly, this argument is very schematic. At the very least, it needs to be filled out with much more factual information. Some of its premises may be mistaken or misleading. But enough has been said to indicate pretty clearly the kind of argument that could be constructed to constitute the second stage of a partial justification of the legal right to AFDC payments that appeals to the human right to social security. The argument is plausible enough. I can see no reasons in principle to deny that this sort of partial justification can be given. It promises to be entirely adequate, if only one can establish the existence of the human right upon which it is grounded.

There is, however, another way of bridging the gap between moral and legal rights that also deserves to be explored. One advantage of this alternative approach is that it would apply, not only to moral rights that hold against the state, but to moral rights that hold against other parties as well. It rests upon the assumption that the state ought to do more than merely refrain from violating the moral rights of the individual; it ought to protect or secure those moral rights. Let us try to reformulate the second stage of the partial justification in these terms.

4. In our society, every eligible individual has a moral right to AFDC payments.

5b. The state ought to protect the moral rights of the individual.

6b. A legal right to AFDC payments is necessary to protect the moral right to such payments.

Therefore, in our society every eligible individual ought to have a legal right to AFDC payments.

Although the logic of the argument is clear enough, the acceptability of its two new premises requires careful scrutiny.

The argument assumes that (5b): The state ought to protect the moral rights of the individual. Why go this second mile? Why hold that the state ought not only to refrain from violating the moral rights of the individual, but also to protect them? One might, I suppose, defend this assumption by pointing out that the rights in question are moral rights and adding that the state ought to enforce morality. There are those who believe that this is a legitimate and proper, even morally required, function of any adequate government. Without pretending to add anything to the debate in which Devlin and Hart have contributed so much, let me merely confess that it seems to me that there are several important areas that are properly private and into which legal enforcement ought not to intervene. Still, even if not all of morality ought to be legally enforced, there might be reason to hold that there is something especially appropriate to the enforcement of that portion of morality concerning the rights of the individual. Philosophers as far apart as Kant and Mill agree on this.

What is it about moral rights that suggests that the state ought to protect them? Several moral and legal philosophers, including Wasserstrom and MacCormick, seem to take social protection as a logically essential feature of rights. In "Human Rights and Civil Rights," Rex Martin has argued that any right not secured to its possessor by social protection is "infirm" or "deficient" *as a right*. His conclusion is that social protection is intrinsic to the very concept of a right. Although his view is plausible, I do not find his argument convincing. Granted that an unprotected right is infirm, it does not follow that it is any less of a right *per se*. Many sick patients are very infirm, some even terminally ill and almost totally disabled, but still possessed of their mental faculties and human beings in the full sense. Something like Martin's argument might be sound for institutional rights. Legal rights and the rights of conventional morality depend for their existence upon social recognition, and one might argue that "recognition" without social protection is not genuine recognition at all; at best it is a misleading pretence of recognition. But the existence of moral rights depends, not upon social recognition, but upon those reasons in which they are grounded. I am not aware of any argument to show that these grounds must include social protection in any form. I doubt, then, that the analysis of the concept of a moral right can establish the view that the state ought to protect the moral rights of the individual.

More promising is some sort of argument to prove that social enforcement is appropriate to and morally called for by the nature of a moral right. John Stuart Mill advances such an argument when he claims that the violation of moral rights necessarily involves the most serious harms to the individual and a threat to the security essential to any society. Hart argues that the social protection of moral rights is necessarily appropriate because rights concern that part of morality dealing with the proper allocation of freedom and, therefore, with morally justified coercion. My own suggestion is somewhat different. The very language of rights presupposes a context in which the will of the right-holder might conflict with the will of some second party; every right necessarily holds against someone and is possessed by someone. Thus, moral rights concern whose will should prevail in some confrontation. If one will grant that it is a proper and even urgent function of the state to settle disputes between its members and to maintain the public peace and domestic tranquility in a manner consistent with morality, then it seems to follow that the state ought to protect the moral rights of the individuals subject to its jurisdiction. My suggestion is tentative; any adequate argument would require much fuller development. What really concerns me here are two points. First, the second stage of this partial justification of the legal right to AFDC payments can be carried through in this manner only if some justification can be given for the premise that the state ought to protect the moral rights of the individual. Second, there are lines of reasoning that may very well justify this assumption.

Can the same be said for the assumption that: (6b) A legal right to AFDC payments is necessary to protect the moral right to such payments? At first glance, it might appear that other forms of protection would be equally possible. Recall that the moral right at stake here is the eligible individual's moral claim-right against the state welfare agency to be provided with AFDC payments. This claim-right of the individual implies a correlative duty of the welfare agency to provide AFDC payments to the eligible individual. Now this moral duty of the state to the individual could be adequately protected simply by enacting and enforcing effectively a legal duty of the welfare agency to make such payments. Why would anything more be necessary?

If all that were required was preventing the state agency from violating the individual's moral claim-right, then perhaps nothing more would be necessary. But the present argument assumes that the state ought to *protect* the moral *rights* of the individual. How a moral right, even a claim-right, is more than, and not reducible to, any correlative moral duty it may imply. Its core consists of that moral duty together with the ethical power to claim performance or remedy in the event of threatened or actual nonperformances of that duty. And around this core ethical claim are clustered a number of associated ethical elements that confer autonomy over that core upon its possessor. Only a legal claim—a legal duty together with a legal power of claiming performance or remedy—could be sufficient to protect a moral claim as a claim. Taking the argument one step further, only a legal right that confers some sort of autonomy upon the possessor of that legal claim could be sufficient to protect the individual's moral right as a right. Thus it is that the nature of a moral right implies that the state's obligation to provide protection can be fulfilled only by means of a similar legal right. In this way, the second stage of this sort of partial justification of a legal right to AFDC payments by appeal to the human right to social security can be completed.

We have now explored three versions of this sort of partial justification. All are two-stage arguments. In the first stage a moral right to AFDC payments is derived by logical subsumption from a postulated human right to social security. Although the precise logic of this stage remains to be worked out in detail, it seems to offer no serious difficulties. It is the second stage in which the state obligation to create and enforce a legal right to AFDC payments is justified by appeal to a corresponding moral right that poses the theoretically important problems. Since the Benthamite analysis of moral rights in terms of what ought to be legal rights is untenable, this transition cannot be accomplished by mere conceptual definition. This sort of partial justification can be carried through only if one assumes either that the state ought not to violate the moral rights of the individual or that the state ought to protect the moral rights of the individual. Both of these are normative, presumably moral, premises. The first assumption is more obviously true than the second, although I have suggested a way in which the latter might be defended. On the other hand, it will be far easier to explain why a legal right is necessary to protect a moral right than to explain why such a right is necessary to prevent violation of the same moral right. While an effectively enforced legal duty seems adequate to prevent the violation of the moral right to AFDC payments, a set of legal elements that confers autonomy on the possessor of a legal right would be necessary to protect a moral right as a right, as a set of ethical elements that confer a system of ethical autonomy upon its possessor. On balance, the argument *via* the state's moral obligation to protect moral rights appears more promising.

Either way, any partial justification of a legal primary welfare right by appeal to a human right must overcome two additional hurdles. First, although it is probably true that the enforcement of moral rights is more appropriate than the enforcement of some other parts of morality, such as the moral virtues, it is surely true that there are some moral rights that ought not to be legally protected. This is one reason to reject the Benthamite analysis of moral rights. But this implies that premise (5b), that the state ought to protect the moral rights of the individual, is acceptable only if it is qualified in some way. One way to do this would be to change the simple "ought" to "prima facie ought" and try to explain what sorts of considerations might outweigh this prima facie obligation. Another way would be to classify the exceptions to this principle of actual obligation and to write one or more "except" clauses into the premise. Important as some such qualification is, I shall postpone this task for another occasion.

Second, it may well be that human rights impose moral obligations across national borders. IF this is so, then the human right to social security of the starving Indian baby or the neglected Polynesian native may well imply some moral duty of United Nations welfare organizations, or private welfare organizations in the United States or of affluent private citizens in the Federal Republic of Germany to provide welfare aid. It is even possible that individuals in the United States eligible for AFDC payments ought to be aided by individuals or organizations outside our country. Should this prove the case, rights embodied in the legal system of a single state might not be the appropriate form of protection for human rights at all. The very universality of human rights, both with regard to the qualifications for their possession and the range of second parties, might dictate a more universal form of protection. In the end, any solution to these and other problems must lie with an examination of the grounds of human rights, for it is the nature of these grounds that will provide reasons for and thus justify any conclusions about what response this or that legal system ought to make to the human rights of any individual.

Should it turn out that human rights are too universal to provide partial justification for a legal right to AFDC payments in our society, there are other ethical rights to which one might appeal. The title of one of the great natural rights documents, the French *Declaration of the Rights of Man and of the Citizen* of 1789, is instructive. Whatever its original intent, it suggests that, in addition to the ethical rights an individual has as a human being, the individual also has certain fundamental ethical rights as a citizen, as a member of an organized society. I am using the word "citizen" here very broadly to refer to any member of a society, whether or not that society confers upon him or her the full legal rights of citizenship. The ethical rights one has by virtue of membership in a society constitute a very important species of special rights. Reserving the traditional label "civil rights" for the legal rights one has as a citizen, I suggest that we call the ethical rights one has as a citizen "civic rights." This designation immediately suggests the class of rights to which it refers and at the same time suggests both its parallel to and distinction from the more familiar civil rights. Memberhip in a society is a very special and ethically significant relationship. Therefore, it gives rise to an important class of ethical rights of the individual citizen in face of the state or of his or her fellow citizens.

If one wishes to ground a partial justification of the legal right to AFDC payments on an ethical right, there might be considerable advantages in appealing to a civic, rather than a human, right. For one thing, civic rights avoid some of the challenges to the social and economic rights mentioned in the United Nations *Declaration*. Some of these rights are formulated in terms most appropriate to modern industrial societies. But human rights are supposed to be universal, possessed by all humans in all ages and in all lands. When economic and social systems vary so fundamentally over historical periods and between different continents, it is hard to identify any plausible candidates for a genuinely universal economic human right. Again, any human economic claim-right would impose a corresponding duty upon some second party to provide the social security or adequate standard of living or whatnot. But many states clearly lack, at least at present, the economic resources to fulfill any such duty. Since ought implies can, there can be no such duty. And where there is no genuine duty, there can be no corresponding claim-right. But a civic right can be formulated in terms of the conditions of the individual society, and there is no theoretical difficulty in holding that individuals belonging to different societies have quite different civic rights. Again, the fact that many societies lack the resources to provide social security does nothing to undermine the reality of a civic right to social security in any society as affluent as the United States.

Another advantage might be that it would be easier to find grounds for a basic economic right in the individual's relationship to his or her society than in naked human nature. The usual move is to ground human economic rights in fundamental human needs. But exactly how the need of the individual implies any right to have the need met remains obscure; the logical connection between a need and a corresponding right, in spite of much speculation, remains mysterious. It might be easier to identify some aspect of the cooperative enterprise of participating in a common society that justifies the allegation that the individual does have some economic rights. Consider, for example, the right to social security. No doubt each individual as human being has a need for security from certain basic threats to his or her well-being as a human being. Although it is easy to see how this makes social security a valuable social ideal and an imperative goal of social policy, it is hard to see how this alone establishes any ethical claim-right of the individual merely as human being to being provided by society with social security. It is easier to imagine how the individual's membership in a society might ground such an economic right. Participation in our industrial commercial capitalistic society exposes the individual citizen to certain risks, such as poverty caused by widespread unemployment or by the breakdown of the traditional family stability in our age, to which the individual would not be exposed were he or she living in a different sort of society. Since these risks are imposed by our social organization and since the society as a whole prospers through such organization, it might be argued that the unlucky members of our society have an ethical right to social security provided by those more fortunate than they. This is, of course, only the hint of an argument; it may well prove little or nothing upon critical examination. But it does suggest that it might be much easier to justify alleged human rights if they are construed as civic rather than human rights.

Finally, there is the problem of identifying the bearer of the duty or duties implied by any economic ethical right. Even granted a human right to social security, who is it that has the corresponding moral obligation to provide such security? It might be the individual's family, a private welfare organization, the state, some international political body such as the United Nations, or individuals living in the same or in other countries. Postulated economic rights can have definite implications for action only if the duty-bearers can be identified. In the case of a civic right, an ethical right possessed by an individual *as a citizen*, the range of plausible duty-bearers is vastly reduced. Presumably civic rights hold against the state or one's fellow citizens. And if one possesses a civic right as a member of a society, than it would be easy to argue that the society as a whole and as politically organized, that is the state, is the primary duty-bearer. Accordingly, there seem to be a variety of reasons to explore a partial justification of the legal right to AFDC payments grounded in a civic right.

Although there are quite a number of civic rights with which one might begin, let me mention only the most promising candidates. 1) The individual's ethical right to social security, now interpreted as a civic rather than a human right, would obviously do the trick. But there seems little to be gained by examining this choice in detail, for the partial justification grounded upon it would presumably be very similar, if not identical, to that we have already discussed. 2) The civic right to the equal protection of the laws is another attractive option. Several jurists have been trying to show how legal welfare rights might be derived from the equal protection clause of the Constitution. They are seeking, so far with no clear success, to capitalize on the gradual reinterpretation of that clause by the courts. A clause that was once taken to require only procedural equality or equality of all citizens before the law later came to be read as requiring substantive equality or the absence of unjust discrimination in the law and is now coming to mean, at least so they argue, that the law must secure some sort of social and economic equality for all its citizens. Quite possibly one could move from the legal to the ethical level, postulate a civic right to equal protection interpreted to impose upon the state some sort of a duty to secure social and economic equality, and then derive from this a moral right of eligible individuals to AFDC payments. 3) In *Right and Wrong*, Charles Fried has recently suggested that one can derive moral rights to welfare benefits from the primary positive right to a fair share of the community's scarce resources. He has given us a very plausible account of the ground of such a right and has given a very helpful, although vague, definition of its content. 4) William Nelson ("Special Rights, General Rights, and Social Justice") has argued that the principles of distributive justice can best be interpreted as defining the content of a civic right to a fair share of the benefits of social cooperation. Since this argument is so highly plausible and so richly suggestive, I shall begin with his conclusion and carry the argument forward by applying it to the partial justification of the legal right to AFDC payments.

One way to formulate such a partial justification, and a way that provides an illuminating alternative to the lines of reasoning we have just explored, is as follows:

1. Every member of a society has a civic right to a fair share of the benefits of social cooperation.
2. Our state has violated this right of each individual eligible for AFDC payments.

Hence, (3) each eligible individual in our society has a moral right to an appropriate remedy from our state.

4. AFDC payments would be such an appropriate remedy.

Hence, (5) each eligible individual has a moral right to AFDC payments.

6. Our state ought to protect this moral right of the individual.

7. A legal right to AFDC payments is necessary to protect this right.

Therefore, every eligible individual in our society ought to have a legal right to AFDC payments.

Fortunately, not all of these steps in the argument require critical scrutiny. Let us look briefly at those that do.

If any detailed conclusions are to be drawn from this postulated civic right to a fair share of the benefits of social cooperation, this right must be defined with some precision. Presumably this civic right is an ethical claim-right of the individual citizen as citizen holding against the state. But what is the ethical duty it imposes upon his or her state? Not, one would suppose, any duty to provide a fair share of the benefits of social cooperation to each and every individual citizen, for most members of society receive their shares of such benefits through the operations of the economic system without any intervention by the state. Only the needy have any ethical claim that the state provide them with welfare benefits. What every citizen may claim, then, is merely that the state act in a way that will result in each citizen receiving his or her fair share. This implies an ethical duty of the state to pursue economic policies that will generally bring about a just distribution of the benefits of social cooperation. Only in cases where this result does not come about in the usual manner does the state have any duty to *re*distribute such benefits in a more fair way.

Granting for the sake of discussion that a civic right to a fair share of the benefits of social cooperation may be postulated, or better yet established, let us turn to premise (2): Our state has violated this right of each individual eligible for AFDC payments. The ordinary processes by which economic goods and services are distributed in our society have left these needy individuals, possibly with a very few exceptions, well below the poverty level. Their share of the benefits of social cooperation is judged to be less than their fair share in each individual case. But just how is this to be known? To hold that Jones or Smith has "less than" his or her fair share suggests that one has some quantitative conception of what that just portion of benefits would be and to notice that the share actually enjoyed is less than this amount. On the substantive conception of the right to a fair share, this would indeed be the logic of the argument. In principle, this sort of argument seems possible, but it would require the formulation of quantitative principles of distributive justice by which to measure the fair share of each member of a society.

I must confess that I am unable to identify, much less establish, any such principles. Therefore, it is very likely that my own thinking operates with a procedural conception of the right to a fair share. I recognize that individuals eligible for AFDC payments have less than their fair share, not by comparing their share with the quantity of benefits due to them, but by noticing that they have been unfairly excluded from the usual processes of economic distribution. For example, needy dependent children lack adequate shelter, clothing, food, and medical care primarily because their parents are unemployed or their remaining parent has been left without support. Surely it is not the fault of these helpless children that they live in families with incomes vastly less than that in most American families. Children in middle and upper-class families have done nothing to earn their much greater share of the benefits of our cooperative economic system. Since individuals eligible for AFDC payments in fact do not enjoy their fair share of the benefits of social cooperation and since they have a civic claim-right against the state that it act in such a way to ensure that they do have such a fair share, it follows that the state has violated their civic right by its failure to act in a manner to ensure this result. Moreover, by a moral principle analogous to a central principle of the law of torts, this violation by the state of a primary ethical right of the individual gives rise in the individual of a claim-right to remedy against the state.

The next step in the argument is that: (4) AFDC payments would be such an appropriate remedy. This certainly seems a most plausible assumption. The wrong done to each eligible individual is state action resulting in that individual receiving less than his or her fair share of the benefits of social cooperation through the ordinary distribution of economic goods and services. Since AFDC payments would constitute a supplementary income for the wronged individual, it would bring the share enjoyed by that individual closer to his or her fair share. (This assumed, of course, that the level of AFDC payments is not so high that it will increase the income of AFDC recipients beyond their fair share. Given the present level of welfare benefits, this is generally a safe assumption. There may be exceptions, however, in which this is not true. If so, eligibility requirements ought to be changed for such individuals. Meanwhile, the argument is unsound for these exceptional cases.) Moreover, it is appropriate that the AFDC payments should be made by the party that violated the individual's civic right to a fair share and to the party whose right has been violated by the state. Roughly, at least, a strong case can be made for the appropriateness of this remedy and, accordingly, for the moral right of the eligible individual to be accorded this remedy.

We have thus arrived by a new route, *via* the principle that the party whose primary right has been violated thus acquires a secondary right to remedy, at the moral right of the eligible individual to be provided with AFDC payments. In one way or another the principles of distributive justice will enter into the definition of any civic right to a fair share of the benefits of social cooperation. Still, there are significant differences between this sort of partial justification and the kind we considered in the previous section of this chapter in which the appeal was directly to such principles. That argument centered on the premise that the state ought to promote distributive justice. Just why and how urgently stood in need of considerable explanation. Why the violator of a right ought to remedy that violation is less in need of explanation.

This remedial line of reasoning has other advantages as well. Notice that this first stage of the argument begins with a civic right of every citizen to a fair share of the benefits of social cooperation and concludes with a moral right of eligible individuals to AFDC payments. Obviously, it would be preposterous to allege any moral right of every citizen to such welfare benefits. But what singles out some subclass of citizens as possessors of this ethical primary welfare right? It is the fact that, in their cases but not in all, the state has violated their civic right to a fair share. This sort of reasoning seems particularly appropriate to public welfare programs. It has often been noted that these programs *re*distribute goods and services. Now what would ethically require that goods and services, already distributed through the regular economic institutions, be redistributed by the state? Well, a most plausible explanation would be that the original process of distribution has violated the rights of one or more citizens, who now have a right to remedy. Finally, one would like an argument that justifies AFDC payments even though it is very likely that the present levels of welfare benefits are unjustly low. A partial justification using the notion of a right to remedy would seem to accomplish this. A partial remedy is ethically called for when no full or complete remedy is presently available. Thus, this sort of argument can justify a legal right to AFDC payments under our present program without undercutting the moral reform of this program by those who demand higher and more adequate levels of welfare benefits.

The second stage of this partial justification, the argument from the moral right of eligible individuals to the obligation to create and enforce a corresponding legal right to AFDC payments, moves forward as in the case of the reasoning from the human right to social security. The crucial premise is that the state has an obligation to protect the moral rights of the individual. Although the logic of the argument remains the same, it is possible that this premise is somewhat easier to establish when one moves from a human right to a civic right. There is some reason to suspect that universal human rights might best be protected by an international organization like the United Nations, but each state seems the obvious organization to protect the civic rights of the members of the society for which it is responsible and over which it exercizes the ultimate political authority. In any event, there is surely no reason to imagine that this sort of partial justification will be any harder to complete than one appealing to a human right. Therefore, it provides a promising alternative sort of partial justification for the legal right to AFDC payments.

In opposition to a variety of partial justifications of the legal right to AFDC payments that appeal to ethical rights, there can be counter-justifications that also appeal to ethical rights. The obvious example would be an application of Robert Nozick's line of reasoning to our Aid to Families with Dependent Children program. His crucial objection is to the fact that any such welfare program will inevitably involve the compulsory redistribution of wealth within a society. "From the point of view of an entitlement theory, redistribution is a serious matter indeed, involving, as it does, the violation of people's rights" (*Anarchy, State and Utopia* p. 168). Although the full articulation of this sort of argument would appeal to several ethical rights, I shall consider a simplified formulation hinging entirely upon the individual's ethical right to property.

1. Every citizen in our society has an ethical property right to his/her justly acquired holdings.

2. Having a legal right to AFDC payments in our society would necessitate compulsory taxation of these holdings.

3. Such taxation would violate the property rights of the taxpayers.

4. No state ought to violate the ethical rights of its citizens.

Therefore, our society ought not to have a legal right to AFDC payments.

Nozick argues for the first premise in terms of his entitlement theory of justice. On his view, what provides a moral justification for one's holdings is simply the history of how one came to hold this or that good or service, not whether one's holding it conforms to some overall pattern of holdings within one's society. "The general outlines of the theory of justice in holdings are that the holdings of a person are just if he is entitled to them by the principles of justice in acquisition and transfer, or by the principle of rectification of injustice (as specified by the first two principles)" (p. 153). To say that a citizen is entitled to his or her holdings is to say that that individual has a property right in or to that which he or she holds. Although Rawlsians will wish to challenge this conception of justice, I will grant it here for the sake of discussion.

The second premise, that having a legal right to AFDC payments in our society would necessitate compulsory taxation of those holdings, calls for somewhat more discussion. Two points need to be noted. First, since the AFDC program is a public welfare program, the revenues it must have in order to provide welfare benefits must come from taxation. There is no other source of public revenue large enough to finance such an ambitious and costly program. This is simply the recognition that the governmental mechanism of redistribution consists of two parts: collecting taxes and providing benefits.

Unfortunately, the latter is impossible, at least in our society, without the former. And that taxes are imposed by the state upon the citizen, often against his or her will, and that tax laws are enforced with legal sanctions are obvious facts of political life. Second, most of the wealth taken from the citizens by such taxation will be taken from holdings they have justly acquired. Only a very small fraction of what is collected in taxes would happen by chance to come from holdings to which the taxpayer has no property right. Although Nozick does not argue this in any detail, it is clear that he believes it to be true. He does go so far as to write: "I believe that the free operation of a market system will not actually run afoul of the Lockean proviso" (p.182). We will return to this point later. But at least we may grant him that most of the income taxed in our society was not acquired in obviously and undoubtedly unjust ways, as by theft or fraud.

If Nozick can defend the first two premises of this counterjustification, then it is only a single, but not small, step to assert that: (3) Such taxation would violate the property rights of the taxpayers. Whether we are to take this step with Nozick will depend upon whether we accept his conception of the ethical right to property. Although he gives no complete and precise definition of this right, he does explain the crucially relevant part of it for our purposes. "The central core of the notion of a property right in X, relative to which other parts of the notion are to be explained, is the right to determine what shall be done with X; the right to choose which of the constrained set of options concerning X shall be realized or attempted" (p. 171). It is this core right that seems clearly to be violated by compulsory taxation of just holdings. If the state compels me to contribute a portion of my earned income in order to finance its public welfare program, then it is the state and not I that determines what shall be done with this portion of my rightful property. My right to choose whether to spend this amount of money on my personal satisfaction or to use it to send my child to college or to give it to a private charitable organization is denied. I have no free choice on this matter; I am forced, under threat of legal penalty, to use my earnings in part to support the Aid to Families with Dependent Children program. Granted that the state ought not to violate the ethical rights of its citizens in this manner, it follows immediately that our society ought not to have a legal right to AFDC payments.

What are we to say of this counterjustification? Well, it is certainly a very plausible line of reasoning and cannot be dismissed without serious consideration. In the end, however, I believe that there are strong reasons to doubt its soundness. I readily grant that: (1) Every citizen in our society has an ethical property right to his/her justly acquired holdings. Whether this be a universal human right or a civic right determined in part by our economic institutions, I am not disposed to challenge its existence or moral importance. One must not be too quick to suppose, however, that most of the wealth that most of us now hold in our society has been justly acquired. In fact, if anything like the previous partial justification that argued to a moral right to AFDC payments as a remedial right is sound, then this is not the case. I am not, of course, hinting darkly that most of us are thieves or swindlers, but there are other possible sources of unjust acquisition. Rawls notes that voluntary market transactions will not result in a just outcome unless the structure of the market is itself fair. Some argument is needed to establish this crucial presupposition of the whole line of reasoning. Against this presumption, it could be pointed out that the existence of extreme economic inequality in our society forces many transactors to bargain from an essentially unequal and adverse position.

Another worry about the justice of acquisition in our society is the Lockean Proviso that there remain "enough and as good left in common for others" (p. 175). Nozick does write: "I believe that the free operation of a market system will not actually run afoul of the Lockean proviso" (p. 182), but the very existence of the needy persons eligible for welfare in our society might imply the opposite. Where is the common pool of goods and services left for their taking, and why have they not bothered to acquire some of this wealth? Looking back in history at the institution of slavery or around the world at societies in which a favored child may inherit all the family estate leaving other children to fend for themselves, we judge that unjust forms of acquisition have been socially accepted at other times and places. What assures us that we are not today practicing unjust forms of economic acquisition also? It is time to return to and expand the quotation with which I introduced the Nozickian line of reasoning. "From the point of view of an entitlement theory, redistribution is a serious matter indeed, involving, as it does, the violation of people's rights. (An exception is those takings that fall under the principle of the rectification of injustices)" (p. 168). As Nozick himself admits, the soundness of this sort of counterjustification hinges on whether public welfare programs fall within this exception. My point is not that most of us may have no ethical property right to our holdings. It is, rather, that the governmental taking of our holdings to finance an AFDC Program need not be unjust, even on Nozick's own theory.

I also grant that: (2) Having a legal right to AFDC payments in our society would necessitate compulsory taxation of these holdings. Any legal claim right of eligible individuals against welfare agencies that they provide AFDC payments would impose upon these state welfare agencies a legal duty to pay out very large sums of money. There is no way in which this would be possible without collecting equal amounts of revenue, and obviously there is no alternative manner of collecting these huge sums without the imposition of compulsory taxation. These taxes would take from the individual citizens earned income to which, I gladly agree, they have an ethical property right.

The more serious question is whether: (3) Such taxation would violate the property rights of the taxpayers. This depends, of course, on the precise nature of these property rights. On this score, Nozick himself has almost nothing to say. Recall his single relevant sentence: "The central core of the notion of a property right in X, relative to which other parts of the notion are to be explained, is the right to determine what shall be done with X; the right to choose which of the constrained set of options concerning X shall be realized or attempted" (p. 171). How shall we construe that core right to determine what shall be done with X. Although it might be an ethical liberty of determining use, it might equally be an ethical power of performing some action that determines the moral permissibility of use. Of course, it might be an ethical claim against interferences with one's use of X or even some sort of ethical immunity. This is no mere quibble, for until the nature of this core right is explained, one simply does not know how, if at all, compulsory taxation invades this core right. Does taxation divest the owner of his property so that it violates his or her ethical immunity against divesting, or does it force the owner to use his or her property to pay taxes and so infringe the liberty to use it in some other chosen manner? Whatever might be the nature of this core right to determine use, is it absolute or prima facie? If the latter, then it may well be that taxation does not actually violate it at all. Nozick seems to assume, with no argument discernible to the naked eye, that the right to property, whatever it may be, is absolute. This is far from obvious.

Even Nozick admits, however, that the core right to determine what shall be done with X holds only within limits. It is equated explicitly with the right to choose which of "the constrained set of options" concerning X shall be realized or attempted. Even this staunch defender of libertarian property rights notes that I do not have any ethical right to "leave my knife in your chest." He seems to assume that the only constraints upon the exercise of a moral right are the moral rights of other parties. But why not grant that one's exercise of one's rights is also limited morally by one's moral duties? Accordingly, if I have a duty, as a member of the society, to pay taxes, then this might constrain my right to choose what shall be done with my taxable income. To prove that a citizen does have a moral obligation to bear his or her fair share of the burdens required to further social well-being stands in need of argument, of course. But so does any denial of this duty.

However one might in the end define the central core of the notion of a property right, precisely what are all those "other parts of the notion" to be explained by their relation to this core? Presumably one is some sort of ethical immunity against divestiture. One wonders whether this immunity, if it exists, holds valid throughout infinite time. Imagine that the Lockean proviso is satisfied at the time when some individual citizen acquires a holding but that, because of social and economic developments, it later ceases to be satisfied. Does the immunity against divestiture remain unaffected? Suppose that a property owner somehow has an absolute ethical liberty of using the property as he or she chooses. Does he or she also have an ethical power of disposing of the property as he or she wishes? And are there no moral constraints upon the exercise of this ethical power? Although Nozick's theory of rights is very different from my own, we agree that they are complex. Just how this complexity of moral rights affects any Nozickian argument against compulsory taxation to redistribute wealth in a society remains, alas, completely unexplained.

No doubt one could, if one took the time and trouble, explicate a Nozickian conception of the right to property so thoroughly individualistic and libertarian that it would follow that compulsory taxation to support welfare programs would indeed violate this ethical right. But why on earth should any humane moral philosopher accept any such conception? As Honoré and others have pointed out, there are various ways in which one might conceive of a right to property. Indeed, anthropology shows that different societies define the individual's right to hold and use property very differently (Honoré, pp. 113–115). Some argument, and a strong one at that, is needed to establish the adequacy of any Nozickian conception of private property. Offhand, I can imagine no reason whatsoever to adopt that conception myself, and certainly Nozick has given his many readers no clue as to his own reasoning on this issue. Until someone both defines the Nozickian conception of the individual's ethical right to property and provides some argument in favor of it, there is no reason to agree that taxes to support welfare programs violate the property rights of the owners.

Even if taxation to support the AFDC program did violate the property rights of the taxpayers, the counterjustification could not be completed without the additional premise that: (4) No state ought to violate the ethical rights of its citizens. What ought a state to do when confronted with a situation in which the ethical rights of some of its citizens conflict with the ethical rights of other citizens? Samuel Scheffler has argued convincingly that the very ground Nozick proposes to support his favorite libertarian rights would equally well establish a fundamental natural right to welfare (Scheffler, pp. 68–71). Any Nozickian will, of course, deny that there could be any such right. "The major objection to speaking of anyone's having a right *to* various things such as equality of opportunity, life, and so on, and enforcing this right, is that those 'rights' require a substratum of things and materials and actions; and *other* people may have rights and entitlements over these" (Nozick p. 238; italics his). But to argue that there cannot be any rights to welfare benefits simply because the enforcement of these would require the taking of individual property is to assume, completely without argument, that ethical rights never conflict. To be sure, there are those who firmly believe, and argue in support of their view, that fundamental ethical rights never do or can conflict. If this position can be maintained, however, one must be careful to define such rights narrowly. The opposite view, that ethical rights often do conflict, is at least as widely held. I do not propose to settle this issue here; it is complex and difficult. But I do suggest that until it is settled by careful reasoning, one is in no position to defend the proposed sort of counterjustification of the legal right to AFDC payments.

Nor need one presuppose that basic moral rights do conflict to undermine the assumption that the state ought never to violate any of the ethical rights of its citizens. Nozick himself admits that it might be morally permissible to violate some individual right in order to avoid "catastrophic moral horror" (footnote, p. 30). To my mind, the unrelieved suffering of the millions left so desperately needy in our society that they qualify for welfare benefits is precisely such a moral outrage. In any event, whether or not ethical rights ever conflict, they might still be permissibly overridden in extreme situations. I very much doubt that the violation of an ethical right is always and inevitable wrong. No doubt the violation of the rights of an individual is very serious indeed. So are the malnutrition, inadequate medical care, and personal suffering of needy dependent children.

The reader may not be astounded to discover that I remain unconvinced by this sort of counterjustification of the legal right to AFDC payments. As it stands, the premises of the argument are lamentably unexplained and left without the supporting argument they so badly need. This does not demonstrate, however, that no partial counterjustification of this sort is possible. In spite of its many defects, this version has considerable plausibility. It remains open to others to improve upon it or to substitute others along similar lines. If and when these are put forward, they must be assessed in their own terms. I cannot imagine any way to rule out all such arguments in advance. In principle, both partial justifications and counterjustifications of legal rights to welfare benefits that appeal to basic ethical rights appear to be possible.

Conclusion

Advocates and opponents of a variety of proposed or actual legal rights to welfare benefits abound in the political arena. The debate leaves the moral philosopher, not to mention the voter, wondering whether the society really ought to establish and enforce this or that primary welfare right. Since a legal right is a complex structure of Hohfeldian elements, any complete answer would be almost unmanageably complicated. But partial justifications and counterjustifications, arguments to show that some such legal right ought or ought not to exist, can be more briefly formulated and at least tentatively assessed for soundness.

At least three quite different sorts of justifications and counter-justifications seem to be entirely possible. These appeal to utility, justice, and ethical rights respectively. These are possible in the sense that logically valid arguments of all three sorts can, provided one is careful to render the logical structure of the argument explicit, be formulated. In this chapter, I have examined a few of the more plausible examples of each.

The more difficult question is whether any instances of any such arguments are sound. Once the logic of the argument is straightened out, the question of which premises are true remains open. I have certainly not managed to produce sufficient evidence to establish the premises of any of the partial justifications of the legal right to AFDC payments we have examined. However, I have indicated the kind of argument that would be needed. Provisionally, it seems to me that both factual and ethical premises for some of the justifications can be supported with strong arguments and that it will be much harder, if at all possible, to defend the presuppositions of the more usual sorts of counterjustifications. Whatever the final verdict, all three sorts of argument deserve the more careful philosophical examination. It is obviously not the case that all, or even most, justifications of legal welfare rights are sound and that no, or almost no, counterjustifications are equally sound. Even if our society ought to have some primary legal welfare rights, there are many others we ought not to have. And different societies, with their very different sets of institutions and economic circumstances, surely ought to have different sets of welfare rights. The philosopher's task is not to accept or reject these sorts of arguments wholesale. His or her task is to clarify the sorts of arguments that are possible and to indicate how one might go about criticizing any such argument that may be proposed. This much we have gone far toward accomplishing.

4

Ethical Welfare Rights

One way to justify the recognition and enforcement of a legal right to some welfare benefit is to argue from the existence of a fundamental ethical right to welfare, such as the human right to social security or the civic right to a fair share. We have explored and assessed arguments of this sort in the previous chapter. But exactly how should such primary ethical welfare rights be conceived? Before we begin to look for grounds for such rights, we must define their core claims with considerably more precision and see what associated ethical elements they also contain. This is the primary task of this chapter.

But in the process, we would do well to recall that there are also secondary ethical welfare rights. These are not ethical claim-rights to some welfare benefit, but other ethical rights that concern the interactions between the individual welfare claimant and the person or persons upon whom fall the moral duty of making available some welfare benefit. Secondary ethical welfare rights are relevant to any welfare program, not so much as a justification for its existence and for the legal rights to welfare it may contain, as by limiting the morally permissible operations of the welfare agency. One example would be the human right to fair welfare treatment. This right is, in Nozick's terminology, a side-constraint upon the actions of the state as it provides or fails to provide some welfare benefit or benefits to the individuals subject to its jurisdication. Although the state welfare agencies may have considerable moral, as well as legal discretion, they must not treat any individual welfare claimant unfairly. Let us, then, seek to achieve a clearer and fuller understanding of these three sample ethical welfare rights—the human right to social security, the civic right to a fair share, and the human right to fair welfare treatment.

114

The Right to Social Security

One of the ethical rights most obviously relevant to a variety of specific welfare programs is the human right to social security. If this frequently affirmed right is genuine, it surely calls for the creation of welfare programs in many societies and probably justifies the creation, recognition, and enforcement of specific legal welfare rights. It is far from clear, however, just what the content of this right is supposed to be. The language in which the existence and practical import of this human right is debated is lamentably vague and ambiguous, as well as various. What I shall propose, then, is a precising definition of this right—a definition that remains true to its central meaning but draws a clearer line around its borderline significance.

The human right to social security is obviously the right to some sort of security. The Oxford English Dictionary defines security as "the condition of being protected from or not exposed to danger." But as normally interpreted, social security does not encompass security from every kind of danger, including the risk of being bitten by a wild animal or the peril of personal loneliness. Article 25 of the *Universal Declaration of Human Rights* specifies the range of security in the words "security in the event of unemployment, sickness, disability, widowhood, old age or other lack of livelihood. . . ." What links unemployment, sickness, disability, widowhood, and old age together is that these are normally events or circumstances that cause one to be deprived of one's livelihood. At least in modern industrial societies, these are the most common events that interrupt or terminate an individual's income by preventing him or her from earning a living.

It would, however, be a mistake to define the universal human right to social security in terms of security of income, as the highly influential *Beveridge Report* does (p. 120). The *American Declaration of the Rights and Duties of Man* also falls into this error when it affirms "the right to social security which will protect him from the consequences of unemployment, old age, and any disabilities . . . that make it physically or mentally impossible for him to earn a living." So defined, the right to social security could not possibly be a universal human right, an ethical right belonging to all human beings simply by virtue of their humanity. For one thing, in many societies the individual members do not derive their livelihood by earning a living, at least if this is interpreted to mean earning an income by working at some job for which one is paid in cash, credit, or kind. For another thing, even in our kind of society most children, many women and some men derive their livelihood from their place in a family rather than by earning an income. Any genuine human right to social security must be defined in universal terms as the right to security of livelihood. Livelihood, as defined by the Oxford English Dictionary, refers to "the means of living," which may or may not consist of some income, revenue, or stipend.

If the kind of security contained in the human right to social security is security of livelihood, then the *Equality of Treatment (Social Security) Convention* of 1962 overreaches itelf when it includes medical care and family benefits, without qualification, as "branches of social security." This is not necessarily to deny that human beings may have some sort of ethical right to medical care and child allowances, but only to point out that any such right is not part and parcel of the right to social security. Aid to Families with Dependent Children is quite properly included in social security coverage because the dependent child is one dependent upon parents unable to provide a livelihood for him or her. It is very misleading to include family benefits or child allowances paid to fully employed and self-supporting parents within social security, for the purpose of such payments is not at all to protect the child from any lack of livelihood. Again, it may well be that Medicare and Medicaid are properly classified as forms of social security, for they are available only to those unable to provide medical care for themselves because they are deprived of an income sufficient to provide all the means of sustaining life. Any program of universal compulsory medical insurance or general public health care, however, would go far beyond social security in providing medical care equally to those who lack a livelihood and those who earn an adequate income.

In what sense is this a human right to "social" security? One view is that this is a right to security from dangers that originate in or are caused by society. A very common sort of argument is, for example, that the individual has a right to unemployment compensation because, in our economic system, unemployment is the result, not of individual laziness, but of the failure of society to provide a sufficient number of jobs or education adequate to train the individual for the jobs that do exist. The 1947 Constitution of Venezuela defines the right to social security as "the right to be protected against the risks of a social nature which might affect them and against the want which results from them." This is only one of many documents that suggest this interpretation.

Tempting as this conception may be, it is a deviation from the mainstream of political and philosophical thinking about the right to social security. Social security as usually interpreted clearly covers financial aid to the aged and to the disabled, but neither old age nor physical and mental disability are normally caused by society. Again, many insecurities, such as the dangers of crime or epidemics, that do originate in large measure in society are not normally covered by the concept of social security. Finally, the limiting factor emphasized in most formulations of the human right to social security is the negative fact that the loss of livelihood is beyond the control of the individual rather than the positive fact that the event causing the lack of livelihood originates in society.

Social security is social in a very different sense. It is a security of livelihood provided by society. What is social is not the origin of the event that deprives an individual of his or her normal livelihood, but the substitute livelihood that replaces in whole or part the income or other means of living that has been temporarily or permanently terminated by unemployment, disability, old age, or some such untoward event.

To how much security of livelihood does the individual have an ethical right? How large must the substitute income or means of living provided by the society be in order to satisfy the human right to social security? Clearly the minimal interpretation would be that the means provided must be just sufficient to sustain the life of the individual. If the substitute means of living were inadequate to enable the recipient to remain alive, then surely it would be a mockery to call it "a livelihood" or "means of living" at all. The *Beveridge Report*, in fact, defines social security in terms of "subsistence." Very likely some of those who affirm a human right to social security mean to affirm more than this; they use expressions like "a basic income," "an adequate income," or even "sufficient to sustain a fully human life." I propose, however, to give the minimal interpretation to the human right to social security for several reasons. No more generous and humane conception is generally accepted and widely reflected in the language of those who discuss the right to social security, and there is no obvious basis for opting for one conception rather than another once one moves above the ground floor of subsistence. Given the widespread scepticism about the existence of any human economic rights at all, it seems wiser to see whether this modest ethical claim to a livelihood can be justified before considering any stronger and more dubious ethical claims. Finally, it is illuminating to contrast this minimal right to social security with a differently defined right to an adequate standard of living.

The human right to social security, as I define it, differs from the human right to an adequate standard of living in at least two important ways. a) The right to social security has at its core an ethical claim to a bare livelihood, to the minimal means of sustaining life. The right to an adequate standard of living claims more goods and services, the means to enjoy a decent, basically satisfactory life in which the individual can exercise his or her human capacities and not be reduced to living on a merely animal level.

b) The right to social security centers on a conditional ethical claim. It is a right to be provided with a substitute livelihood "in the event of"—if and only if—the individual lacks a livelihood through circumstances beyond his or her control. It is a residual right, a right of last resort. It presupposes that the individual normally has a livelihood provided to him or her in other ways. The individual earns a living at some gainful employment, or is a member of some family supported economically by some breadwinner. If some event causes temporary economic hardship to the individual, a livelihood is supposed in the first instance to be provided by other relatives or by some private charitable organization, such as one's church. Only when these background social institutions fail to provide one with the means of sustaining life does the individual have any ethical claim against the state to step in and provide social security benefits. In contrast, the human right to an adequate standard of living is an initial or original, not merely residual right. It is not a right that comes into operation when one loses or lacks a livelihood provided in the usual manner; it has at its core an ethical claim against any and all parties providing one with a livelihood that they provide one that is adequate. It implies that one's employer has a duty to pay one adequate remuneration. It requires that the parent supply the child with adequate food, shelter, and medical care. And it calls upon the state to adopt and carry out economic policies that will result in an adequate standard of living for all the members of the society.

The human right to social security is also often confused with the human right to protection by society. Thus, it is not at all clear how Principle 2 of the *Declaration of the Rights of the Child* differs from Principle 4. The former affirms that "the child shall enjoy special protection, and shall be given opportunities and facilities . . . .to enable him to develop . . . in a healthy and normal manner"; the latter asserts that "The child shall enjoy the benefits of social security" and "shall be entitled to grow and develop in health." Still, a distinction can and should be made between these two rights. a) The right to social security has at its core an ethical claim to security from one very special sort of danger, the lack of a livelihood. The right to social protection has at its core a much broader claim. Although the individual surely has no ethical claim against the state to protect him or her from every sort of danger, including the risk of dying from lung cancer and the threat of divorce, his claim to protection by society quite clearly covers police protection and fire protection and probably extends to pure food and drug laws and truth in advertising legislation. Thus, the human right to social protection extends far beyond the more narrowly defined right to social security.

b) Although the words "protection" and "security" overlap in much of ordinary language, they have distinct meaning in this special context. The difference is revealed by the paradigm cases of what is required by each of these human rights. The main function of police and fire protection is to *prevent*, completely or in part, crime and fire, but the purpose of social security benefits is to *replace* a livelihood that has been lost. The core of the right to social protection is an ethical claim that society do what it can to prevent the occurrence of certain dangers; the core of the right to social security is an ethical claim to provide a substitute livelihood in the event that a certain danger, the loss of one's normal livelihood, should occur. The relevant or analogous duty arising from the right to social protection would be the duty of society to carry out an economic program that would prevent unemployment or to enact and enforce regulations that would reduce the incidence of disabling accidents on the highways and in the factories.

Now that I have explained in general terms what I mean by "social security," I can go on to explain fairly briefly my conception of the human right to social security. At its core is an ethical claim of the individual human being against his or her society to be supplied with a minimal livelihood in the event that he or she lacks the means of sustaining life because of circumstances beyond his or her control. This core claim consists of two simpler normative elements. First, the state has a moral duty to provide a substitute livelihood to the individual, but only under certain conditions. The individual must be deprived of a livelihood provided through the usual economic institutions, such as employment or the family, and the deprivation must be such that the individual cannot unaided provide a substitute livelihood for himself or herself. I am not suggesting that the state is the only party with a moral obligation to give financial assistance to the economically needy. Individual members of the needy person's family may have a perfect duty to provide assistance, and private institutions or even unrelated individuals may have imperfect duties to help. But the moral duty to provide "social" security falls upon the state because this is a right to security from society and the state is the society as a corporate political body.

Second, the core ethical claim contains an ethical power of the individual rightholder to claim performance or remedy in the event that the state threatens or fails to perform its moral duty of providing a substitute livelihood. This ethical power is the ability of the individual to perform an action with ethical consequences. The specific act involved here is the act of claiming or demanding a substitute livelihood from the state. The performance of this act has as a consequence a new obligation of the state not to fail or refuse this justified claim. This obligation coincides with and reenforces the state's original moral duty to provide a substitute livelihood, for it has the same content or requires the same state action. Its ground, however, is different, for it arises from the changed relationship between the state and the claimant. What would before have been merely neglect of a duty to the individual citizen becomes, after the individual has claimed social security, an act of rejection and disrespect for the citizen. Together, the moral duty of the state to provide a substitute livelihood and the ethical power of the needy individual in certain circumstances to claim performance of or remedy for nonperformance of this duty constitute the core ethical claim of the human right to social security. This is an ethical claim-right of the individual, as human being, holding against his or her state.

An ethical right, like a legal right, cannot be reduced to its core. The human right to social security contains, in addition to the core ethical claim of the individual against the society, a number of associated ethical elements.

1) The bilateral ethical liberty of the right-holder to exercise or refrain from exercising his or her ethical power of claiming perform-ance or remedy in the event that the state threatens or fails to fulfill its moral duty to provide a substitute livelihood under the appropriate circumstances. This implies the ethical liberty of the individual in economic need to petition or demand of his or her society that it provide him or her with a substitute livelihood. That is to say that it is not morally wrong to seek and even insist upon receiving social security benefits from the state. Those who conceive of welfare benefits as charity typically believe that it is wrong for any human being to demand what should be freely and spontaneously given out of love; but to think of social security as a right is to recognize that it is morally permissible and ethically entirely proper for the needy indi-vidual to take the initiative in claiming what is due him or her as of right.

2) The ethical liberty of the individual possessing the right to social security to accept and make use of the substitute livelihood provided to him or her by the state. Recall that this human right is operative only in the event that the individual lacks the means of living because of circumstances beyond his or her control. To assert this ethical liberty is to deny that under these circumstances it is morally wrong for the needy individual to "live off society." This has, of course, not always been admitted by those influenced, or infected, by the Protes-tant Work Ethic. No doubt those capable of earning a living by productive economic activity ought to work for their livelihood, but the ethical liberty at issue here is limited to those abnormal situations in which the right-holder is incapable of providing for his or her own economic needs and is not being taken care of by any private individual or organization, such as a friend, the family, or a private welfare organization. This ethical liberty, like the previous one, confers upon the right-holder, if respected, some measure of freedom with respect to the enjoyment of the core claim of the human right to social security.

The next associated ethical element, on the other hand, confers upon the right-holder, if respected, some measure of control over the enjoyment of the core claim to social security: 3) The ethical power of the possessor to waive his or her claim against society to social security. That is, if the right-holder informs the state that he or she chooses not to be provided with a substitute livelihood in spite of lacking a livelihood through circumstances beyond his or her control, then the moral duty of the state to provide a substitute livelihood to this individual is extinguished. This is an ethical power of the individual because the individual's act of exercising it has ethical consequences, specifically the consequence of suspending a preexisting moral duty of the society to him or her.

Notice, however, that the possessor of the human right to social security does *not* have the ethical power to renounce or transfer his or her right to social security. Although he or she can waive this core claim to be provided with a substitute livelihood on any given occasion, no act that the individual human could perform would completely and permanently terminate his or her ethical claim against the state throughout the remainder of the individual's life. Again, there is no way in which one individual human being can transfer his ethical claim to social security to another person, as I can transfer my property right in my car by selling or giving my car to another party. There simply is no comparable procedure by which, for example, a husband could transfer his claim to social security to his wife so that she would then have a double claim upon the state to be provided with double the means to sustain human life. It is the absence of these two ethical powers, the powers to renounce and to transfer the core claim to social security, that specifies the sense in which this human right is "inalienable."

4) The bilateral ethical liberty of the right-holder to exercise or refrain from exercising the power of waiving the core claim to social security. To assert that the possessor has the ethical power of waiving his or her right is to say that, if he or she performs a specific action, then the state no longer has any moral duty to provide a substitute livelihood on this occasion; this is simply to assert that his or her action does, if and when performed, have certain ethical consequences.

In contrast, to assert that the right-holder has the ethical liberty of exercising this ethical power is to presuppose the former assertion and to go on to assert that it is not wrong for the possessor to perform that action that, when performed, has these ethical consequences. Some would deny this additional assertion. It could be argued, for example, that to refuse a substitute livelihood under circumstances that deprive one of the means of sustaining life would be, in effect, to commit suicide and thus morally wrong. The circumstances that make one ethically eligible for social security are not always, I would argue, such as to make death inevitable for anyone who waives his or her claim against the state to be provided with a substitute livelihood. The right-holder may have some unexhausted assets he or she could use to tide himself or herself over a short economic emergency, or some individual or organization other than the state might step in to provide the needed means of subsistence.

5) The ethical immunity of the right-holder against having his or her core ethical claim to social security extinguished by any act of the state. The legal claim of a creditor against some second party, either a natural person or a corporate body, can be terminated by the legal act of formally declaring bankruptcy. It may be (although this is often denied) that the moral claims of the creditor against the debtor are also terminated by this legal action. But there is no legal or political action that the state can perform that would have the ethical consequence of terminating its moral duty to provide social security to one of its individual members. To be sure, a society has no duty to provide social security benefits to its members when circumstances genuinely render it incapable of fulfilling any such obligation; genuine obligation presupposes ability to perform one's duty. But the moral obligation to provide a substitute livelihood to an individual right-holder cannot be cancelled or extinguished by any state action, except, of course, the act of actually providing social security. It is in this sense that the human right to social security is, in the language of the French *Declaration of the Rights of Man,* "imprescribable."

No legislative, judicial or administrative action that would purport to terminate the individual's core ethical claim to social security would actually have this ethical consequence. This is crucial, not merely to the continuing existence of this core claim, but to the *right* to social security. The language of rights necessarily presupposes some actual or possible confrontation between two parties, the right-holder and the party against whom the right holds. The point of a right is to determine which party should prevail in some such conflict of wills. Now if the second party, the party against whom the right holds, could cancel the core of the right by its unilateral action, then possession of a right—legal or ethical—would be pointless, for it would cease to hold against the second party just when the right-holder wishes to and needs to appeal to his or her right.

The human right to social security, as I conceive it, contains at least the ethical claims, liberties, powers and immunities I have listed. These ethical elements are analogous to the legal elements defined by Hohfeld's fundamental legal conceptions, but their existence depends upon the existence of grounding reasons rather than legal norms or other social institutional elements. It is in this sense that ethical rights may be said to be natural rather than institutional. These elements are not so many isolated constituents merely aggregated together, for they combine to form a single structured whole. At the center of the human right to social security stands the ethical claim of the human individual against his or her society to be provided with a substitute livelihood in the event that he or she lacks the means of sustaining life because of circumstances beyond his or her control. Around this central core stand a number of associated ethical elements, each essentially related to the core claim to social security. Each of these associated elements, if respected, confers upon the possessor of the core claim some sort of freedom or control over the enjoyment of that claim to social security. Thus, the structure of ethical elements as a whole constitutes a system of normative elements that, if respected, confers upon the right-holder autonomy concerning the ethical claim to social security.

The Right to a Fair Share

While advocates of legal welfare rights have traditionally appealed to human rights, such as the right to social security or the right to an adequate standard of living, some recent discussions have shifted to a civic right to a fair share. William Nelson has suggested that the individual member of society has a moral right to a fair share of the benefits of social cooperation ("Special Rights, General Rights, and Social Justice," p. 427). Charles Fried holds that the principal positive right we have against those with whom we live in general communities is a right to a fair share of the community's scarce resources (*Right and Wrong*, p. 110). Although they disagree about what is to be shared, they agree that this is an ethical right the individual possesses as a citizen or as a member of a society, not simply as a human being, and that the content of this right can be defined by the principles of distributive justice.

Let us see how one might define a civic right to a fair share in terms of John Rawls' two principles of justice. For our purposes, the most directly relevant principle is his Difference Principle that governs permissible economic inequalities in a just society. "Social and economic inequalities are to be arranged so that they are both: (a) to the greatest benefit of the least advantaged, consistent with the just savings principle, and (b) attached to offices and positions open to all under conditions of fair equality of opportunity" (*A Theory of Justice*, p. 302). It is noteworthy that the least advantaged hold a special place in this theory of just distribution. Thus, Rawls' two principles of justice define a minimal fair share of the benefits distributed by the economic institutions of any society. It is that share of the wealth that the least advantaged individual would receive under ideal conditions where the social institutions conformed perfectly to the two principles of justice. If, under the actual conditions prevailing in any society, the individual finds himself or herself with less than this minimal fair share, then corrective justice demands that the society provide welfare benefits to redistribute wealth up to that point where the individual actually possesses a minimal fair share of the economic benefits distributed by the society. This Rawlsian conception of a moral right to a fair share defines the amount of that share in terms of the Difference Principle and grounds the individual's right to that share upon the moral demands of corrective justice. Although Rawls does not himself affirm the existence of any such right, it is a promising suggestion that might well be derived from his theory of justice.

Should we adopt such a moral right to a minimal fair share as a fundamental right to welfare benefits? A serious, and for all practical purposes fatal, deficiency in this conception of a right to a minimal fair share is the impossibility, at least in the present stage of our psychological and economic knowledge, of specifying the amount of the minimal fair share. To precisely how much in the way of goods and services is the least advantaged member of a society entitled? I doubt that a purely Rawlsian theory can answer this question. The reason such a theory cannot specify the economic floor in quantitative terms is that it is an ideal procedural theory of justice. The minimal fair share is the share the least advantaged individual would receive if the social institutions of his or her society conformed perfectly to the two principles of justice. The share is not defined in terms of any specified result of the process of distribution. Any result whatsoever is just provided it results from the operations of fair institutions. But how can one know what the results of a perfectly just set of institutions would be? What happens in any actual society with its imperfect institutions is surely no basis for judgment here. And we lack the scientific theory necessary to construct an ideal working model of any society and run the model through its distributive procedures. But if there is no way of quantifying the level of goods and services constituting the minimal fair share, this conception of a right to a fair share will not enable us to know what welfare benefits are required to fulfill such a moral right. This empties the right of all practical implications for the design and reform of actual welfare programs.

There is another difficulty with the purely Rawlsian conception of a moral right to a minimal fair share of the economic benefits distributed in one's society. If this is supposed to be a primary welfare right, it must be some sort of a claim-right of the individual against the state. As a welfare right, it is a right possessed only by those in economic need, specifically those who have not in fact received their minimal fair share of goods and services through the actual operations of the social institutions of the society. It is a right to be provided with goods and services sufficient to bring the individual's share up to the minimal fair share required by justice. Thus, it is a remedial right, a right demanded by corrective justice under circumstances where distributive justice has not been done. Precisely at this point there are two huge gaps in the Rawlsian theory of justice. That theory is primarily a theory of justice under ideal circumstances and says very little about the principles of corrective justice. Also, it is explicitly a theory of just distribution, including the distribution of rights, but it does nothing to explain how justice might itself give rise to any new rights. There may well be some sort of essential connection between justice and rights. But what is this connection? And is it of the sort to explain how some specific rights, such as the right to a fair share, can be grounded in distributive justice? One reads and rereads *A Theory of Justice* in vain seeking the answers to these questions.

This is precisely where William Nelson has tried to develop the theory in a most original and suggestive direction.

Many moral and political philosophers are interested in the attempt to discover correct principles of social justice. The kind of principles I mean are principles for assessing the distribution of goods in a society. . . . What puzzles me is that I do not know what the *scope* of such principles is supposed to be, i.e., I do not know under what conditions people come to have reciprocal rights and obligations in accordance with these principles. (p. 410)

Nelson's suggestion is that these principles of justice should be regarded as governing the just distribution of the benefits of social cooperation within a society. Thus, the rights to which they give rise or which they define are not universal human rights, rights of the individual merely as human and holding against the world, but rights of the citizen, the individual as a member of a society and holding against the society as a whole or against the fellow citizens as members of a common society. Again, the goods whose just distribution is to be assessed are not every sort of natural resource or product of individual labor, but those social benefits which result from the social scheme of cooperation as a whole.

If we look at a society as a cooperative enterprise in which "at least some of the advantages which accrue to those living in the society will be advantages which are in part attributable not to their own diligence, but to the cooperation of their fellows," we can explain how membership in a society can give rise to a claim-right of individuals with less than their fair share holding against those who have more than their fair share of the benefits of social cooperation.

But my general point is just this: the relation of interdependence among the participants in a cooperative endeavor is the kind of relation which could serve to ground the application of principles of justice with redistributive effects if those principles are regarded as principles specifying the content of special rights and obligations. (p. 429)

In short, the moral relation between welfare right-holder and the duty-bearer of the moral obligation to redistribute social benefits is grounded in their economic relationship as mutual participants in a cooperative economic system. The moral principle to which Nelson appeals is Rawls' principle of fair play, the principle that those who accept and intend to continue accepting the benefits of cooperation have an obligation to do their part, to share the burdens of the cooperative enterprise, when it is their turn to do so. Just as accepting the benefits of a cooperative enterprise imposes upon one a moral obligation to share its burdens, so, Nelson suggests, "a willingness to comply with one's obligations of fair play" is a necessary and sufficient condition of one's having a moral right to that share of the benefits of cooperation prescribed by the principles of justice (p. 427).

What are we to say of Nelson's conception of a civic right to a fair share? It does, I believe, point in exactly the right direction. At the core of every primary welfare right stands a claim of the right-holder against some duty-bearer to be provided with some economic good or service or set of goods and services. Nelson has recognized clearly that any such claim of one party against a second party must be grounded in some special relation between them. He has posed the crucial question here: what kind of a relation could ground this sort of a right? His answer to this question, on the other hand, is not quite on the mark. It is close. The solution to this problem of grounding a right to a fair share probably does lie in the individual's relationship to an economic system shared by all the members of the society. But the ethical claim of the individual against the state, against society as a whole, to a fair share is not grounded in the relationship between one individual and other individuals engaged in a cooperative enterprise, and the underlying moral principle is not that of fair play. This fair play conception of a right to a fair share will not serve as a fundamental right to welfare.

One difficulty is that this fair play conception of a right to a fair share does not define a right to welfare. Although this does not matter for Nelson's purposes, which were to identify the scope of principles of distributive justice and to explain how they can define a right to the redistribution of wealth, it is of importance for our purpose, which is to identify and define some sample welfare rights. A welfare benefit is some economic benefit provided to an individual because of the individual's need, but need does not enter into this conception of a right to a fair share. It is not simply that the word "need," and all synonyms, are missing from the definition of this right. The fair play conception has no essential connection with economic need at all. To be sure, if an individual finds himself or herself in dire poverty because he or she does not have a fair share of the social benefits in the society, then providing a fair share would be to provide a needed benefit. But the right to have a fair share is not limited to, nor does it have any special relevance for, those in need. One might be in need, even though one in fact has one's fair share of the advantages of social cooperation, because of one's lack of goods and services arising in other ways in the economic system, benefits occurring as natural resources available to the society or products of individual diligence and labor. On the other hand, one might not be in genuine economic need but still be deprived of one's fair share of the advantages of social cooperation. If one has borne a disproportionate share of the burdens of the scheme of cooperation, then perhaps one's share of the benefits of cooperation ought, according to the principle of fair play, to be larger than that of others. If so, an individual with a comfortable income might still have a right to be provided with even more goods and services to complete his or her fair share.

To be sure, one might be able to derive moral rights to welfare from an economic civic right, like this one, that is not itself a primary welfare right. But I very much doubt that this fair play conception of a right to a fair share could even serve in place of a right to welfare. The crucial question is whether those in need of welfare benefits through no fault of their own would qualify for the right to a fair share as defined by Nelson. Presumably retired workers, whether breadwinners or homemakers, would possess a moral right to their fair share of the benefits of social cooperation. After all, they have borne their share of the burdens of the economic system; they have worked hard and long in the cooperative endeavor. Hence, the principle of fair play requires those who continue to accept the benefits of the system to take their turn at sharing the advantages they enjoy with those whose cooperation made these social benefits possible. But what about the large numbers of unemployed youth in our society who cannot find jobs, either because of massive unemployment or because their education has left them almost unemployable at any of the jobs available in our complex society? Since they have not borne the burdens of our cooperative economy, how does the principle of fair play give them any moral claim upon its benefits? Nelson suggests that a mere "willingness to comply with one's obligations of fair play" is a sufficient condition of having a moral right to a fair share. I must confess that I do not understand how mere willingness to play fair on the part of someone who has not actually played the game is sufficient to give one an ethical claim on the game benefits enjoyed by those who are playing, but let that pass. Very young children dependent upon parents unable or unwilling to provide for their economic needs are as incapable of being willing to play fairly in any economic game whose activities, rules, burdens, and benefits are as yet unknown to them as they are incapable of actually playing the game. What of feeble-minded adolescents or brain-damaged adults, equally incapable for psychological reasons of being willing to play our economic game? One fears that many of those classes of individuals most in need of welfare rights would not possess a right to a fair share if this is interpreted according to Nelson's fair play conception.

Finally, this fair play conception is just as inapplicable in practice as Rawls' minimal share conception of the right to a fair share. Nelson suggests that the principles of distributive justice do not concern all of the goods, benefits or advantages distributed in a society; their scope is limited to the benefits of social cooperation. He specifically excludes the distribution of natural resources and the products of personal industry from their scope. To specify an individual's fair share, then, one must be able to distinguish that surplus of goods and services resulting from the society's scheme of social cooperation from other goods and services. How on earth could one measure each of these in any actual social economic system? I cannot imagine how, and Nelson gives us no hints. Not knowing how much is to be shared fairly among the players in the game, one can hardly guess what share ought to fall to the lot of each individual according to the principles of justice. Surely one cannot begin to apply the principles of distributive justice until one discovers to what aggregate of goods and services they are supposed to apply. Even if Nelson has identified and defined a genuine civic right, this right will be of no use in the design, operation, or moral criticism of any actual public welfare program.

Our goal, then, should be to define a conception of a right to a fair share that is relevant to welfare benefits and applicable in practice. A good place to begin is to notice that there are a number of different ways in which the distribution of goods and services in a society can be unfair or unjust.

1) Unjust reward. If the economic institutions of a society are such that negligence, fraud, and coercion tend to "pay off" in terms of the goods and services one receives, while the practice of conscientiousness, honesty, and a respect for the rights of others reduces one's income, the economic system may well be branded as unjust in this respect. One sort of justice insists that virtue ought to be rewarded and vice punished. Although this is not a specifically economic conception of justice, probably no conception of justice is economic *rather than* moral. Still, the notion of just rewards is applicable to economic activity just as to any other sort of human action simply because the economic man is also and at the same time a moral agent.

2) Unjust remuneration. The normal adult is both a productive worker in the economic system and a recipient and consumer of economic goods and services. This is equally true of those breadwinners who receive wages or a salary from some employer and homemakers who share in the family income and perform unpaid services for the family. Another aspect of justice demands that there be some proportion between one's economic contribution and the share of goods and services one receives. One need not agree with the Marxist theory that all those who sell their labor are exploited by the capitalists in order to recognize that some workers, whether paid or unpaid, are exploited because they contribute much more of value to the economy than they receive back from it.

3) Unjust exclusion. Some individuals appear to be entirely or largely excluded from sharing in the wealth produced in the society in an arbitrary and inequitable manner. It is not so much that these

persons receive the wrong size share—a share smaller than their virtue or productivity merits. Rather they are denied anything like a genuine share because they are not provided for by the economic institutions that shape the process of economic distribution. The crux of the injustice is that others similarly situated receive a full share, while these individuals are left without a share through no fault of their own. I suggest that we might conceive of the right to a fair share as a reflection of this sort of distributive unfairness.

Let me begin to clarify the distinctions I have just drawn with an artifically simple model of a distributive system. Imagine that a church holds a pot-luck dinner. Anyone who wishes to participate is asked to bring a dish (main dish, salad, or dessert) adequate to serve four persons. The church will supply bread, butter, and beverages. The members of the church bring their goodies, and these are divided, distributed, and consumed. Now one can imagine several different ways in which the process of distribution might be unjust.

1) Unjust reward. One lady works very hard and for long hours to produce a very difficult dish, perhaps Peking duck or an elaborate fruited braided bread. An elderly and impecunious widower sacrifices mightily to buy ingredients for a dish that the average member of the church could easily afford to make. Even if justice does not dictate that their virtue be rewarded with larger-than-normal portions, it would surely be unfair for these persons to receive no sort of reward, at least some special recognition or a word of thanks. It would also be unfair for a selfish individual to produce a scanty unappetizing dish but to receive large delicious helpings.

2) Unjust remuneration. If one person brings two dishes or an exceptionally large and desirable dish while another brings a very small and unappetizing one, it seems unfair for two individuals who have contributed so unequally to receive equal portions of the total food available.

3) Unjust exclusion. Although it might be fair enough to prevent all those who have not contributed any dish from sharing in the church meal, it would be unfair to exclude some individuals who appear without any dish to contribute but to permit others to eat without contributing. Or suppose that the participants are required to form a single line and to help themselves one by one, but that the organizers provide no control to restrain the greed of those near the head of the line. It might turn out that the last few individuals in line would find only a few crumbs of bread and scraps of food remaining. This would be a clear case in which the institutions shaping the distributive process unfairly excluded some individuals. It is not so much that their share of the meal was smaller than it should be to match their patience in waiting in line or their contribution to the meal; the requirement that they stand in line and wait their turn led to their being deprived of a share in the meal. It is no reply to point out that

there were a few crumbs of bread and a few scraps of salad left; these do not constitute a genuine share at all.

Now let us see how these distinctions between different sorts of distributive injustice might apply to our economic system.

1) Unjust reward. A doctor's sense of moral duty and compassion for those lacking adequate medical care might move him to give up a lucrative suburban practice and open an office in an urban ghetto or in a small rural community not served by any physician. It seems unfair that this virtuous action should so dramatically lower his income. Suppose that a university professor is denied promotion and annual raises in salary because she has publicly protested against what she regards as sexual discrimination or an unjust war. The plant worker whose salary is reduced because he tried to improve the working conditions of his coworkers by trying to unionize them is also being economically punished where, from a moral standpoint, he ought to be rewarded for his virtue. It seems especially unfair if the economic system rewards the salesman who misrepresents his product or the contractor who makes a large profit by shoddy workmanship and the use of inferior materials but manages to evade any liability for the defective product.

2) Unjust remuneration. Migrant workers are often paid far less than native workers performing similar tasks, and typically far less than their labor is worth. The sweatshops springing up in and around New York City in recent years pay unfairly low wages, as the large profits realized by some employers of such shops reveal. Estimates of the amount a husband would have to pay in order to employ workers to shop, cook meals, clean clothes and the home, care for children, etc. suggest that many housewives, who may have to satisfy their own needs and desires out of a very limited household budget provided by the husband, receive much less in goods and services than they contribute to the domestic economy. Children employed in fast food restaurants, to do odd chores around some small stores, and to perform yard and lawn work are often paid much less than their labor is worth, at least if the amount that adult labor can command in the economic marketplace for doing the same or comparable work is taken as a rough measure of just remuneration.

3) Unjust exclusion. Needy dependent children differ from other dependent children, for all young children are dependent upon others for the goods and services they consume, only in that they have had the misfortune to be born into families that are unable or unwilling to support them. They are thereby virtually excluded from sharing in the process of economic distribution in our society, at least in the absence of any welfare program to cover them, while the majority of dependent children, who are no more productive economically than they, do receive a share of the goods and services produced in our society through the institution of the family. Simi-

larly, elderly individuals, most of whom have been productive throughout most of their adult years, may be deprived of a genuine share of the social wealth because they have no children to support them or because their children cannot or will not care for them in their old age and/or because their savings have become totally inadequate to meet the rising costs of our inflationary economic system. It is unfair for these individuals to be denied a share of current productivity when other individuals similar to them in all relevant respects are provided for by the normal processes of economic distribution in our society that feature one or more breadwinners who then support other dependent members of the family. In periods of massive unemployment or in periods of rapid technological and social change, large numbers of individuals may lack any income because they were not lucky enough to obtain gainful employment or have been left virtually unemployable in modern society by virtue (or vice) of the inadequate education they have received in our public schools. Yet other individuals no more willing to work, but more lucky in job-hunting or better prepared for our society, share fully in the process of economic distribution.

Thus it is that some members of our society are, for all practical purposes, excluded from the usual processes of economic distribution, not by any actions of their own for which they are responsible, but because of the nature of the social institutions that govern distribution. What is unfair about this exclusion is that it is arbitrary and inequitable. It is arbitrary because these individuals are excluded for no relevant reason; it is inequitable because other individuals similar in all relevant respects are not similarly excluded from sharing in the process of economic distribution in our society.

If we are to conceive of a right to a fair share in terms of unjust exclusion, we must become more clear about the nature of this sort of distributive injustice. I conceive of this as a sort of social injustice in Rawls' sense; that is, it is an injustice of social institutions. More specifically, the individual member of society is excluded from sharing in the goods and services of the society by the nature of the social institutions that shape and control the processes of economic distribution in that society. More than such overall institutions as communism or capitalism, production in the home or in the factory, tax structures, and investment institutions are involved here, for much economic distribution takes place through the family, the church, private welfare organizations, and public programs.

Now these social institutions might exclude the individual from the distributive process in a variety of ways. Governments might actively exclude citizens from certain occupations by licensing requirements that are arbitrary and serve no useful social purpose. A more common active form is discrimination, racial or religious, that handicaps some members of society so severely that they are kept, in spite of their best eforts, from participating in the normal distributive process. Passive exclusion takes place when the social institutions simply do not provide for the economic needs of the individual. Even though the individual is not actively kept out of the economy, the individual is left out of the process of economic sharing. Many individuals who are thus left out are incapable of taking action to become included, for example infants, seriously handicapped adults, and terminally ill patients. One way or another, the social institutions that control the processes of economic distribution are such that the individual is left without a share of the goods and services of the society.

What is it to be excluded? How might one distinguish between the individual who does not receive a share and the individual who receives a small share, one less than average and certainly less than that received by the more fortunate members of the society? It seems to me that the line dividing those who have a share, greater or lesser, and those who lack a share is the poverty line. To be among the poor in a society is not merely to have less than most others, it is to have so little that one may properly be said to lack a genuine share at all.

The Oxford English Dictionary defines being poor as "having few, or no material possessions; wanting means to procure the comforts, or the necessities, of life; needy, indigent, destitute." Notice two aspects of this definition. It is comparative; one has few rather than more possessions. Also, it suggests that one has very few, perhaps none at all. One may be left destitute, without the bare necessities of life. For my purposes, however, it is essential to insist that poverty be defined in terms of the relevant comparison class. We, living in an affluent society, might judge that most or all inhabitants of a much poorer society are living in poverty. But clearly it would be foolish to suggest that most of the members of that society are excluded from its processes of economic distribution. It is merely that there is less to distribute in that society. To be excluded the individual must have very few goods or services relative to the norms of his or her own society. In a very egalitarian society, it might be the case that no one, or only a very few, are poor by its standards. But when an individual is poor in comparison with the norms of his or her society, then it can properly be said that that individual lacks a real share of the wealth of the society. And when the individual is impoverished by the social institutions of the society, then that individual is excluded from sharing in the processes of economic distribution. Provided, of course, the impoverishment continues for some length of time. A worker may lose his job or an entrepreneur may lose her business and become poor. But if the individual is still in a position to obtain gainful employment or to receive goods and services in some other way, then that individual is not excluded from the processes of economic distribution. I take as my criterion of exclusion, then, continuing impoverishment by the social institutions.

Not all such exclusion is unjust. Suppose that the economic institutions of a society make no provision for the economic needs of individuals able, but unwilling, to work. Or suppose that the society does not provide food, clothing, shelter, or medical care for the worker who gambles away his or her earnings every payday and so, in one sense, remains in continual poverty. (In another sense, this gambler is not excluded from the distribution process; he or she merely consumes his or her share in a different manner.) This need not be unjust, for this sort of exclusion is not arbitrary. There are reasons to justify leaving out those who could, but refuse to, care for themselves. Only when the impoverishment by the social institutions is arbitrary and inequitable is it unjust. Another way of putting this point is to say that the wrong done to the citizen is not merely being excluded, but the wrong of being treated unjustly in the process of distribution of goods and services. To be sure, every excluded individual is thereby harmed, at least in a broad sense of that term. But only when the harm is unjustly inflicted is the individual also wronged.

That the individual who suffers unjust exclusion is wronged implies that the individual citizen has an ethical right not to be unjustly impoverished by the social institutions of his or her society. This is not a human right—not a right one possesses simply as a human being—but a civic right, an ethical right the individual possesses as a citizen, as a member of some society. At its core is the ethical claim of the individual member of a society holding against the state not to be unjustly impoverished. Since this ethical claim of the right-holder against the duty-bearer is clearly relational, it is presumably grounded in or conditional upon some special relationship between the citizen and the state. What might this relation be? The short answer is that the individual member of a society is economically dependent upon the state. Any answer as short as this, however, requires a somewhat more lengthy explanation.

What confers upon the individual right-holder this ethical claim not to be impoverished by the economic system is the citizen's economic dependence upon the economic institutions of his or her society. If the individual were born an adult in a state of nature, fully capable of producing all the goods and services he or she would consume, this would not be so. Robinson Crusoe, whatever he might reasonably fear from a lack of resources or an unkind nature, was lucky enough to be independent of any social system, at least until he found his man Friday. One might imagine social systems so loosely organized and so economically blessed that the individual would be largely independent of society, at least after childhood and before old age and excluding periods of illness or disability. But in a society anything like ours, where natural resources are someone's legal property and most production is cooperative and social, no individual is independent of the economic institutions of the society. Thus, to be excluded by these institutions from the process of economic distribution is necessarily to be impoverished and thereby to be seriously harmed. And to be unjustly excluded is to be unjustly harmed and thereby wronged. Individuals who are not members of this society, however, do not stand in this same relation to its economic institutions. To be sure, the price I pay for coffee may be affected by the economic system of Columbia or Brazil, but this impact is indirect and concerns me only as filtered through the economic system of my own society; and my having a share of goods and services is hardly dependent upon any other economic system.

The citizen's ethical claim holds against the state. Why the state? The economic system of a society, specifically the social institutions that distribute goods and services within that society, include much more than the state, (i.e., the society as legally and politically organized). Farms and factories, stores and consumer cooperatives are not typically public enterprises or operated by the state, although they might be in a socialistic country. Private welfare organizations and individual charitable giving serve to distribute wealth in various ways. Within each family, it is usually the case that several members are economically dependent upon the earnings of one or two relatives who are gainfully employed. Each family is also a small-scale economy in which goods and services are produced, meals cooked and medical care tendered, and distributed to the members of the family. Given the complexity of our economic system, what fixes responsibility for not unjustly impoverishing the citizen exclusively upon the state? It is partly the fact that the many and diverse institutions within the society are shaped, although not produced *ex nihilo*, by the state. Their existence is permitted and regulated by the law of the land, and the policies of the government modify them in very basic ways. The state may outlaw sweatshops in the garment industry or change the ways huge factories operate by labor legislation. Policies of taxation and credit limits have a great impact upon investment and the structure of the economic system. Changes in child-labor laws or in divorce laws may affect the structure of the family. Even when the state has not given definite shape to some social institution, it still claims the authority to do so. In a society like ours, although not in every society, the state is sovereign. It asserts and maintains a monopoly on the control of permissible force and establishes its authority over every other institution. Therefore, the state is ethically responsible for the operations of the entire economic system. Hence, the ethical claim of the individual holds against the state.

The core of the civic right not to be unjustly impoverished is an ethical claim of the individual member of a society against the state not to be rendered poor for any extended period of time by the social institutions that shape its processes of economic distribution. Around this core claim stand other associated elements that confer upon the claimant autonomy concerning the enjoyment of this claim. I shall not stop to spell these out, however, because this right is only a stop along the way to my conception of a right to a fair share. This right is not itself a welfare right. It is not an ethical claim to be provided with any welfare benefit or benefits at all; it is a purely negative right not to be unjustly treated in one specific manner, by being excluded from sharing in the process of distribution in one's society.

However, a positive right to welfare can be derived from and defined in terms of this negative ethical right. Each citizen has an ethical claim-right holding against the state not to be unjustly impoverished. Accordingly, if any citizen is in fact unjustly impoverished, that individual is wronged by his or her state. As the wronged party, the individual acquires an ethical claim-right to be provided with an appropriate remedy. Since the wrong that has been done to the individual is unjust impoverishment, the remedy is relief from his or her poverty. Thus, the remedial duty that now falls upon the state is to provide welfare benefits, economic goods and/or services, to the individual claimant sufficient to remove the unjust impoverishment. Since a genuine remedy must be adequate to the wrong it is intended to make right, the remedial right is defined in terms of the individual's right not to be unjustly impoverished. The content of this remedial right can be described in other, but equivalent, terms. The individual has been wronged in that he or she has been unfairly excluded from a share in the goods and services distributed in the society. Hence, there arises an ethical claim-right of the wronged individual to be provided with a fair share, that is with the amount of goods and services he or she would have had had he or she not been thus unfairly excluded. Here is a third conception of the ethical right to a fair share. As a remedial right derived from the more basic right not to be unjustly impoverished, I christen it my "unjust impoverishment conception" of a right to a fair share.

Since the ethical right not to be unjustly impoverished is a civic right, this right to a fair share is also a civic right. Still, it is based upon a somewhat different relation between the citizen and the state. The original right not to be unjustly impoverished is grounded in the economic dependence of the individual upon the state insofar as the state shapes and has ultimate authority over the various social institutions that control the processes of economic distribution in the society. This is why the individual possesses this right as a citizen and why the claim-right holds against the state. Simply because the right not to be unjustly impoverished holds against the state, and the state only, only the state is in a position to wrong the individual by unjustly impoverishing him or her. In the event that the state does in fact wrong the individual claimant in this manner, there arises a remedial right to a fair share. This is a welfare claim-right that is possessed by the individual as the wronged party and holds against the state as the party who has inflicted the wrong upon the claimant. But because the individual has been wronged as a citizen, for it is only as a citizen that the individual possesses the right not to be unjustly impoverished, the remedial right is also a civic right one possesses as a citizen, albeit a citizen who has been wronged. To the purist who objects that one does not possess this right purely as a citizen, I can reply that actually every citizen, whether wronged or not, does possess as a citizen simpliciter a conditional ethical right to be provided with a fair share, specifically the ethical right to be provided with a fair share *if* one has been unjustly impoverished.

Let me sum up briefly my proposed conception of the civic right to a fair share. At its core is the conditional ethical claim of the individual as a member of a society holding against the state that the state provide to him or her a fair share of the goods and services distributed in the society in the event that the individual has been unjustly impoverished by the society. This core consists of the moral duty of the state to provide to the individual welfare benefits sufficient to bring the individual up to that economic level just above the poverty level, together with the ethical power of the individual to claim performance of this remedial duty in the event the state fails or refuses to do so. Around this core claim are a set of associated ethical elements including at least the following: 1) The individual citizen has the bilateral ethical liberty of exercising or refraining from exercising this core ethical power. 2) The individual citizen has the ethical power of waiving the entire core claim against the state. 3) The individual citizen has the bilateral ethical liberty of exercising or refraining from exercising this power to waive the core claim. 4) The individual claimant has an ethical immunity against being deprived of this core claim by any unilateral action of the state. This, in brief, is a sketch of an ethical right to a fair share when an ethical right is taken to be a set of normative elements that, if respected, confer upon the right-holder autonomy with respect to the enjoyment of a core ethical claim.

Can my unjust impoverishment conception of a right to a fair share meet the tests of applicability and relevance any better than Rawls' minimal share conception and Nelson's fair play conception? To begin with, could one use this conception in practice to determine when an individual has an ethical claim to welfare benefits and to specify what those welfare benefits ought to be? An obvious difficulty is that my conception of the right to a fair share is defined in terms of poverty, and the notion of being poor or impoverished is at best a very vague one. On my conception, one could identify individuals with a claim to welfare benefits only if one could identify an individual who is poor, and one could know how much in supplemental goods and services the state out to provide to that individual only if one could tell when the individual rises above the poverty line. Obviously one cannot make either judgment with precision, but it does not follow that such judgments can never be made or that in many cases their correctness is in serious doubt. Imagine some new pure food and drug legislation that creates a legal right "not to be made bald" by any shampoo sold in the United States. Given the vagueness of the word "bald," there will be many borderline instances in which there may be no determinate application of this legislation. But in many cases, a reasonable judge would have no difficulty in deciding whether the plaintiff is indeed bald. Moreover, if one imagines advances in medical technology, it would be possible in practice to decide that the offending shampoo company has in fact relieved the baldness of the claimant. To be sure, some plaintiffs might be borderline cases whose cases are dismissed for lack of evidence of sufficient lack of hair, and from time to time some shampoo company might be legally required to grow a few extra hairs on some individual's scalp. But in many cases a right defined in vague terms is clearly applicable, and other cases can be dealt with in ways that are not grossly unjust precisely because they are borderline cases. Much the same is true of the ethical right to a fair share, vague as it is.

Returning to the legal right to have one's baldness remedied, there would be an additional problem of application in practice. Before insisting that some shampoo company remedy the baldness of the individual plaintiff, the judge would need to do more than to assure himself or herself that the plaintiff is in fact bald; it would be necessary to determine that the baldness had been caused by the shampoo sold by the defendant company. Similarly, before knowing that the state has any duty to provide welfare benefits to the individual claimant, one would need to do more than assure oneself that the individual is indeed poor. One would need to show that the individual had been unjustly made poor, that the poverty resulted from the social institutions of the society unfairly excluding the individual. Now I did suggest my criterion of unjust exclusion; exclusion is unjust when it is arbitrary and inequitable. Neither of these notions is very clear or precise. Unfortunately, I have no more precise analysis, and certainly no developed theory comparable to that of John Rawls, to offer the reader. My criterion, and consequently judgments made upon it, will be controversial in many cases. Still, two things can be said. In some cases, there is a considerable degree of agreement on the justice or injustice of excluding this or that individual or class of individuals from some specified sort of coverage in a system of economic distribution. And, at least as important, where disagreement does exist, there are ways of arguing for and against the injustice of this or that instance. I do not pretend that the situation is satisfactory. I would dearly love to be able to present an articulate theory of justice in precise quantitative terms. Still, even without that, the situation is not hopeless. Judgments can be made in practice and these judgments are typically reasonable rather than arbitrary. Thus, judgments of justice or injustice of this sort are not completely impossible in practice. To this degree, but admittedly to this degree only, my conception of an ethical right to a fair share is applicable in practice. Recall that several legal systems operate rather comfortably with the concept of unjust enrichment. To be sure, most judges hesitate to render any judgment of unjust enrichment in borderline cases, but in other cases such judgments are rendered and, as a rule, upheld if appealed.

If my unjust impoverishment conception of the civic right to a fair share is applicable in practice, then it seems clearly relevant to welfare programs and policies. Ethical claims that the state provide goods and services to the individual—claims grounded in the unjust impoverishment of the claimant—are claims to welfare benefits, to goods and services provided to the needy individual and on the basis of need (i.e., poverty). I propose as my second example of an ethical welfare right—an example in addition to and partial contrast with the human right to social security—the civic right to a fair share.

The Right to Equitable Welfare Treatment

The "Bill of Welfare Rights" asserts the existence of "the right to fair and equal treatment, free from discrimination based on race, color or religion." While the National Welfare Rights Organization is asserting the existence of a legal right within the United States, I intend to try to define a corresponding ethical right that may well be possessed by the citizen of any society. The importance of fair treatment to applicants for and recipients of public welfare is obvious and undeniable. Precisely what distinguishes fair from unfair welfare treatment is much less obvious and more debatable. Surely it cannot be taken for granted that equal treatment is fair and unequal treatment unfair. Many argue that it is unfair to provide equal old age assistance to individuals living in states where the cost of living differs drastically, and most agree that parents with several children should receive more Aid to Families with Dependent Children than those with only a single child. Again, discrimination based on race, color, or religion is not the only form of unjust welfare treatment. Unemployed fathers denied benefits available to unemployed mothers and unmarried mothers denied benefits available to married mothers are treated unfairly even when such denials are not based upon race, color, or religion. In order to have a convenient label that begs as few questions as possible, I will speak of "the right to equitable welfare treatment."

This is a secondary, rather than a primary, welfare right. It is not an ethical right to some welfare benefit, for equitable welfare treatment is not itself a welfare benefit; it is not some good or service provided to the individual because of need. Still, this is a welfare right in the broad sense because it is a right concerning the treatment accorded individuals by state welfare agencies relating directly or indirectly to the provision of welfare benefits. This secondary welfare right functions, in Nozick's terminology, as a side-constraint, limiting the morally permissible ways in which public welfare officials may deal with individual citizens.

How can we best conceive of this practically important and theoretically interesting right? I suggest that its defining core is the ethical claim of the individual citizen against the state not to be treated worse concerning welfare benefits than others who are similarly situated without a justicizing difference. This long and complicated formulation is hardly intelligible without considerable explanation.

This is an ethical right of the individual citizen, that is, a right an individual possesses as a citizen. Since only a fraction of the citizens in any society are on welfare, one might imagine that the right to equitable welfare treatment is possessed only by those citizens who interact with the welfare agencies, but this cannot be so. Clearly this right, if genuine, is possessed by every recipient of welfare, for it would be a violation of any recipient's right to equitable welfare treatment to be provided with smaller welfare benefits than another recipient with no greater qualifications. Just as clearly, this right must extend to unsuccessful applicants for welfare because it would violate an applicant's right to equitable welfare treatment to be denied a welfare benefit provided to others no more qualified. By the same sort of reasoning, it would be a violation of any citizen's right to equitable welfare treatment to be arbitrarily denied the opportunity to apply for welfare in the first place. Here the argument stops, however. Individuals in other countries are not treated inequitably if they are not permitted to apply or considered qualified to receive public welfare provided by the United States. For the moment, I appeal to my reader's intuitions of equity to achieve agreement. When I examine the notion of a legitimate comparison class, I hope that an explanation of our prephilosophical judgments will become apparent. However, I must explain that I am using the expression "the citizen" in a very broad sense to refer to any individual member of a society. I assume that in this extended sense resident aliens are citizens but that foreign tourists are not. I do not presume to draw any finer conceptual boundaries than that for present purposes.

Although I have followed tradition and chosen a positive name for this valuable right, it is actually a negative right. The core of the right to equitable welfare treatment is not an ethical claim to be treated in some specifiable manner (the equitable one) but a claim *not* to be treated in any *in*equitable way. Here, as in other species of justice, it is the concept of injustice that is primary. This is revealed by an examination of the logic of the concept. How does one recognize that A's treatment of B is equitable? Not by noticing that it is similar in all relevant respects to A's treatment of all others who are similarly situated, for one hardly knows when one has reviewed *all* relevant respects, much less identified the *entire* class of persons similarly situated. Let me put the same point otherwise. Perceived equality of treatment does not create any real presumption of equitable treatment, for a single inequality of treatment in any unexamined respect could completely overturn the judgment of fairness in this case. On the other hand, any sort of perceived inequality of treatment that is both disadvantageous to the patient and unjusticized is inequitable, no matter how equal it may be in other respects. As a consequence, a judgment that some form of treatment is equitable is defeasible in a way in which the negative judgment that it is inequitable is not. "That treatment is equitable" is refuted by the introduction of new evidence revealing unexamined features of the conduct or the persons compared, but "that treatment is inequitable" can be refuted only by showing that the alleged inequality is not in fact worse treatment for the patient or that there is a justicizing reason for inequality in this respect. Accordingly, this civic right is a negative one; it is a right *not* to be treated in any way that is *in*equitable.

Inequitable treatment, as the very word implies, consists in inequality of treatment, but it is inequality of a very special sort. A treats B inequitably only when A treats B worse than A treats some comparable individual C. To say that A's treatment of B is worse than A's treatment of C is, of course, to make a judgment of comparative value. Thus, equity is a matter of comparative, rather than noncomparative justice, to borrow a useful distinction of Joel Feinberg's (*Rights, Justice, and the Bounds of Liberty*, p. 266). Comparative justice essentially involves comparisons between persons because in the contexts in which it is applicable, one can determine what is due to a person *only* by reference to his relations to other persons. The inequality that gives rise to a presumption of unfair treatment is the inequality of the value of the treatment accorded B and C. Granted that B has been treated worse than C, it follows that both patients have been treated unequally by A. Only B, however, has been treated inequitably. One is not treated unfairly by being treated better than others, only by being treated worse. Moreover, it is only the value of the treatment to the patient, to the individual subjected to it, that is relevant. That A's treatment of B paid off handsomely for A or that it was of great social utility is beside the point. It is presumably inequitable treatment provided it is worse for B than A's treatment of C was for C. Inequitable treatment is always unfair *to* the individual subjected to it. Hence, the comparative value judgment involved in inequitable treatment is a judgment of the comparative value impacts of the two treatments upon the two patients. In this way, inequitable treatment is always worse treatment.

Not every conceivable comparison, however, is to the point. Laclede Gas Company pays my neighbor handsomely; it pays me not a cent. It thereby treats me worse than it treats him, but this unequal treatment gives rise to not the slightest presumption of inequitable treatment because my neighbor and I are not similarly situated. He is an office manager for Laclede Gas; I teach at Washington University. To be sure, we are both customers of Laclede Gas Company. Thus, I would be inequitably treated by the gas company if I received poorer service or were charged higher rates for the same gas-with-service received by my neighbor. Why is it that with respect to the fairness of the payment of salaries or wages only employees are similarly situated and that the class of customers is not a legitimate comparison class? The reason is that it is as an employee, not as a customer or in some other capacity, that one has a claim to be paid wages or a salary. To be similarly situated, then, is to have some status that gives one standing to claim the benefit, or freedom from the burden, provided or imposed by the kind of treatment being judged equitable or inequitable. There inevitably will be some benefit or burden accruing to the patient whenever equity is at stake because only if there is some such value or disvalue imposed on the patient can the treatment possibly be worse in the relevant sense.

Only within a relevant comparison class does the fact that A treats B worse than A treats C create any presumption of inequitable treatment. B and C belong to a relevant comparison class only if they are similarly situated, that is only if they share some status by virtue of which both have a claim to some benefit or freedom from some burden involved in A's treatment. Notice that this is a claim B and C have against A. Accordingly, to be similarly situated the members of a genuine comparison class must stand in the same relation to A, the agent "treating" the patients being compared. Our son complains bitterly that it is unfair that he receives an allowance much smaller than the allowances of almost all of his friends. He insinuates that since he and his friends are about the same age, live in the same neighborhood, share many activities, and so need about the same amounts of spending money, he and his friends are similarly situated. Our children have an ethical claim against us to provide them with spending money until they become able to earn their own spending money. Each of his friends, as a child of other parents, has a similar claim against his or her parents of the same sort. But since they have no such claim against us, the way their parents treat them with respect to allowances has no bearing on the fairness of our treatment of our son. In a way, our son is correct. *It* (notice the pronoun) may well be unfair that he receives so much less than his friends, but *we* are not thereby treating him inequitably. Only if we gave him a smaller allowance than we give to our other children would we be treating him inequitably. Since only our children have any ethical claim to be provided with an allowance by us, the

comparison class relevant to determining the fairness of our treatment of one of our children concerning allowances consists only of
our dependent children. The parallel with public welfare payments is
clear. Since only citizens of the United States have any legal or moral
claim to be provided with welfare benefits by our government, it is
not inequitable for welfare legislation in this country to exclude
foreigners from eligibility for such public welfare.

Consider another situation. It is alleged, probably correctly, that I
grade more harshly than the majority of the faculty here at Washington University. If this is true, then, with respect to grades, I often
treat my students worse than other professors treat the students
enrolled in their courses. Is this unfair? My students have a claim
against me to receive the appropriate academic credit for work
performed in my course by virtue of having enrolled for credit in that
course and having paid the required tuition or fees. Since other
students at Washington University lack the status of paid enrollee in
my courses, they have no such claim against me. Accordingly, they
do not form part of the comparison class relevant to judging the
equitability of my grading. Students who have not enrolled in my
courses simply do not have the relationship to me upon which any
relevant claim against me could be grounded. It follows that *I* am not
unjust in grading my students more harshly than many of my faculty
colleagues grade theirs. Still, it remains true that Washington University is treating some of its students inequitably if it operates an
educational program in which some professors, acting as its agents,
grade more harshly than others. For all tuition-paying students in the
College of Arts and Sciences form a single comparison class with
respect to academic treatment by the institution against which they
have such claims, as claims to accurate academic credit for assignments completed. Once more the parallel with public welfare payments is clear. The State of Mississippi does not treat its residents
inequitably simply because it provides lower AFDC payments to its
residents than New York or New Jersey pays to theirs. But the United
States may well treat its citizens residing in Mississippi inequitably by
operating a federal welfare program in which one state agency
provides lower levels of welfare than other state agencies provide to
other no more qualified citizens of the United States.

Just as it takes two to tango, so it takes two patients similarly
situated with respect to the same agent to constitute a genuine
comparison class. It would appear, then, that interactions between
two individuals alone could never be unfair in this way, but this is not
so. Let us imagine that I am lucky enough to have two beautiful and
industrious wives. Obviously, I can treat one wife inequitably by
providing her with less spending money or assigning her more
household chores than I do my other, and more favored, wife. Less
obviously, but just as genuinely, I treat my one and only wife

inequitably by giving her less spending money than I reserve for myself or insisting that she perform more of the family chores than I undertake myself. This is possible because in this situation I am both agent and patient. I am providing spending money to my wife and to myself, allocating chores to myself and my wife. And my action is unfair to my wife because I am treating her worse than I am treating myself. Although I hold most of the power in our little family, we share a common status as members of the family that gives both of us claims against the head of the family, me, to be provided with spending money and protected from hardships. It is not possible, however, to take the next step and treat oneself inequitably without introducing some second person who is similarly situated with oneself, for the smallest possible comparison class must have two members.

Two individuals are similarly situated with respect to some specified mode of action of some agent only when they share some common status that gives them both a claim against the agent to the value involved in that kind of treatment. This explains why equity is applicable in some contexts and not in others. An employer treats one worker unfairly by paying him or her less than some other worker for the same work performed because both workers possess the status of being an employee that gives both a claim to payment for work performed. But I do not treat one neighborhood grocer inequitably by spending less of my money at his or her store than I do at another neighborhood grocery that offers no better goods and no more reasonable prices because possessing the status of vendor does not confer upon either grocer any claim to my trade or my money. Again, I treat one of my children inequitably if I provide for him or her less protective, comfortable, or attractive clothes than I provide for a sibling because their common status as my children gives them both a claim against me to be provided with clothing until they are old enough to take care of their own economic needs. But I do not treat someone collecting for the Multiple Sclerosis Society inequitably if I give her a less generous contribution than I give to someone collecting for the Cystic Fibrosis Foundation, for their common status as medical charities gives neither any claim to a donation from me.

The fact that two parties are similarly situated only when they have the same relevant claim-grounding relation to the same agent also helps to explain why we are ambivalent about whether certain sorts of treatment are unfair. Is it inequitable for me to bequeath a much larger share of my estate to one of my children than to another simply because he is my favorite? If one thinks of the act of bequeathing one's estate as the act of providing for one's children, then one judges my treatment of my less-favored child as inequitable because both my children as my children have a claim against me to be provided for as far as I comfortably can do so. On the other hand, if one thinks of the act of bequeathing one's estate as the act of giving away one's own property after one's death, then no unequal division is inequitable because no one has any claim to be given one's own property. Is it unfair of me to tip more or less depending upon my mood and with no regard for the quality of service rendered? If one thinks that the waiter has earned a reasonable tip by serving the diner quickly and well or that the waitress has a claim to the customary tip because of an implicit understanding between servant and served, then one judges that I treat Jane inequitably by leaving her a smaller tip than I leave John, even though her service was as good and as customary as his. But if one thinks of tipping as a gratuitous act of largesse to which the status of servant gives the recipient no claim at all, then no inequality in tipping is judged to be unjust treatment. Since Jane and John's shared status grounds no claim to a tip from the diner, they are not similarly situated in the sense relevant to comparative justice.

Whenever an agent A treats some patient B worse than he or she treats some similarly situated party C, then there is a presumption that A is treating B inequitably. Fortunately, this presumption can often be rebutted. But to do so, it is not sufficient, as many moral philosophers allege, to advance just any sort of reason to justify this difference in treatment. As Frankena argues ("The Concept of Social Justice," in Brandt, pp. 4–5):

Not all moral principles are "principles of justice" even if they are valid—for example, the principles J. S. Mill calls generosity and beneficence are not. . . . If this is correct, however, then right-making characteristics or justifying considerations must be distinguished from just-making or justicizing considerations. Just-making considerations are only one species of right-making considerations.

Only a justicizing reason can rebut a presumption of inequity. Let us try to discover what sort of reason that must be.

The obvious place to begin is with some examples to illustrate Frankena's distinction between justifying and justicizing reasons. Imagine that I storm into my chairman's office to protest the fact that I received a smaller raise this year than Professor Jones, a colleague with a similar length of service to the department and comparable philosophical reputation and abilities. Arguably, my chairman might justify his treatment of me by replying that Jones has a larger family and so has been harder hit by inflation than I or that Jones has had exceptionally heavy medical expenses during the year. But these reasons would at best show that my chairman's actions were not wrong; they would do nothing to show that they were not inequitable. To reply that Jones has willingly taught an extra course for the department or that he has enhanced the standing of the department by publishing more than I during the year would, on the other hand, justicize the department's giving me a smaller annual raise.

Another example might be a welfare system in which unemployed persons are provided with much less generous benefits than retired persons in order to motivate the unemployed to seek work. The social utility and personal benefit of a system in which unemployed persons move more quickly back into productive and rewarding employment might be a justifying reason for such unequal treatment, but it is hardly a reason to show it equitable or fair. But to point out that unemployed persons typically have less economic need because they do not yet face the medical problems of the retired might be a justicizing reason for this difference in treatment. Finally, let us imagine that Washington University decides that for one year it will tenure no junior faculty at all. The administration might be able to justify this treatment of those members of its faculty facing a tenure decision this year by appealing to the harsh realities of economic necessity, but this would not be any reason to conclude that its treatment of individuals denied tenure in spite of their meeting all the usual criteria and having proven themselves as fully as those receiving tenure in recent years is at all just or equitable.

Other examples come readily to mind, but let us try to generalize from those at hand. If our sample is typical, there are two sorts of justicizing considerations. A justicizing reason either shows that apparently adverse treatment is really, when judged by the appropriate standard of comparison, not worse treatment or that A is justified in treating B worse than C because of a justicizing difference between B and C. Imagine that our older son alleges that we treated him unjustly because we gave him a smaller allowance than we now give our younger son. To point out that inflation has lowered the value of the dollar is to show that our treatment of him, in terms of real income, is not in fact worse than our treatment of his younger sibling. To point out that his younger brother differs from him in that he has economic needs, such as paying for the materials to make reeds for his oboe, that he did not have is to point to a justicizing difference between the two children that makes our different treatment of them equitable (provided that our older son has had at least the opportunity to play the aboe or other instrument).

By a circuitous route, we have arrived at the most obdurate problem in the theory of just treatment. Most contemporary discussions of equitable treatment assume that formal justice consists of treating similar cases similarly and different cases differently. To move from formal to material justice, alas, one needs some criterion to distinguish between relevant and irrelevant similarities and differences. Frankena has taught us that to identify relevant differences is not sufficient, for we must also sort out justifying differences from justicizing differences. Fortunately, my explanation of what renders two parties similarly situated also suggests a way to identify a justicizing difference. Two parties are similarly situated with respect to some mode of treatment only when they each have some claim to the benefit involved in that treatment or claim against the burden imposed by it. A justicizing difference, accordingly, is some difference between the parties being compared that grounds such a claim. Thus, if my claim to an annual raise is grounded in my service to the department and the university, then my lower raise would be justicized by my lesser service in comparison to Jones who receives a higher raise this year.

Claims to benefits or to freedom from burdens can be grounded in very different ways. The existence of a social practice or institution with established rules gives those subject to it a claim that the rules be followed. This is why many cases of equitable or inequitable treatment involve the uniform or irregular application of rules. But not all problems of just treatment can be assimilated to situations in which rules are applied to individual cases. Some claims to receive benefits arise from understandings or social customs that generate reasonable expectations. One advantage of my interpretation of the notion of a justicizing difference, in addition to its truth, is the way in which it can provide a single explanation for an apparently diverse range of situations in which we apply the ethical right to equitable treatment.

At last, we are in a position to comprehend the ethical right to equitable welfare treatment. Its defining core is the ethical claim of the individual citizen against his or her state not to be treated worse concerning welfare benefits than others who are similarly situated without a justicizing difference. This is a civic right because it is a right possessed by the individual as a citizen. It is a welfare right because only treatment concerning public welfare benefits is covered by its core claim.

An ethical claim-right, however, is more than a single core claim. It is a system of normative elements that, if respected, confers freedom and control over the enjoyment of this core claim upon its possessor. Among the associated elements that together make up the ethical right to equitable welfare treatment are the following: 1) The right-holder's bilateral liberty of exercising or refraining from exercising his or her ethical power of claiming performance or remedy in the event of threatened or actual inequitable welfare treatment by the state. This means that it is not wrong for the right-holder to insist upon equitable welfare treatment, or fair remedy in the event of inequitable treatment, but that the right-holder may rightly refrain from so insisting if he or she so chooses. (2) The right-holder's ethical power to waive his or her core claim against the state. This means that the right-holder is able to cancel the state's duty to refrain from treating him or her inequitably. At first, it sounds strange, even perverse, to suggest that the citizen could by any action render it morally permissible for the state to treat him or her unjustly. But if my conception of the ethical claim to equitable treatment is correct, this is only to be expected. The claim to equitable welfare treatment is a piggy-back claim; it presupposes some prior and independent claim to some benefit involved in welfare treatment to ensure that some judgment of comparative justice is applicable in this context. Accordingly, if this prior claim might be waived, then presumably the claim not to be treated worse in this respect than anyone else similarly situated would thereby also be waivable. Imagine that an unemployed citizen has an ethical claim to some form of unemployment benefits but waives his or her claim in order to avoid an undesired dependency upon the state. Surely it would not then remain unjust treatment for the state to provide no unemployment benefits to this individual even though it continued to provide such benefits for others similarly situated. (3) The right-holder's bilateral liberty of exercising or refraining from exercising this ethical power of waiving his or her claim to equitable welfare treatment. Morally speaking, the individual citizen is free to choose whether to waive the core claim or not; he or she is morally permitted but not morally required to do so. (4) The bilateral ethical liberty of the right-holder of resisting or refraining from resisting inequitable welfare treatment in any way that is not seriously immoral. This is a more modest analogue of one's liberty of using all necessary force in self-defence. It is morally permissible for the right-holder to resist inequitable welfare treatment by complaining to a higher official in the welfare agency, requesting a welfare hearing, suing the welfare agency or bringing political pressure to bear upon the welfare official responsible for the inequitable treatment. Such a liberty of action does not go without saying, for it is typically wrong to interfere in the activities of a government agency in such ways, especially to try to force the authorities to act in ways advantageous to oneself. But such normally impermissible actions become permissible when one is resisting inequitable treatment. Still, they are not required; the right-holder has no duty to resist in these ways. Naturally, there are limits upon one's liberty of resisting. One may not act in ways that are seriously immoral, such as bribery, battery or threatened murder. (5) The right-holder's immunity against having his or her core claim extinguished by any unilateral action of the state. Without this protection, the right to equitable welfare treatment would not hold against the state in any genuine and important way. Each of these associated elements confers, if respected, some sort of freedom or control concerning the core claim upon the possessor of that claim. Hence, the complex of ethical claims, liberties, powers and immunities constitutes a normative system that, if respected, confers autonomy concerning the enjoyment of equitable welfare treatment upon the individual citizen.

Conclusion

The central purpose of this chapter has been the intepretation of three alleged ethical welfare rights: the human right to social security, the civic right to a fair share, and the civic right to equitable welfare treatment. Since all three are claim-rights, the emphasis has been upon a clear and precise formulation of the ethical claim at the core of each right. I have defined these respectively as the ethical claim of the individual human being against his or her society to be supplied with a minimal livelihood in the event that he or she lacks the means of sustaining life because of circumstances beyond his or her control; the ethical claim of the individual citizen against the state that the state provide to him or her a fair share of the goods and services distributed in the society in the event that he or she has been unjustly impoverished by the society; and the ethical claim of the individual citizen against his or her state not to be treated worse concerning welfare benefits than others who are similarly situated without a justicizing difference. The obvious gain is that the ambiguous and inarticulate names of these rights have been expanded into definitions that make the contents explicit and considerably more precise. In addition, I have specified some of the more important associated elements that make up each of these ethical welfare rights.

My conclusion is that my general conception of a right applies helpfully to ethical welfare rights. Just as a legal right can be best conceived of as a structure of Hohfeldian legal elements that, if respected, confers legal autonomy concerning some core upon the right-holder, so an ethical right can most fruitfully be thought of as a structure of ethical claims, liberties, powers and immunities that together, if respected, confers ethical autonomy concerning some core upon the possessor of the right. That I can analyse ethical rights in terms of my theory proves nothing. One can always misdescribe the facts to fit one's prejudices. What is illuminating are the ways in which this interpretation clarifies our understanding of these rights. It spells out the content of these ethical rights in much more detail and with more precision than is usual. It displays the internal structure of each right in a way that is obscured by the short labels we usually use to refer to them. Most importantly, it reveals the practical import of each right. Because each ethical element specifies some action that must, may, can, or cannot be done according to ethical norms, this way of conceiving of ethical rights makes it clear just how they apply to human conduct and social practice.

Reflecting upon the practical import of these three ethical welfare rights assures us that they have an important bearing upon public welfare programs. Accordingly, these rights are of exceedingly great importance IF they are genuine. But are these alleged ethical welfare rights real? Their existence depends upon their grounds, the reasons that can be advanced to establish the ethical norms that create and define them. Our next task, then, must be to inquire into the possible grounds of ethical welfare rights.

5

The Grounds of Ethical Rights

We have seen that it is possible to conceive of several ethical welfare rights that, if genuine, have important implications for any morally justified public welfare program. But do these conceivable rights actually exist? All those, and they are many, who believe that the act of providing welfare is an act of charity, at most the performance of an imperfect duty of benevolence, will deny that the recipients have any ethical right or moral claim to the benefits they receive. The existence of any right depends upon the validity of the norms that define its content and confer it upon the right-holders. Ultimately, the validity of a legal norm depends upon its recognition and application by the institutions of the legal system. Much the same is true for the conventional norms of positive morality and conventional etiquette. But ethical norms are independent of human institutions, an independence that does not imply their inapplicability to such institutions. The validity of an ethical norm depends upon the reasons that can be given for it, upon its rational justifiability. Hence, the reality of any alleged ethical welfare right can be defended only by establishing the grounds for it, the reasons that justify the assertion that there is such a right.

Are there any grounds for ethical welfare rights? If so, what kinds of grounds are adequate to establish their existence? These are large questions and not easily answered, but I can hardly ignore them in a book such as this. The best I can do is to begin to answer them. In an area where speculative generalization and sweeping denial are rife, a few careful steps forward constitute more of an advance than a long daring leap to some conclusion that raises two questions for every one that it answers. Accordingly, I shall cut my treatment of the grounds of ethical welfare rights down to modest, and let us hope manageable, proportions by limiting it in two ways. First, I shall consider only two sample welfare rights, the human right to social security and the civic right to a fair share. Both are primary rights, but they differ considerably in content, and their possession hinges on very different statuses. Having defined their contents in some detail, we should be in a position to identify their possible grounds more precisely. After all, just what might ground a right depends essentially upon the nature of the right to be grounded.

Second, I shall discuss only the grounds of the core of each ethical right to welfare. To be sure, an ethical right is more than its core; it contains also associated elements that, if respected, confer autonomy concerning this core upon the right-holder. But if I can show that there are adequate grounds to support an ethical claim to social security or to a fair share, then this goes a long way toward establishing ethical rights to social security and a fair share. Although this limitation will simplify my task, and my argument, considerably, it still leaves some measure of complexity. An ethical claim of x against y consists of a duty of y together with an ethical power of x to claim performance or remedy from y. The grounds of any ethical claim are likely to be correspondingly complex. I must look for the grounds of y's duty plus the grounds for x's power to claim. Although they could turn out to be the same, they might be quite different. Let us see.

The Right to Protection

The first example of an alleged ethical welfare right for which we need grounds is the human right to social security. At its core is an ethical claim of the individual human being against his or her society to be provided with a minimal livelihood in the event that he or she lacks the means of sustaining life because of circumstances beyond his or her control. The very name of this right suggests that the central function of any public system of social security is to protect the individual from some sort of insecurity. This in turn reminds us of the venerable tradition in political theory that holds that the central end of government is security and that the primary duty of any state is to protect its citizens, at least against the threat of foreign military attack and internal criminal activity. If the state really does owe protection to its citizens, then the individual citizens have a right to such protection. And if justice demands equal protection of the laws, this is because each citizen has a prior ethical claim to the protection of the state. Now if the individual does have an ethical right to protection by society and if the scope of this right reaches to protection from economic dangers, then the ground of the human right to social security might well be the more basic, or at least more traditional, human right to protection. Presumably, the core of any such right would consist of an ethical claim of the individual human being against the state to be protected to some specifiable degree against some specific range of dangers. To establish the reality of this core ethical claim, one must identify adequate grounds for an ethical duty of the state to protect the individual and also adequate grounds for an ethical power of the individual to claim protection, or remedy for lack of protection, from the state.

Paradigm instances of the protection the state ought to provide for the individual are military protection from aggression by foreign states and police protection from acts like murder, assault, rape, arson, or theft. What might be the grounds of the state duty to provide protections of this sort? (For the moment I shall make no attempt to define the sort of protections that define the scope of this duty. Later, however, I shall inquire whether the scope of this duty reaches to protection against the lack of a livelihood.) What reason is there to assert any duty of the state to provide military defence and police security for its citizens?

The obvious reason is the utility of such protection, utility reflecting both the interests of the individuals protected and the public interest. The individual benefits from state protection in various ways. Clearly, acts of foreign aggression or criminal attacks upon the individual are harmful to that individual. To the degree that state protection is effective, it benefits the individual by preventing these harms to him or her. It also saves the individual from having to provide some measure of protection for himself or herself, efforts that would be more costly than the taxes paid to finance state protection and less effective also. Finally, the security provided by state protection improves the quality of life for the individual by lessening fear and anxiety and preserving the freedom of movement of those who need not hide in the relative security of their own homes for fear of attack on their persons or burglary of their homes should they leave. The public also have an interest in the protection of the individual. If a breadwinner or homemaker is killed or disabled, it is often the state that must take up the burden of caring for the family. If some are exposed to murder, assault or robbery, then all must live in fear and the restricted freedom that goes with it. Thus, state protection is useful to the individual and to society alike.

Given some such utilitarian reasons for protection, I presume that the state *ought* to protect the individuals within its jurisdiction whenever the act of protecting by the state is desirable. There seem to be three sorts of situation in which state protection is desirable: (1) when the benefits of state protection outweigh the costs; and only the state can effectively protect the individual; (2) when the benefits of state protection outweigh the costs, and the state can best provide the protection and state protection will not duplicate unnecessarily existing protections; and (3) when the benefits of state protection will outweigh the costs, and the state can provide the protection and although other parties might do so as well or even better, these other parties will not and cannot easily be made to do so. Ideally the state ought to provide protection to the individual in all such cases. But not every action the state ought ideally to perform constitutes an ethical duty, an action the state has a moral obligation to perform. The state has a duty to protect the individual only when the state ought to do so and failure to provide protection will result in serious harm or at least a great loss of utility. Military aggression and the sorts of crimes I have mentioned do result in serious harm to the victims, so that the state duty to provide military and police protection can be grounded in utility.

It might be objected, however, that this utilitarian ground is not strong enough, or perhaps not distributive enough, to establish any state duty to protect *each individual*. Surely if the human right to protection is genuine, the core of any individual's ethical claim against the state must include a state duty to protect the individual right-holder, not just people in general. But it seems easy to imagine individuals, such as incorrigible criminals or disabled persons who will always be a burden upon society, the protection of whom would advance the social utility very little, if at all. I suggest that one might close this apparent gap between the duty to protect the individual and social utility by reflecting upon four considerations. a) Even in the most favorable instances, there will be a state duty to protect the individual on utilitarian grounds only when the individual is threatened with serious harm, for only then will the benefits of protection outweigh the costs of providing it. This serious harm to the victim remains to weigh heavily in the utilitarian scales no matter who the victim may be.

b) The nature of the state duty to protect limits the costs of performing this duty. Notice that the state's duty is not in each and every instance to prevent the threatened harm from external aggression or internal criminal action. This would be impossible to achieve, and any attempt at perfect prevention would be far too wasteful of scarce resources to be desirable, much less dutiful. The content of the duty of the state is to provide a reasonable level of security for each individual. Although this may not be inexpensive, it may be a burden the state can afford to shoulder in every case.

c) There is a strong public interest in individual security. In addition to harming one or more individual victims, each criminal act undermines the law and order essential to the preservation of any viable society. Even more obviously, foreign aggression is as much a threat to the society as to the individuals who happen to be injured by it. When anyone is left exposed to such dangers, many others live in reduced security and with the anxiety of feeling insecure. Thus, individual insecurity has ripple effects that spread widely in society. For this reason, it is a mistake to imagine that in establishing the state duty to protect any individual one should weigh the usefulness of protection to that single individual in one balance and the utility to all others in the other balance.

d) Most state actions of providing protection have an umbrella effect that shelters many individuals. It is not quite true that police protection is an indivisible whole that must be provided to all or to none in the way that military defence may plausibly be taken to be. One can assign extra bodyguards to important public officials or refrain from sending police patrols into certain sections of the city at night. Still, state protection is not provided to each individual in separate and independent parcels or portions. The policeman who patrols my block, alert for anyone attempting to break into my home or in the act of mugging me, is protecting a number of homes and anyone who happens to be in the area he is patrolling. The crime lab and the communications system are there to deter any criminal who might be tempted to attack any individual in the city or town. It is at least as true to say that the police protects the public as that it protects this individual or that one, but in protecting the public it is, of course, protecting the individuals that make up the public. When all four of these considerations are taken into account, it appears that there can be an adequate utilitarian ground for the state duty to protect each and every individual.

Could this same utility serve also to ground the individual's ethical power to claim performance, or remedy for nonperformance, of this state duty? Some philosophers allege that this is so, and one can readily understand why they believe this. Since the purpose of claiming performance is to cause the duty-bearer to actually do the morally required action, all the useful consequences of the dutiful act are indirectly consequences of the act of claiming itself. And if the utility of these consequences is sufficient to justify the dutiful action, they should be equally sufficient to justify the act of claiming. Plausible as this line of reasoning is, it is doubly invalid. First, the utility of the act of claiming is seldom if ever the same as the utility of the act of performing the duty claimed. To be sure, the consequences of the dutiful act are contained in the consequences of the act of claiming performance if, but only if, the act of claiming is successful. There is no assurance that any given act of claiming will in fact cause the second party to perform the demanded action, and hard experience reveals that claiming is often in vain. Even if successful, an act of claiming performance may have side-effects that reduce its utility. It may induce resentment or resistence in the second party, who may then perform the duty less willingly and less well than he or she would have done had the first party not insisted on standing on his or her rights. Claiming one's rights can even transform an intimate and loving relationship into a more impersonal and formal one, a transformation that can be very harmful to the lives of a husband or wife, a parent or child.

Second, even if the utility of the act of claiming could be derived from the utility of the duty claimed, this would do nothing to ground the ethical *power* of claiming. What ethical conclusion could one validly draw from the knowledge that the act of claiming is useful? Assuming that utilitarianism is correct, one could infer that at least the right-holder has the ethical liberty of claiming performance and possibly that he or she has an ethical duty to do so. But all of this is beside the point. What we are seeking is the ground of the ethical power of claiming. To assert that the right-holder has an ethical power to claim performance, or remedy for nonperformance, is to say that the right-holder is able by claiming performance or remedy to create a new duty of the state to perform the prior duty claimed or to remedy the injury done by its nonperformance of this duty. To show that the act of claiming, the exercise of this ethical power, is morally justified is one thing; to show that the claimant actually has this power, that he or she really does have the ability to bring a duty of performance or remedy into existence simply by demanding performance or remedy is quite another.

One might be able to identify a utilitarian ground for this power of claiming by reflecting upon the philosophy of Hobbes with sufficient imagination, that is to say without too much fidelity to the text. Each individual is naturally exposed to countless threats to life, limb, and property. Therefore, the welfare of the individual is dependent upon obtaining security from such threats. Since the individual lacks the power to protect himself or herself from these dangers, a necessary condition of achieving security is subjecting oneself to a sovereign who can protect one. Submitting to the sovereign implies limiting one's freedom of acting to protect one's own vital interests. Therefore, the authority of the sovereign over the subject lasts only so long as the sovereign retains the power to protect the individual. At this point, the philosophy of Hobbes throws new light upon the state duty to protect the individual. It is not just that the state ought morally to provide such protection because of the utility of state protection for the individual protected and for the public at large. In addition, performance of this duty is necessary in order to preserve the relation of subject to sovereign, the relation between an individual who accepts the authority of the sovereign and a ruler who makes rules binding upon the subject.

What gives the individual standing to claim state protection, then, is standing at one end of the subject-sovereign relation. It is the relation between ruled and ruler that explains how the very act of claiming protection from the state imposes upon the state an additional duty to provide such protection. To be sure, the state has an antecedent duty to protect the individual grounded in the utility of such protection. In the absence of any act of claiming performance, nonperformance by the state constitutes a failure to protect the individual. But nonperformance in the face of an act of claiming protection is a refusal to provide protection. Thus, by the linguistic act of claiming protection from the state, the individual subject transforms a failure into a refusal. Although the claiming does not change the state action in itself, it does change the meaning of this action. A state failure to provide protection for the individual is cause for concern about the future and may weaken the relation between subject and sovereign. But a refusal to protect serves notice to the individual that he or she is thrown upon his or her own resources and cannot continue to rely upon state protection from threats to life, limb, or property.

At precisely this point, Hobbes reminds us that no reasonable individual will continue to accept the authority of the sovereign or to consider himself or herself morally bound by its laws. And, since actual subjects are purposive beings endowed with some degree of rationality, this will in practice modify their interaction with the state. In this way, a refusal to protect the individual is far more destructive of the subject-sovereign relation than a mere failure to protect. Given the tremendous importance of the subject-sovereign relation for individual security and public order, the individual's act of claiming performance of the state duty to provide protection can indirectly change dramatically the utility of such protection and the disutility of its absence. In this *change* of utility, we discover the ground of the *power* to claim protection from the state. Although this is a utilitarian ground of sorts, it is not at all the same kind of ground as that of the state duty to protect. The state duty to protect the individual is grounded in the utility of the act of providing such protection. The individual's power to claim protection from the state is grounded in the way in which the act of claiming changes the utility of the performance or nonperformance of the duty claimed.

Having identified utilitarian grounds for the state duty to protect the individual and for the individual's power to claim performance of this duty, we have revealed the grounds of the individual's core claim against the state to be provided with protection. But does this core of the individual's right to protection reach to protection against the lack of a livelihood in circumstances beyond one's control? If not, it will prove impossible to derive any right to social security from this right to protection.

What is the scope of the individual's ethical claim to state protection? If the Hobbesian line of reasoning is accepted, this claim will reach to all protections necessary to make submission by the individual subject to the authority of the sovereign rational. The individual cannot be expected to forgo legally forbidden acts of self-defence against threats to life, limb, or property unless the sovereign protects the individual against such threats. Although this reasoning concerns natural dangers independent of society, it has double force when applied to risks arising from social arrangements such as the division of labor or a military draft. If it is unreasonable for the individual to leave himself or herself exposed to natural dangers by accepting the authority of the sovereign, it is even more unreasonable to incur new and additional risks by such acceptance. The relationship upon which the individual's claim to protection hinges is that of subject to sovereign. This is primarily a legal relationship of the lawmaker and judge to the individual subject to the law. But the state, if genuinely sovereign, has the authority to regulate a wide variety of social institutions, including economic ones. This generalizes the relation to that of ruled to ruler, where the practice rules of various social institutions are also covered. In accepting the authority of the sovereign, the individual subject is accepting the validity of a wide variety of rules governing the acquisition, retention, and conveyance of property. If the operation of these rules, economic and legal, may at some point leave the individual without any means of sustaining life, it is unreasonable to expect the individual to continue to submit to the restriction of these rules, among other things forbidding theft as a means of obtaining a livelihood, unless the state protects the individual subject from this danger. If the state refuses to provide a substitute livelihood under these circumstances, it will be undermining the valuable relation of subject to sovereign. Reflect upon the alienation felt by the destitute and the antisocial action that so often results, and observe the partial breakdown of law and order in areas of intense poverty when the state refuses to protect the individual against economic threats. I suggest, then, that the Hobbesian line of reasoning that establishes the individual's ethical claim to police protection covers minimal economic protections as well. Accordingly, it should be possible to ground a right to social security in the right to protection.

But does this line of reasoning establish any human right to protection? The crux of the reasoning is the value and nature of the subject-sovereign relation. Primarily, this is a relation between the individual citizen and his or her state. Thus understood, the corresponding ethical right would seem to be a civic right, a right possessed by the individual *as a citizen*. But only a human right to protection, a right possessed by the individual *as a human being*, could ground a human right to social security. Does the right to protection extend beyond citizens to other human beings? In the broad sense in which I am using the term "citizen," resident aliens are citizens; they are members of the society. Illegal aliens and tourists, however, are not full members of the society. They are, however, subject to its laws. A visitor to a country becomes a temporary subject, for he or she is subject to its jurisdiction temporarily. Accordingly, for that period of living within the borders of the state, any human being stands in the relation of subject to sovereign and has the standing to claim protection from the state. The grounds are precisely the same as those of the ethical claim of the permanent and full citizen.

This does not imply, however, that the right to protection is a human right. Quite the contrary. A genuine human right is universal, but the right to protection holding against some state is possessed only by those human beings subject to its jurisdiction. More fundamentally, the right to protection is not possessed by the individual as human, but as subject. What gives the individual standing to claim protection from a given state is standing at one end of the subject-sovereign relation. This implies that the right to protection is a civic right, an ethical right one possesses as a citizen. If this right extends beyond full citizens to illegal aliens and tourists, this is because they are temporary citizens. This has an important practical implication. While the alien or tourist remains within the jurisdiction of the state, the state has a duty to provide protection for the individual. But the state can extinguish this moral obligation, should it become onerous, by deporting the individual and thereby terminating his or her temporary and partial citizenship.

If my argument is accepted, it is not possible to ground any human right to social security in the human right to protection. At least, I have been unable to discover any grounds for any universal human right to state protection. At the same time, I have advanced what seem to me adequate grounds for an ethical claim of any individual subject to the jurisdiction of a given state against that state for protection from certain threats to life, limb, and property. This may well be the core of a civic right to protection, and upon this right one could ground a civic right to social security. Although this is not exactly what we were seeking, it is enough to establish the existence of a very important ethical right to welfare.

The Right to Life

Several writers have suggested that the right to life implies an ethical claim against society for sustenance in an emergency (See Bedau, "The Right to Life," pp. 550-51). Since the core of the human right to social security is an ethical claim of the individual against his or her state to be provided with a minimal livelihood in the event that he or she lacks the means of sustaining life because of circumstances beyond his or her control, this suggests that the right to social security can be grounded in the right to life. Presumably, the right to life, a right possessed by all human beings simply as human, could ground a universal human right to social security. The only conclusive way to assess this suggestion would be to identify the grounds of the human right to life and define the content of this right in just those terms justified by those grounds. Unfortunately, I have no new insight into the grounds of the right to life. Accordingly, I will simply assume for the sake of argument that there is a human right to life and explore less sure avenues to the definition of its content.

The right to life, at least if one accepts the conception suggested by Bedau's article, seems to be what Feinberg calls a rights-package. It is a cluster of rights concerning life rather than a single homogeneous right. Its least controversial component is an ethical claim-right of the individual human being holding against the world not to be killed. Presumably the ethical claim at the core of this right not to be killed is suitably qualified so as to exclude morally permissible killings, but such complications are not important for our present purposes. Probably another component of the right to life package is the ethical liberty-right of the individual human to defend his or her life with all necessary force. Although one normally has a moral duty to refrain from killing or even battering another human, such actions are morally permissible if they are really necessary to save one's life in the face of some attack upon one. For our purposes, the essential question is whether the right to live also contains an ethical claim-right of the individual human holding against one or more second parties to have one's life sustained by all necessary means. If there is such a claim-right, it might well ground a claim to social security, to a substitute livelihood in the event that the right-holder lacks the means of sustaining life because of circumstances beyond his or her control.

Granted that the human right to life contains a claim-right not to be killed, what reason is there to believe that it also contains a claim-right to have one's life sustained? I can think of three plausible arguments for taking this controversial step. First, reflection strongly suggests that any ground sufficient to establish a claim not to be killed would equally establish a claim to sustenance. Consider some sample grounds. The right not to be killed might be grounded in God's creation. But God's love of His creature or his property right in His creation is surely as much a reason for moral agents subject to the will of God to sustain each image of the Divine as to refrain from destroying it. Again, some ground the right to life on the supreme, even infinite, value of each individual life. But the fact that each human life is precious is as much a reason for preserving each life as not to destroy it. Others ground the right to life in respect for persons. But knowingly to allow a person to perish when one might have sustained his or her life seems to show as little respect for the person as intentionally to terminate his or her life. By some such reflective induction one might conclude that there is as much reason to accept an ethical claim to have one's life sustained as to accept the generally acknowledged ethical claim not to be killed.

Second, recent discussions of the morality of euthanasia sometimes argue that the distinction between killing and letting die has little if anything to do with the rightness or wrongness of euthanasia. These arguments designed to prove that active and passive euthanasia are morally equivalent (at least with respect to duty if not with respect to virtue) apply equally to the interpretation of the human right to life, the right primarily at stake in cases of contemplated euthanasia. If valid, they show that there is no reason to accept a claim-right not to be killed but to deny a claim-right to have one's life sustained.

Third, a powerful reason to grant a human right not to be killed is that this explains, or perhaps reflects, the moral difference between killing a human baby and drowning a kitten. It is not just that it is worse to kill a child than to kill an animal, as it might be worse to destroy a priceless work of art than to destroy a painting of modest esthetic value; the two acts of killing are wrong in radically different ways because a human life has a very different moral status than an animal life. But surely this is equally true of the acts of letting a human baby and a kitten starve to death or die from a curable disease. It is not just that the child feels more pain than the animal; the human child has a very different moral status from the tiny animal. Recognizing a human claim-right to have one's life sustained, an ethical right not possessed by any brute animal, explains, or at least recognizes, this morally crucial difference. I do not pretend to have developed any of these arguments fully enough to prove its conclusion. I do suggest that there are reasons to take very seriously the suggestion that one component of the human right to life is an ethical claim-right that others sustain one's life when one is unable to do so by one's own efforts.

Although some argue that there is as much justification for asserting a human right to have one's life sustained as to affirm a human right not to be killed, many others, including myself, remain sceptical. If we take the right not to be killed as our model, the right to have one's life sustained is a universal human right holding against the world. If this right is a genuine human right, it must be possessed universally by every human being. And if it has any practically important bearing upon such widespread threats to human life as unemployment, old age, dependent childhood, world hunger, and epidemics of disease, it must impose correlative duties upon all individuals, organizations, and governments in a position to sustain life. But this conception of a human right to have one's life sustained raises two serious theoretical problems.

If the claim-right is really a universal human right, then each potential duty-bearer finds himself or herself confronted with vast numbers of claimants, all of whose lives require sustenance. This raises the problem, or pair of problems, of scarce resources. If the individual, organization or state lacks sufficient resources to sustain the lives of all the claimants, then the addressee of so many claims can have no duty to do the impossible. And since claim and duty are logical correlatives, there can be no genuine claims where there are no actual duties. Even if the number of claims confronting a single second party is limited enough so that sustaining all the lives of the claimants is possible, to do so might demand excessive sacrifices for the potential duty-bearer. In such cases, to respond positively would be action above and beyond the call of duty. Once more, the limited resources rule out any real duty and, thereby, undermine the alleged ethical claims. From the perspective of a single claimant, however, the situation at first looks more promising. If there is a human right to have one's life sustained, then each individual human whose life requires sustenance is in a position to claim such sustenance from every individual, organization, and state in the entire world. There is no lack of resources there to sustain one individual life. Here the theoretical problem is just the opposite. If the individual really does have an ethical claim against the world to have his or her life sustained, then every individual, organization, and state has a duty to provide sustenance to this individual. But if all perform their respective duties, there will be a vast duplication of effort. Surely there can be no genuine duty to perform such redundant and pointless actions. Hence, not all potential parties can have any duty to respond positively to each claim for needed sustenance. But if not all these duties are genuine, then not all the corresponding claims can be genuine either. Thus, taking the right to have one's life sustained to be universal raises the problem of scarce resources, and taking it to hold against the world raises the problem of pointless duplication. Can these problems be solved in theory or in practice?

Before exploring possible solutions, it will be revealing to notice why comparable problems do not arise concerning the human right not to be killed. It is never impossible, and very rarely imposes any undue sacrifice upon any duty-bearer, to refrain from killing each and every human being in the entire world. When it does call for undue sacrifice, perhaps the sacrifice of one's own life, then the right to self-defence takes priority over the duty not to kill the attacker. Accordingly, there is nothing like the problem of scarce resources raised by the universal extent of the right not to be killed. Each second party can meet all human claims and without excessive personal sacrifice. Nor is there any pointless duplication arising from the fact that each individual's right not to be killed holds against the world. The fact that many, even all but one second party, refrains from killing an individual human being does not make the action of some additional individual or organization or state of refraining from taking his or her life redundant. Quite the contrary, the individual's life is spared only if the entire world—every second party—does his or her or its duty to spare the claimant's life. It is this asymmetry between positive and negative claim-rights that makes one much more reluctant to admit any right to have one's life sustained than to accept the more traditional right not to be killed.

How might one limit the moral demands imposed upon each moral agent—natural person, private organization, or state government—

by the ethical claims to sustenance of all the human beings who would lose their lives without sustenance? One cannot solve the problem of scarce resources by limiting the number of claimants without abandoning the universality essential to every genuine human right. But one might make the claim conditional on the ability of the addressee to meet it without undue sacrifice. This conditional claim would be possessed by every human being, but it would impose an actual duty upon some second party only when performance of that duty is possible for that party and without making morally excessive demands upon the duty-bearer. But this limitation by itself will not solve the problem of scarce resources, for no second party has resources sufficient to sustain the lives of all human beings who stand in need of sustenance at any given time. Suppose, then, an additional condition that the second party know that the claimant's life will be lost without sustenance. Since any given agent will presumably be ignorant of most human beings who need sustenance, this will reduce considerably the number of conditional ethical claims that actually impose duties upon him or her. The effectiveness of this conceptual move depends upon precisely how it is construed.

First, to know that some human's life will be lost without sustenance may not be sufficient to generate a duty upon a given agent, for some other addressee might act to sustain the individual's life and thus render one's own action morally unnecessary. But how often can any moral agent be in a position to know whether or not some other agent—person, organization, or state—will act to sustain a life in danger? Second, must one know the individual and that just this individual's life stands in need of sustenance or is it sufficient that one knows there are humans, whom one cannot name or label with definite descriptions, who will die unless provided with sustenance? If the latter, most moral agents know in a general way of the existence of more lives in danger than they individually have the resources to sustain; if the former, most human claimants will find themselves with no potential second party possessing both a knowledge of his or her individual predicament and the resources to sustain his or her life. Besides, it seems morally unsatisfactory to solve the problem of scarce resources by appealing to our ignorance of human beings who are supposed to possess the human right to have their lives sustained by us.

I strongly suspect that it will prove impossible to formulate the knowledge condition tightly enough to solve the problem of scarce resources yet loosely enough so that there will be some second parties with an actual duty to sustain the lives of all those who need social security. Those closest to the unemployed, aged, needy dependent children, and handicapped will know of more claimants than their resources could possibly sustain, while those more removed from and unfamiliar with these classes of humans will have no duty to provide aid because of their ignorance. Nor is this problem solved by addressing the ethical claims for sustenance to states only. No state has the resources to sustain all the human lives it knows in general terms to be in danger, and no state knows each individual within its jurisdiction who stands in need of social security. Hence, this strategy of saving the universality of the ethical claim to have one's life sustained by making it a conditional ethical claim does not promise to solve the problem of scarce resources. Worse yet, if it were to succeed, the defender of the human right to have one's life sustained would have won a Pyrrhic victory. This move succeeds in limiting the demands imposed upon each potential party by the claims of all humans only by inserting into the ethical claim conditions that will be satisfied so rarely that most conditional claims will impose no actual duties. Thus, what purports to be a universal human claim-right must be empty of practical import in almost every instance. A conditional ethical claim that seldom implies any actual duty to sustain a human life is hardly worth possessing by any right-holder. This strategy saves the theoretical universality of this alleged human right by depriving it in practice of almost all human value.

Let us now turn from the problem of scarce resources to the problem of pointless duplication. If each individual's human right to have his or her life sustained really does hold against the world, then it imposes on each other individual, private organization, and state government a correlative duty to sustain the life of the individual right-holder. But if all second parties perform their duty to the right-holder, presumably a morally desirable thing, there would be tremendous duplication of effort to no practical advantage or moral purpose. Thus, not all potential second parties can have an actual duty to sustain the life of any given individual human whose life is threatened. And if not all correlative duties are real, then not all the ethical claims against the potential second parties are genuine either. In the end, then, it seems that this alleged human right cannot hold against the world.

At this point, too, one is tempted to construe the ethical claim and its correlative duty as conditional in another way. To say that "*all* other individuals, private organizations and states have a duty to sustain this human being's life" really means that "*each* other individual, private organization and state has a duty to sustain this human being's life *unless* such sustenance is rendered unnecessary by the action of some other individual, organization, or state." But this does not really solve the problem of pointless duplication, for before the first moral agent has acted, this construal also implies that all potential second parties have a moral obligation to act. This move solves the problem of duplication only after some party's action has terminated the ethical claim that gives rise to the problem. I will not stop to consider the several theoretical contortions that one might be tempted to engage in to preserve the human right to have one's life sustained as holding against the world.

A little reflection reveals that neither in theory nor in practice does one really want any such right to hold against the entire world. No doubt one would like the claim to have one's life sustained to be universal, to be possessed by each and every human being. But one hardly wants each individual's claim to hold against every second party; what one wants is that each individual's ethical claim should hold securely against some second party. Still, it will not do to say that it holds only against the second party in the best position to save this individual. This provides no solution to the problem of pointless duplication when two or more parties are equally well situated to sustain an individual life. And should the best situated party fail to perform his or her duty, one wants that duty to fall on other shoulders. One does not really want to say that only the best situated party has any moral obligation to save a life in danger. Thus, the parents of a dependent child ought in the first instance to feed it, shelter, protect it, and provide medical care for it. But should they fail to do so, this duty falls upon some other relative or upon some private welfare organization, and ultimately upon the state. But none of this is explained by postulating a human right of the child that is supposed to hold against the world.

My conclusion is that neither theoretical problem can be solved. The problem of scarce resources arises if one insists that the individual's right to have his or her life sustained is a universal human right. This virtually guarantees that the many demands imposed upon each agent will exceed the available resources or those that can be morally demanded of that party. Such excessive demands cannot be admitted as genuine ethical claims holding against that second party. This suggests that a more significant claim-right must arise from something less universal than a human right, at most a civic right. The problem of pointless duplication arises if one assumes that any individual's right to have his or her life sustained holds against the world. If every person, private organization, and state government acted simultaneously to sustain the life of any individual claimant, their actions would largely duplicate one another. Surely there are not duties to act in such a pointlessly redundant manner. To avoid this pointless duplication, one must fix the responsibility for sustaining the life of any individual much more narrowly than upon everyone. By what principle might it be possible to determine which, out of all potential second parties, have the duty to sustain each individual life? Only, I believe, appealing to some special relation between the individual claimant and the second party against whom the claim holds. Once more our conclusion must be that a significant ethical claim-right to have one's life sustained will be some sort of special right, not a general human right. Hence, I do not believe that the human right to life contains any human right that others sustain one's life. If not, then the remaining components, of this rights package, the human right not to be killed and the human right to defend one's life, are not sufficient to establish any human right to social security. The alleged human right to social security cannot be grounded in the human right to life.

Human Needs

One who lacks the means of sustaining life itself obviously lacks the means required to meet one's most basic human needs for food, clothing, shelter, medical care, etc. Many philosophers assume that human rights, especially welfare rights, are grounded in human needs. Only a few of them, however, have attempted to explain just how needs might ground rights. Let us examine the most plausible suggestions.

A traditional and illuminating classification of theories of rights divides them into will theories and interest theories. If one accepts some version of the interest theory of rights, one might try to ground the human right to social security in the fundamental interests of the individual in fulfilling his or her human needs for food, clothing, shelter, and medical care. But, as James Nickel reminds us ("Is There a Human Right to Employment," p. 159), "Interests are too numerous for there to be a right to everything that one has a substantial interest in having. If there is a linkage between interests and rights it will have to be only within some subset of interests." He goes on to specify this subset and to explain how they ground human rights in this way:

One obvious approach to take here is to say that it is only the most important and most nearly-universal interests that generate universal rights. This approach uses the premise that when resources are available all interests having a certain level of importance and universality generate corresponding universal rights. . . . On Mill's view, to have a right is "to have something which society ought to defend me in possession of," and society should provide such defences in areas where the imperatives of utility are strongest and most constant. (Nickel, pp. 159–160)

This appears to be a utilitarian line of reasoning. The importance of the interest to the individual guarantees the utility of the protection a right affords. The universality of the interest explains why such interests generate universal human rights. Accordingly, the essential human needs for food, clothing, shelter, and medical care might well ground a human right to social security.

In assessing this approach, I begin with the reminder that my theory of rights is rather different from and more complex than Mill's. Still, I shall not demand that this utilitarian sort of argument justify all the associated ethical elements in the human right to social security. I shall ask only that it be adequate to establish its defining core claim to be provided with a substitute livelihood. Even this is questionable. Does the importance of the interests in food, clothing, shelter, and medical care to the individual guarantee the social utility of providing for these needs? Does the universality of these basic human interests assure that it will always, in each and every instance, be useful on balance to provide a substitute livelihood? It is not obvious that the answers to these questions are in the affirmative. Still, there is a plausible argument from marginal utility to support the conclusion that society can best maximize utility by providing the necessities for everyone before allowing the more fortunate to enjoy the luxuries of life. Accordingly, I will grant the utility of the state action of providing social security. (Whether utility is maximized by each state providing social security for its own citizens or by having the more affluent states provide more extensive social security is an issue I shall bracket here.)

Let us suppose that the state action of providing a substitute livelihood to the individual has great utility because this enables the individual who lacks a livelihood in circumstances beyond his or her control to satisfy his or her human needs for food, clothing, shelter, and medical care. It is also plausible to assume that the state has a duty to promote the common good or public welfare. In this way human needs of the individual could serve as the grounds of a state duty to provide social security. But the individual's core claim against the state to provide a substitute livelihood consists of more than this duty of the state regarding the individual; it also contains the ethical power of the individual to claim performance or remedy in the event of threatened or actual nonperformance of this duty by the state. Can this ethical power also be grounded in the human needs of the individual? The utility of providing for these needs is no guarantee of the utility of claiming such provision, for these distinct actions may have rather different consequences. Even if it did, this would establish only the moral permissibility, or even duty, of exercising the power to claim. But what is it that confers this ethical power upon the individual human being in the first place? Conceivably, the importance to the individual of fulfilling one's human needs gives the individual standing to claim provision for them, but just how this might be explained remains mysterious. On this score, Nickel is completely silent. Nor does my own imagination speak to me more helpfully. Therefore, I must conclude that this approach to the grounding of the right to social security in human needs fails to explain the logical link, if any, between needs and rights.

A very different way of linking human needs to welfare rights is proposed by Stanley Benn in his *Human Rights—For Whom and For What?* He begins by noting that human beings are axiotima, things it is appropriate to value or esteem, and defining their basic needs as the conditions without which they could not live or retain the features by virtue of which we perceive them as axiotima. He then goes on to argue:

If human beings were *only* objects of value, then the moral language of benevolence would be adequate to account for our duties; and this was sufficient for medieval Christian theology. The new development was the individualism of seventeenth-century England and its American colonies—epitomized in Colonial Rainborough's "the poorest he that is in England hath a life to live as the greatest he," amounting to an assertion of the moral personality of every English natural person. . . . The second stage was the growth of public responsibility for welfare services in the economically developed nations of the West. If it was within the power of a government to treat its GNP as a pool, from which resources could be allocated to meet social needs, the poor were getting less than their due if, at the very least, their basic needs were not being met. . . . Human welfare rights arise, then, not directly from a right that needs—even basic needs—should be satisfied, but rather from a right to equal consideration and fair treatment. If anyone's needs are to be satisfied, then no one's need for the less basic should be satisfied before everyone's need for the most basic, since we are all alike axiotima. (p. 70)

If I understand this argument correctly, its logical structure is something like this formulation.

1. As a thing of value, each human has basic needs.
2. As a person, each human has an ethical right to equal consideration.
3. When a state allocates goods and services to meet the needs of some, if it does not meet the basic needs of any human individual, it is not according that individual equal consideration.

Therefore, every individual as a human being has an ethical claim-right holding against the state that it meet his or her basic needs provided it allocates goods and services to meet any needs of others.

Since providing a substitute livelihood to one who lacks a livelihood under circumstances beyond his or her control is meeting the basic needs of that recipient, this line of reasoning could readily be applied to the human right to social security.

Is this sort of argument sound? It is, or could easily be made, logically valid; the conclusion does indeed follow from the premises. Moreover, I am willing to grant the first two premises. I am tempted to grant the third premise also, but unfortunately, I can see no clear reason to accept its truth. Why is the state not according an individual human equal consideration when it allocates some goods and services to meet some needs of others but fail to meet the basic needs of this individual? Why could this allocation not take place after and as a result of equal consideration? Suppose that it allocates relatively few goods and services and these on the basis of reasonable criteria. Suppose also that it does not render the individual claimant ineligible on the ground of any arbitrary or discriminatory criteria. It is hard to understand why these suppositions are inconceivable or, if conceivable, why the resulting allocation would constitute unfair treatment. I am not prepared to deny flatly this third premise, but I do believe that Benn must explain more fully precisely how the individual's human right to equal consideration is violated in this sort of situation.

Assuming that Benn can fill out his argument more completely, his proviso remains worrisome. At best, his approach to grounding human welfare rights in human needs could establish the existence of a provisional human right to social security. Any human being lacking the means of sustaining life under circumstances beyond his or her control would have an ethical claim against the state that it provide him or her with a substitute livelihood if, but only if, he or she is lucky enough to live in a society that already has at least a rudimentary system of public welfare. Those unfortunate enough to find themselves living under governments that have not assumed any responsibility for meeting human needs at all would, alas, have absolutely no ethical claim against their state to meet any of their basic human needs. This surely deprives any ethical claim-right grounded in human needs by using Benn's approach of the universality essential to any genuine human right.

Even more distressing is the manner in which Benn's approach renders human welfare rights, even when applicable, redundant. Let us imagine an individual unfortunate enough to find himself or herself lacking the very means of sustaining life under circumstances beyond his or her control but lucky enough to live in a society that does redistribute some goods and services to meet some human needs. Benn's argument would prove that that individual does have an ethical claim against the state that it provide him or her with a substitute livelihood adequate to meet his or her basic needs. The individual could, accordingly, appeal to this human right to demand social security as his or her due. But what is to be gained by invoking any such human right to social security. Were there no such right at all, the needy individual could appeal directly to the human right to equal consideration and, using Benn's argument, make his or her case for social security. Thus, this way of grounding welfare rights in human needs seems to make them entirely redundant and of no theoretical or practical importance at all. I conclude that Benn's approach is not a satisfactory way to ground the human right to social security in human needs, although it may well be a very powerful argument grounded in the human right to fair treatment for legal welfare rights.

Joel Feinberg's writings suggest, even if they do not explicitly contain, a third approach to the grounding of human welfare rights in human needs. A succinct statement of his position is found in *Rights, Justice, and The Bounds of Liberty* (p. 153).

Natural needs are real claims if only upon hypothetical future beings not yet in existence. I accept the moral principle that to have an unfulfilled need is to have a kind of claim against the world, even if against no one in particular. A natural need for some good as such, like a natural desert, is always a reason in support of a claim to that good. A person in need, then, is always "in a position" to make a claim, even when there is no one in the corresponding position to do anything about it. Such claims, based on need alone, are "permanent possibilities of rights," the natural seed from which rights grow.

Feinberg is, of course, trying to explain how human needs are, or imply, moral claims according to his conception of a moral claim. Since my conception of an ethical claim is rather different from his, what I propose to do is to see whether his approach to grounding claims in needs could be applied to the ethical claim to social security as I have defined it.

On my conception, one component of the individual's ethical claim to social security is the state's duty to provide a substitute livelihood to the individual who lacks one under circumstances beyond his or her control. Now Feinberg suggests that this state duty can be grounded in the basic needs of the individual for food, clothing, shelter and medical care. But how? A clue is provided by his analysis of a need.

The concept of a "need" is extremely elastic. In a general sense, to say that S needs X is to say simply that if he doesn't have X he will be harmed. A "basic need" would then be for an X in whose absence a person would be harmed in some crucial and fundamental way, such as suffering injury, malnutrition, illness, madness, or premature death. (*Social Philosophy*, p. 111)

If one assumes, as Feinberg probably does, a general moral duty to prevent avoidable harm, at least when one can do so without undue sacrifice, then the existence of a human need implies a duty to satisfy that need, and the existence of a basic human need implies the existence of an especially stringent duty to do so. Many philosophers can accept a duty to prevent harm more readily than any alleged duty to promote welfare. For them, Feinberg's way of grounding the duty to meet a human need in harm will be preferable to Nickel's way of grounding that duty in the utility of meeting the need. At the very least, this is a most plausible suggestion.

The individual's ethical claim to social security is, however, more than the correlative duty of the state to provide a substitute livelihood. It also contains an ethical power of the individual to claim performance of this duty from the state or to the claim remedy for nonperformance from the state. How might Feinberg ground this ethical power in the basic needs of the individual? Perhaps this question can be answered by juxtaposing two brief passages.

Having a claim to X is not (yet) the same as having a right to X, but rather *having a case*, consisting of relevant reasons of at least minimal plausibility, that one has a right to X. (*Social Philosophy*, p. 66)

A natural need for some good as such, like a natural desert, is always a reason in support of a claim to that good. (*Rights, Justice, and the Bounds of Liberty*, p. 153)

What confers upon an individual the ethical power of claiming X is having a need for X because every need is a reason and to have a reason to support a claim is to have the standing to make that claim. But precisely how does having a reason give one standing to claim? Feinberg follows Hohfeld in assuming that a claim simply is the correlative duty seen from the other end of the relation between claimant and duty-bearer. Naturally, he would presume that the ground of the duty would be identical with the ground of the claim. But on my conception of a claim, an ethical claim is more than the correlative duty seen from a different perspective; it also contains an ethical power of creating an additional duty of performance or remedy simply by the act of claiming. How might having a reason confer this sort of an ethical power?

Let us assume, for the sake of discussion a Kantian principle that there is a fundamental duty to respect every person as a rational agent. Now if someone has presented reasons to me why I ought not to treat him or her in some manner, but I fly in the face of those reasons and do treat this person in that manner, then surely I am failing to respect that person's rationality by ignoring or acting contrary to the reasons he or she has presented to me. Accordingly, by the very act of presenting those reasons to me that person has imposed upon me a duty I would not have had without this action of the individual. In this way, combining Feinberg's suggestion that needs are reasons with a Kantian respect for persons, one might be able to explain how human needs ground an ethical power to claim their satisfaction. No doubt this third approach to grounding human welfare rights in human needs goes beyond what can be found in Feinberg's writings, and probably beyond anything lurking in the back of his mind. But it is a theoretically interesting way of explaining what is usually asserted without explanation, the logical link between needs and rights. What is especially promising about Feinberg's approach is the way in which he supplies two links. Human needs are linked to the duty to meet them *via* the harm that results from leaving them unmet, and human needs are linked to the power to claim their fulfillment *via* the notion that to have standing is to have reasons. What are we to say about the adequacy of this approach?

Like most moral philosophers, I can readily accept the moral principle that one has a duty not to harm others. I am even willing to add that one can harm another through acts of omission as well as by acts of commission, although it is not easy to specify exactly when refraining from action constitutes an act of omission. Thus, Feinberg's way of grounding a state duty to provide social security in human needs is entirely acceptable to me. To my mind, it is both less open to question and more compelling than the approach of either Nickel or Benn.

I am not satisfied, however, with Feinberg's way of grounding the power to claim in human needs by noting that to have an unmet need is to have a reason why others should meet that need. 1) Having a reason to present in support of a claim does not in and of itself give one the power to make a claim because there may be no second party there to whom one can present that reason. To be in a position to claim one must be "close enough" to some addressee so that one's demand can be heard. At this point Feinberg is unfaithful to his own insight that the nature of a claim can best be understood by reflection upon the process or activity of claiming; this is a transitive activity that necessarily involves both a claimant and an addressee. This relational aspect of claiming is essential to anyone who, like Feinberg himself, wishes to borrow the Hohfeldian logic in which claim and correlative duty are two sides of the same relation. Feinberg admits that human needs ground human rights only in some weaker "manifesto sense" because needs are only "permanent possibilities of rights." For the same reasons he ought to add that to have a reason to support a claim is to have only a permanent possibility of acquiring the power to claim.

2) The view that having reasons to support a claim confers the power to claim does not explain why it is that only the right-holder, or some agent of the right-holder, has standing to claim performance or remedy. Many persons may be aware of the unmet needs of some dependent child, unemployed adult, or retired aged individual. Are all of these persons in a position to claim from the state fulfillment of these needs? Feinberg might reply in the affirmative, for he argues that others have the power to exercise the rights of the infant on its behalf. Perhaps parents or guardians are, but would any and every person aware of the needs of the child, and thus having a reason to support a claim on that child's behalf, have standing to make its claims for it? This strikes me as a license for the intruding busy-body, precisely one of the moral evils that individual rights exclude. We would all be unhappy with the notion that a mere stranger can waive the rights of a child or a senile adult. I suggest that the concept of a right as a system of normative elements that, if respected, confers autonomy upon its possessor requires that only the claim-holder, or someone acting as agent of, the claimholder, has the power to claim

performance or remedy. Feinberg has not explained adequately what limits this standing to make a claim.

3) I am not convinced that human needs are the right kind of reason to support ethical claims. Every claim is a claim of some claimant against some duty-bearer. Now an unmet need may well be a reason for action, as Feinberg asserts. But is it a reason why one addressee rather than another ought to act to meet the need? I do not see that there is anything in the nature of one individual's unmet need that fixes responsibility for meeting that need upon some other determinate party. If not, then it cannot constitute an adequate reason for an ethical claim of the needy individual *against* any determinate addressee. Claims are relational. They are possessed by some first party and hold against some second party. Therefore, any reason that could support a claim must itself be relational; it must justify the demand made by the claimant upon the addressee. Human needs, even dire needs, are first personal; they do not address themselves to any second person. Accordingly, they are not the right sort of reasons to confer any power of claiming upon the needy individual. Feinberg, of course, says that claims arising from needs hold against the world. But this only raises the problem of pointless duplication that I discussed a few pages ago. Since I see no way of solving this problem without grounding the power to claim on some relation between claimant and duty-barrier, I must reject all nonrelational reasons, like human needs, as grounds for the power to claim.

My conclusion is that the alleged human right to social security cannot be grounded in human needs. Too often moral philosophers simply assert that basic human needs imply human welfare rights, but how this might be so is left unexplained. The most plausible approaches to grounding human rights in human needs have been suggested by James Nickel, Stanley Benn, and Joel Feinberg. We have examined all three and found them wanting. Unless someone can carry one of these approaches further or suggest a different approach, this way of establishing human welfare rights will not work.

Wrongful Harm

Having had something less than spectacular success in identifying adequate grounds for the alleged human right to social security, we may be well advised to turn to our other example of an ethical right to welfare, the alleged civic right to a fair share. As before, let us ignore its associated ethical elements and seek only a sufficient ground for its defining core, the ethical claim of the citizen who has been impoverished by the operations of the economic institutions that shape the distribution of goods and services in his or her society holding against the state to be provided with a fair share, that is with an amount of goods and services just sufficient to bring him or her up above the poverty line.

Proclamations of welfare rights are a modern phenomenon. Historically, the belief in the existence of ethical welfare rights has grown out of an increasing recognition of society's responsibility for the plight of the unemployed, the aged, children dependent upon impoverished families, and even the ill and the handicapped. More specifically, the underlying idea seems to be that society is morally responsible for providing social security because it is causally responsible for economic insecurity. Although the idea, or at least its widespread acceptance, is modern, the reality is ancient and universal. In every society, the income of the individual is determined by social institutions created or modified or regulated by state action. This suggests that ethical welfare rights might be grounded in the wrongful harm inflicted upon the individual by the state. To do so, one would need the ethical analogue of the central principle of tort law. An acceptable moral principle of remedy might be formulated as follows: a party wrongfully harmed by the action of a second party has an ethical claim-right holding against that second party to an appropriate remedy. This principle does not, of course, apply to natural harms, harms to the individual that do not result from human actions, for example the destruction of one's home by a tornado or a wound inflicted upon a camper by a wild animal. Nor does it confer any right to a remedy for harms arising from human actions that are not wrongful, such as just taxation that reduces one's wealth or the economic failure of an entrepreneur put out of business fairly by his or her competitors. Only wrongful harm serves to ground any ethical right to a remedy.

This moral principle of remedy is readily applicable to the case of an individual citizen impoverished by the operation of the social institutions that control the processes of economic distribution in his or her society. To be impoverished is certainly to be harmed, indeed harmed very seriously. Since the social institutions that control the distribution of goods and services in any society are formed and regulated by state action, to be impoverished in this way is to be impoverished by the state. And since every member of a society has a civic right not to be unjustly impoverished by the state, such state action, be it acts of commission or omission or both, is a wrongful violation of the ethical rights of the individual. In the last chapter, I have sketched, or at least hinted at, an argument to establish the existence of this civic right not to be unjustly impoverished. If this civic right is granted, and if one grants the moral principle of remedy, then the civic right to a fair share can be grounded readily in wrongful harm.

The reader wondering whether to accept the civic right not to be unjustly impoverished may be interested to note that its role in my ethical system is analogous to the role played by the Lockean Proviso in the moral philosophy of Robert Nozick, certainly no advocate of welfare rights. If Nozick recognizes the moral necessity to limit original acquisition of private property with the proviso that there is "enough and as good to spare," this is presumably because he recognizes that acquisition of private property can be just only so long as it does not arbitrarily exclude other individuals from similarly acquiring property of their own. Analogously, my civic right not to be unjustly impoverished is the recognition that society wrongs an individual if it arbitrarily excludes him or her from the processes of economic distribution by which individuals in that society acquire goods and services.

But let us suppose that some reader remains unconvinced by my argument for the existence of a civic right not to be unjustly impoverished. There is another way in which the civic right to a fair share can be grounded in wrongful harm. This right to a fair share can still be taken to be a remedial right demanding remedial action of the state regarding any citizen who has been impoverished by the arbitrary operations of the social institutions that determine the distribution of goods and services in that society. If the individual citizen has been reduced to poverty, then the citizen has surely been harmed. Moreover, if the citizen has been excluded from the processes of economic distribution arbitrarily, for no good reason such as his or her refusal to accept available employment, then the citizen has been *unnecessarily* harmed by the state. Sometimes the state harms the citizen necessarily, under duress of compelling reasons. The state must tax away some of the citizen's wealth if it is to continue to function and perform its duties to the citizens. The state may have to conscript a citizen to defend itself and its very existence from military attack. But to inflict harm upon the citizen unnecessarily is wrongly to harm the citizen. Thus, arbitrary exclusion from the processes of economic distribution constitutes an action of inflicting unnecessary harm, and therefore wrongful harm, upon the individual member of society. Now a party wrongfully harmed by the action of a second party has an ethical claim-right holding against that second party to an appropriate remedy. The wrongful harm in this case is that of being impoverished by being excluded from the processes of economic distribution. Accordingly, the appropriate remedy would seem to be to be provided by the wrong-doer, the state, with the goods and services one would have received had one not been unjustly impoverished. This is precisely the content of the core ethical claim of the civic right to a fair share, for I have advocated an unjust impoverishment conception of the right to a fair share.

There are, then, two ways in which the civic right to a fair share can be grounded in wrongful harm. Both recognize that the state is responsible for the social institutions that control the distribution of goods and services in the society. Accordingly, if any citizen is left impoverished for no good reason by the processes of economic distribution, then the state has by its acts of commission or omission impoverished the citizen. Such impoverishment inflicts harm upon the citizen because it renders him or her incapable of meeting his or her basic needs. It is wrongful harm either because the individual citizen has an ethical right not to be unjustly impoverished or because the infliction of harm unnecessarily is morally wrong. Either way, wrongful harm serves as an adequate ground for the civic right to a fair share.

A Social Contract

Probably no recent work has influenced contemporary ethical theory more profoundly than John Rawls' *A Theory of Justice*. Rawls argues that his two principles of social justice are rationally justified because they would be chosen by rational individuals in the original position agreeing unanimously to adopt fundamental moral principles to shape their social institutions. Analogously, one might try to ground ethical welfare rights on a hypothetical social contract.

Jeffrie G. Murphy does precisely this in his article "Rights and Borderline Cases." His primary purpose is to argue, contra Nozick, that there are fundamental moral rights to welfare benefits. Let us apply his line of reasoning to the civic right to a fair share. The essential argument goes like this:

1. If a law guaranteeing X to the individual would be chosen by rational agents in the original position, then the individual has a moral right to X.
2. Rational individuals in the original position would contract to guarantee a fair share to each member of society.

Therefore, each individual citizen has a moral right to a fair share.

The logic of the argument poses no problems; it is the two premises that require our critical attention.

Premise (1) is a direct logical consequence of Murphy's Rawlsian-inspired analysis of one species of moral rights, what he calls social contract rights.

An individual should be understood as having a right to X if and only if a law guaranteeing X to the individual would be chosen by rational agents in the original position. (p. 235)

He arrives at this analysis of one meaning of the expression "a moral right" by combining the theories of Mill and Rawls.

I shall argue that we use the language of rights to do at least *two different* (though related) moral jobs, and that a failure to keep clear the distinction between these two jobs is behind a substantial amount of the fruitless controversy surrounding the question of whether borderline cases do or do not have rights. One important function of the language of rights, stressed by such philosophers as John Locke and especially Immanuel Kant, has been to mark out the special kind of treatment (called "respect" by Kant) which is particularly fitting or appropriate to *autonomous, rational persons*. . . . Another quite different tradition in moral and social philosophy, best represented by John Stuart Mill and our contemporary John Rawls, involves the view that rights claims are *not* morally basic. Rather, they are *derivative* from more general moral principles. "To have a right," Mill suggests, "is to have something which society ought to defend me in the possession of." The central idea here is that rights claims function, not to mark some specially fine feature of persons, but rather to mark out which of all moral claims *ought to be enforced by the state;* in other words, which ones *ought to be law.* (pp. 230-232)

Murphy is arguing that the expression "a moral right" is ambiguous and that, although Kant may have captured the sense of the expression referring to autonomy rights, Mill has correctly grasped a second and equally important sense of the expression. He then reformulates Mill's conception in other terms.

On this view, a creature may be said to have a right to X if and only if it is morally reasonable, all things considered, to *guarantee* X to that creature as a matter of law. (p. 232)

He goes on, however, to reject Mill's utilitarian theory of what it is morally reasonable to choose and to substitute for it the theory of Rawls.

As already indicated, Rawls suggests that we use the idea of a social contract as a model of rational decision in morality. That is, we shall regard as rationally justified any moral principle (or any social practice) if that principle (or practice) would be unanimously agreed to, adopted, or contracted for by a group of rational agents coming together, in what Rawls calls the "original position," in order to pick principles and then practices to govern their relations with each other as members of a common society. (p. 233)

Combining this Rawlsian conception of rational decision in morality with Mill's conception of a moral right yields Murphy's social contract conception of moral rights.

What are we to say of this social contract conception of rights? This sort of a conception of moral rights is attractive to many social philosophers because it promises to permit the recognition of rights to welfare benefits more readily than the autonomy conception presupposed by philosophers such as Robert Nozick. I, too, have adopted an autonomy conception of rights and have shown in the previous chapters that this conception of rights does not exclude rights to welfare benefits. Murphy begins by arguing that the autonomy conception of rights defines only one of the two senses of the expression "a moral right." As he puts it, "we use the language of rights to do at least *two different* (though related) moral jobs." The evidence he presents in support of this thesis is, however, unimpressive. He observes that there are two different traditions in moral and social philosophy: autonomy theories of rights, such as those of Locke and Kant, and nonautonomy theories, such as those of Mill and Rawls. Even granted the accuracy of this observation, it hardly follows that the expression "a right" is used ambiguously, even in moral philosophy. A philosophical theory of rights is more often a normative theory about the grounds of rights than an analysis of the language of rights. A proposed definition of the expression "a right" may be mistaken and may not fit any established use of the expression. It can not even be taken for granted that a philosopher, when he or she uses the expression "a moral right," actually and consistently uses it in conformity with his or her own proposed analysis.

A considerably stronger line of reasoning that Murphy might have used (but did not) argues that the expression "a right" must be ambiguous because there are clear cases of moral rights that do not fit the autonomy conception. For example, it clearly makes sense to say that children have a moral right to an education, even when such education is compulsory and they have no choice in the matter at all. My response to this sort of argument is to distinguish between my own autonomy conception of rights and Hart's simpler respected choice or option conception. While the option analysis of rights may have difficulty recognizing what Feinberg has called "mandatory rights," I can explain them in terms of my own theory. Although the child may have no choice whether to attend school, the child may have a choice as to whether to claim performance of the state duty to provide him or her with an education should the state fail to perform its correlative duty. Thus, autonomy may enter into the picture even when the core of the right to an education is not a bilateral ethical liberty. I cannot see that the case for any conception of moral rights other than some version of the autonomy theory has been made by Murphy or by others. At the very least, no convincing argument is presented in "Rights and Borderline Cases."

Even were one to grant that the expression "a moral right" is ambiguous and that the autonomy conception is adequate to only one sense, it would not follow that Mill has correctly defined the other sense. I very much doubt that to say that someone has a moral right to X ever means to say that "it is morally reasonable, all things considered, to *guarantee* X to that creature as a matter of law." Murphy clearly expresses the point of this sort of analysis. "The central idea here is that rights claims function, not to mark some specially fine feature of persons, but rather to mark out which of all moral claims *ought to be enforced by the state*." If this really is all that is included in the central idea of this conception, then it is clearly open to Hart's charge of redundancy. One can talk about which claims ought to be enforced by the state simply by specifying the moral duties of the state; nothing is gained by using the language of rights at all. What is distinctive and theoretically interesting in the language of rights is left out of any analysis that reduces rights to their correlative duties. Every moral claim-right necessarily involves the right-holder who possesses the right and the duty-bearer against whom the moral claim holds. This relationship is not adequately analysed by the proposed definition, for it provides no clues whatsoever as to the second party of any claim-right.

Suppose that the citizen does have a moral right to a fair share. Against whom does this right hold? To be told that the state ought to enforce this moral claim tells us nothing at all, for it replaces state protection of the right for second-party performance of the correlative duty. It might be that the state ought to enforce the duty of affluent individuals to share their wealth with those in poverty, or it might be that the state itself has a duty to provide welfare benefits to the poor. Surely any adequate conception of a moral claim-right will make it clear against whom any moral claim holds. Any definition that omits all reference to the duty-bearer and mentions only the state duty to force the duty-bearer to perform the correlative duty leaves out what is primary and includes what is secondary. In any event, it is hardly sufficient for Murphy to assume that Mill has correctly defined one sense of "a moral right." He must explain why he considers Mill's conception of a moral right to be more adequate for the purposes of moral and social philosophy than its competitors.

Murphy continues his argument by replacing Mill's act-utilitarianism with Rawls' social contract conception of moral rationality. This is not the place for any extended critical assessment of the methodology of *A Theory of Justice*. I will grant, for the sake of discussion, that Rawls can establish his two principles of justice by showing that they would be unanimously agreed to by a group of rational agents in the original position choosing principles to govern the shape of their social institutions. A hypothetical social contract does seem like an appropriate way to determine the moral rationality of social institutions and practices. But it seems inappropriate as a ground for moral rights simply because these are noninstitutional. The existence and content of any moral right are determined, not by the legal norms or moral conventions of a society, but by the considerations that constitute the reasons for the ethical norms that define it. Accordingly, without challenging the use of Rawls' social contract conception of moral rationality for his purposes in establishing the principles of social justice—that is the principles to govern social institutions—I do question Murphy's adoption of this methodology in attempting to ground moral rights. To my mind, all three steps in Murphy's argument for his analysis of a social contract right are defective. He has simply not established the first premise of his central argument for welfare rights.

Still, his second premise calls for consideration in its own right. Is it true that rational individuals in the original position would contract to guarantee a fair share to each member of society? At this point Murphy sketches the following "Rawlsian answer":

Rational persons, in the original position, would want to protect themselves against certain major losses and harms. Thus they would probably agree to a *minimum floor* of security below which no member of society would be allowed to fall. Even selfish people, caring about their own welfare, would want to guard against the kind of destruction of primary goods that would result if they became severely disadvantaged, as people often do, through no fault of their own, but simply through their "bad luck on the social and natural lottery." (pp. 235–36)

The question we must ponder is "how adequate is this Rawlsian answer?"

What evidence is presented to demonstrate that in fact rational individuals in the original position would contract to legally guarantee some specific welfare benefit, such as a fair share? The evidence suggested amounts to the reason or reasons rational agents in such a position would have to enter into such an agreement. It is that they "would want to protect themselves against certain major losses and harms," in this case the harm of arbitrary impoverishment. This is an appeal to the self-interest, or at least expected self-interest, of the individual who is currently behind the veil of ignorance but will (hypothetically) later be living in the society to be governed by the agreement now being made. He or she does not know what position he or she will occupy in that society, but he or she does know enough economic theory to realize that many individuals will probably be impoverished and that there is a risk that this fate will befall himself or herself. He or she will also know that poverty is "destructive of primary goods" such as opportunity, developed skills and abilities, and, of course, wealth so necessary to pursue any feasible life plan to attain personal happiness and well-being. Hence, it is only rational for the potential member of any society to agree to some form of social protection against so terrible a loss or harm to himself or herself. So far, so good.

But it hardly follows that rational agents in the original position will opt for any legal guarantee of a fair share to protect themselves against this dire risk, for any such social arrangement will have its costs. Supplementary goods and services sufficient to relieve arbitrary poverty can be provided by the state to all needy individuals only if the state has at its disposal very considerable resources, and these are normally raised by taxation of the more affluent members of society. Thus, the individuals in the original position must weigh their self-interest in receiving the welfare benefit, should they happen to be arbitrarily impoverished, against their potential loss of spendable income, should they happen to escape the threat of poverty. Unfortunately, the situation is even more complicated than this. Any system of welfare benefits supported by public taxation has, in economic theory, the effect of a double disincentive to work productively; there is less need to work to avoid the misery of poverty, and there is less incentive to earn income that will be confiscated by the government to support its welfare program. Accordingly, contracting to guarantee a fair share to each individual is going to reduce the economic productivity of the society and, thereby, reduce significantly the expected income of most of its members.

It is often argued that welfare programs also weaken the motivation of the individual to accept primary responsibility for his or her own welfare. This undermines moral character and often results in a lower level of well-being for the individual. Welfare programs supported by high rates of taxation also drastically reduce the opportunity for successful individuals to save and thereby reduce the amounts of capital available for the creation of new economic enterprises and the expansion of the more promising ones. A result may well be economic stagnation and a lower standard of living. Surely Murphy cannot simply ignore all these costs. To show that a legal guarantee of a fair share is actually in the expected self-interest of the individual in the original position, he must weigh the value of the protection against the risk of arbitrary poverty against the various expected costs of the legal guarantee of a fair share. It is by no means obvious that the balance of self-interest favors the social contract he proposes. Of course, at this point he might appeal to the maximin principle of rational choice. Given the threat of poverty, and the devastating effects of arbitrary poverty upon the well-being of the individual, the rational individual will wish to protect himself or herself at almost any cost. More specifically, he or she will agree to any arrangement that maximizes his or her welfare should the worst of all possible circumstances in fact befall him or her. Perhaps, but I wonder. It is not obvious that the most rational choice would be that indicated by so conservative a principle. Although Rawls argues that this is so, his argument remain inconclusive and to many unconvincing.

Let us grant that a rational agent contracting for basic principles to govern his or her society would wish to have some sort of social insurance against so grave a risk as the possibility of being arbitrarily impoverished. It does not follow that this insurance would take the form of a legal guarantee of a fair share. To establish this, one must demonstrate that this sort of legal arrangement would be preferable, in terms of the expected self-interest of the parties in the original position, to every alternative social arrangement. Murphy simply fails to specify, much less to consider with care, the options available to rational agents in the original position. They might at least consider a traditional free enterprise system, assuming that it would be more productive than the more bureaucratic welfare state, and rely upon the charity of individuals and organizations to redistribute wealth to the needy. More likely, they would reason that what is needed is a system of insurance against the risk of poverty that could be purchased by those who care to protect themselves against this harm. Another possibility is to opt for a society with an extended family to which are allocated the economic functions of pooling income and distributing it among the family members. This is a method of sharing risk and protecting the individual common in many societies. No doubt sociologists, economists, and anthropologists can suggest still other alternatives that might be adopted to protect the individual member of a society from the risk of arbitrary poverty. I hazard no guess as to which one it would be most rational for agents in the original position to choose. But clearly any argument to prove that they would in fact contract in favor of a legal guarantee of a fair share must show, not only that this social arrangement is advantageous to the individual in the original position, but that it is more advantageous in terms of expected self-interest than any and every available alternative. On this score, Murphy provides no evidence whatsoever.

Clearly, then, Murphy's attempt to ground welfare rights, such as the civic right to a fair share, in a hypothetical social contract is most inadequate. His Rawlsian answer to the question "why would rational agents in the original position opt for a legal guarantee of some specific welfare benefit?" is very incomplete. He is quite right in pointing out the harm that befalls an individual who suffers arbitrary poverty. But he generates no estimate of the probability of this harm in fact befalling any given individual in the original position. He completely ignores the various and significant costs of any legal institution guaranteeing a fair share to the individual. Nor does he consider the relative advantages of the options open to rational agents in the original position choosing between a variety of possible sets of social institutions. To be sure, I have not proven that it is impossible in principle to close these gaps in his argument. On the other hand, he has given us no hints at all as to how his argument could be completed to demonstrate that, in fact, rational agents in the original position would agree to the contract he suggests.

But suppose that they would in fact so contract. Would this serve to ground any civic right to a fair share? I cannot see how. Although a Rawlsian appeal to a hypothetical social contract seems appropriate when justifying principles of social justice (i.e., principles to govern social institutions), the relevance of any hypothetical social contract to moral rights, which are independent of social institutions, is dubious at best. Thus, I will abandon this approach to the grounds of ethical welfare rights myself and leave its further exploration and development to those more familiar with and committed to the methodology of John Rawls.

Conclusion

I have tried to identify and assess some of the most plausible grounds of ethical welfare rights. Although the right to protection is not adequate to ground any human right to social security, it probably could ground a civic right of the same sort. Since the human right to life does not contain any core ethical claim to have one's life sustained by others, its existence does not establish the existence of any human right to social security. Nor can human needs provide any justification for human welfare rights. None of the three strategies of Nickel, Benn, or Feinberg will do the job. Each might well ground a state duty to provide social security, but none explains the ethical power of the right-holder to claim performance of this duty. Hence, none can ground the ethical claim of the individual against the state to be provided with social security. The civic right to a fair share can be grounded in the wrongful harm inflicted upon the individual citizen who is arbitrarily impoverished by his or her society. Once the responsibility of the state for this harm to the individual is recognized, the claim of the citizen against the state for a remedial fair share is established. To my mind, the attempt to ground welfare rights in a hypothetical social contract is most unpromising.

What general conclusions might one draw from this examination of a few proposed grounds for two alleged ethical rights to welfare. The most obvious, and perhaps the most important, lesson to learn is that one should not conceive of our fundamental ethical rights to welfare benefits as human rights. These are not moral rights the individual has simply *as* a human being, for they cannot be grounded in human nature or the general aspects of human existence *per se*. Our most fundamental welfare rights are at best civic rights, moral rights of the individual as a citizen holding against his or her state. Only in this way can the problems of scarce resources and pointless duplication be solved in theory and the responsibility for meeting human need fixed in practice.

In this chapter, I have examined only proximate grounds for ethical rights to welfare benefits. But the civic right to protection and the right to remedy for wrongful harm themselves stand in need of grounds. Presumably, the relevance and adequacy of any proximate ground for a welfare right can be shown only within a more extensive and fundamental ethical theory, such as utilitarianism or a Kantian respect for persons. I would like to be able to explain to the reader just how the proximate grounds to which I have appealed point beyond themselves to the more basic ethical theory needed to justify any and all claims to ethical welfare rights, but I cannot do so. This more fundamental issue in ethical theory must remain open at the end of this more specific and limited exploration of one small, but important, corner of ethics and jurisprudence.

6

Welfare Reform

The previous chapters have formulated and defended a theory of welfare rights. In them, I have explained my conception of a welfare right, shown how my conception would define some sample legal and ethical welfare rights, examined several ways to justify legal welfare rights, and explored some grounds of ethical rights to welfare. But are these theoretical speculations of any practical consequence? This question is doubly important. To understand fully any abstract definition or normative principle one must realize just how it could be applied in human practice, whether to the functioning of social institutions or to the choices of individual moral agents. Also, much of the value of any philosophical theory of welfare rights must surely lie in its capacity to improve public welfare programs. Accordingly, I shall show that my theory of welfare rights does provide practical guidance to anyone considering several currently debated reforms in our federal system of public welfare, especially changes in our Aid to Families with Dependent Children program.

Abandon Categorical Systems

The Social Security Act provides federal financial support to provide welfare benefits to only a very few categories of citizens—members of families with dependent children, the aged, the blind, and the disabled. In addition, federal unemployment insurance provides limited benefits to those who lose their jobs through no fault of their own. Moral reformers have proposed that we abandon this categorical welfare system and adopt, in its place, a general welfare system, one in which all classes of needy individuals would be eligible for welfare. How do ethical welfare rights bear on this proposed change?

The answer lies in an examination of some of the arguments in support of this reform.

1) We ought to abandon our categorical welfare system because the categories defined by the Social Security Act exclude many needy individuals with an ethical right to welfare benefits. An inspection of the existing categories suggests that this is true. For example, the definition of a dependent child leaves families in which the combined earnings of both parents are insufficient to provide a livelihood for one or more children with no legal claim to AFDC or any other welfare aid. Similarly, unemployed, often unemployable individuals, who have never been covered by federal unemployment insurance or who have exhausted their benefits are ineligible for welfare benefits no matter how destitute they may be through no fault of their own. But surely such individuals have both a civic right to social security and a civic right to a fair share. These ethical welfare rights are clearly violated by our limited categorical welfare system.

One response to this argument would be to deny that our social security categories do in fact exclude any individuals with an ethical right to welfare benefits. To be sure, the ethical rights to social security and a fair share are civic rights, not more special rights possessed by more limited categories of citizens only. At the same time, the moral obligations they impose upon the state are conditional duties. Thus, the individual's right to social security requires the state to provide a minimal livelihood only "in the event that he or she lacks the means of maintaining life because of circumstances beyond his or her control." Similarly, the individual's ethical right to a fair share imposes a duty upon the state to provide an amount of goods and services sufficient to remove his of her poverty only "if the individual has been unjustly impoverished." It can be argued that the categories recognized in federal legislation cover just these conditions. But this response is surely mistaken. The classes of citizens mentioned in the previous paragraph as examples of those excluded under our categorical system fall within the conditions under which the civic rights to social security and to a fair share impose a duty to provide welfare benefits upon the state. Statistics suggest that this is true of many other individuals as well. In 1978, only about 14 ½ million individuals were receiving benefits under the categories of our social security system, but the number of poor persons in the United States was approximately 24½ million. Surely large numbers of those 10 million destitute individuals had an ethical claim to social security or a fair share against the United States government.

Another response to the charge that our categorical welfare system violates the ethical rights of many needy individuals to social security and/or a fair share by excluding them from our federal social security system would be to admit the charge but deny that this implies any moral imperative to abandon a categorical system. If our existing welfare categories exclude individuals with ethical rights to welfare benefits, then what is needed is a redefinition of our categories, not a change to a general welfare system. Established categories could readily be improved in any or all of three ways. Federal legislation could enlarge existing categories to take in individuals now excluded. Or new categories could be added to cover each class of citizens with an ethical right to welfare benefits but presently uncovered by our social security categories. Or we could add a residual category to render eligible for welfare benefits every citizen presently ineligible but satisfying the conditions of the ethical rights to social security or a fair share.

In point of fact each and every state does have some such category of welfare, most often called "general assistance." One may even complain that I have been unfair to criticize our federal social security categories when these are only a part of the cooperative federal-state welfare system in our country. This complaint is well-taken. In principle, the addition of a residual category would rebut this first argument for abandoning our categorical welfare system provided, of course, the residual category were defined broadly enough to include all individuals with an ethical right to welfare benefits. In practice, however, general assistance has been provided by the states at a markedly lower level than welfare aid provided in the federally supported categories. This raises the charge of inequitable welfare treatment, a charge to which we must return later.

But first let us look at a third response to the charge that our categorical welfare system violates the ethical rights to social security and to a fair share of many citizens. One can admit that this is the case but maintain that there is a moral justification for thus infringing the rights of some individuals. After all, the individual's right to social security and/or to a fair share imposes upon the state only a prima facie duty to provide a substitute livelihood or to relieve poverty. Unfortunately, the state has many prima facie moral obligations and limited resources with which to meet them. Its actual duty is to meet the most stringent of its moral obligations. With respect to its welfare system, the most stringent duties are imposed upon society by the most urgent needs of its citizens, and our existing categories in fact reflect the most currently pressing needs in our society. Any historical study of welfare legislation will confirm the coincidence between the welfare categories existing in the legal system at any time and the urgency of the contemporary social problems to which they respond. Perhaps, but the urgency of a problem for some society does not always coincide with the urgency of some need for the individual. Since ethical welfare rights are distributive, the ethical claim of each individual depends upon that individual's circumstances alone. And in any society, the needs of large numbers of individuals, especially of those with power in the society, can cause the legal welfare system to neglect the most pressing needs of less numerous classes of individuals, especially of minority groups with less political influence.

This realistic awareness of power politics suggests another justification for a welfare system even though it excludes many individuals with an ethical right to welfare benefits. The state has no moral obligation to do the impossible, and political expediency limits what the state *can* do to provide welfare for its citizens. Any equitable welfare system will be subject to and defined by the law of the land, and legislation is possible only where and as political power can be effectively mobilized. No doubt the ideal is a welfare system in which every individual with an ethical right to welfare will have a legal claim to receive such welfare. But to insist on the ideal or nothing is, in practical politics, to settle for nothing. Any welfare system must be built, piece by piece, with statute after statute modified by judicial interpretation and application. The practical politician begins by recognizing the ethical claims of those classes of individuals for whom political support is present or can be readily created. Then excluded groups can gradually work within the political system for new legislation to extend the coverage of the welfare categories. This means that at any stage of history, the entrenched welfare categories will exclude some individuals with an ethical right to welfare. But to abandon welfare categories entirely and adopt a general welfare system is to make impossible the mobilization of political power by and for identifiable groups in the society. The inevitable consequence is either no welfare system at all or one with benefit levels so low as to fail to fulfill the ethical rights of the recipients. Since the hard realities of politics imply that no society can do better, morally speaking, than a categorical welfare system, any infringements of individual rights incidental to such a system are morally justified. I am not quite sure how to assess this response for two reasons.

First, it is unclear whether the alleged limitations in what is politically possible are real. My inclination would be to try to enact legislation that would provide welfare benefits for all those with an ethical right to welfare and at reasonably adequate levels. If determined efforts in fact fail, then this would confirm the suggested limits on what is politically feasible. But I would not wish to give up without trying, and trying often and hard.

Second, I lack the theoretical grounds to decide which of two alternatives is more unacceptable from a moral point of view. One is the existing situation in which a categorical system of welfare completely excludes some individuals with an ethical right to welfare but provides considerable welfare benefits to those who are covered. The other is a situation in which all citizens with a right to welfare are included but, because of diluted political support, benefit levels are lower and thereby fail to fulfill the rights of any of the recipients. Since rights are distributive, one cannot neglect the rights of some individuals simply to benefit other individuals or increase the general welfare. But in this situation, the choice is between rights and rights, not rights and social utility. Perhaps, although it is only a suggestion, the ethical right to equitable welfare treatment tips the balance so that it is morally preferable to fulfill the rights of all even if incompletely rather than satisfying the rights of some more fully and others not at all. In any event, any welfare system recognizing a number of categories of eligible individuals raises the question of the equitable distribution of welfare benefits among the categories.

2) We ought to abandon our categorical welfare system because the great differences between the benefit levels in the different categories violate the ethical right to equitable welfare treatment of the individuals in the less-favored categories. In 1979, for example, the average monthly amount paid to a blind recipient of welfare was $212.27; to a disabled recipient, $181.71; to a recipient of old age assistance, only $122.67; and to an individual receiving AFDC, a mere $92.67. Surely such gross inequalities in the amounts of welfare assistance provided to individuals in the four basic categories recognized by our social security system constitute inequitable treatment of citizens receiving Old Age Assistance and Aid to Families with Dependent Children.

Certainly such great differences in the benefit levels provided to individuals in the different categories constitute strong presumptive evidence of inequitable welfare treatment. Such a presumption might, however, turn out to be mistaken in the light of additional evidence. The defining core of the civic right to equitable welfare treatment is the ethical claim of the individual citizen against his or her state not to be treated worse concerning welfare benefits than others who are similarly situated without a justicizing difference. Presumably, to be provided with a smaller dollar amount of welfare aid is to be treated worse concerning welfare. But we must remember that not all welfare aid takes the form of monetary payments. In particular, recipients of AFDC typically receive foods stamps and often family services as well. The dollar value of these other forms of welfare assistance would need to be figured in to arrive at an accurate estimate of welfare treatment to the individual. Again, notice that individuals compared are in different welfare categories. Might it be denied, therefore, that they are similarly situated? I think not. Individuals are similarly situated with respect to welfare treatment when they have the same sort of ethical claim to welfare, and the ethical claim-rights to social security and to a fair share cut across all four social security categories.

More plausibly, it might be maintained that there are justicizing differences sufficient to justify the lower amounts of aid provided to individuals in some categories. The much lower amounts paid to recipients of OAA and AFDC in comparison with those paid to the blind and the disabled might be justicized by the fact that blind or disabled persons require much more help, for which they must pay, than sighted or able individuals on welfare. Again, the difference between the average amount paid to an elderly individual and an individual dependent child might be justicized by the fact that members of families with dependent children typically live in family units of three to five, which afford opportunities for economizing ruled out to elderly persons usually living alone or in couples. My guess is that such justicizing differences partly, but not completely, rebut the presumption of inequitable treatment of citizens in the less-favored categories of our social security system. What is clear is that inequity cannot be established merely by citing statistics of the average amounts paid in the different categories. Moreover, if a fuller examination of the evidence, including a consideration of all justicizing differences, does reveal actual inequity, the individual's ethical right to equitable welfare treatment might well call for a revision in the amounts paid in the several categories rather than for abandoning our categorical welfare system.

3) We ought to abandon our categorical welfare system because the welfare categories are used to violate the ethical right of many black citizens to freedom from racial discrimination in welfare. Although I have given no philosophical analysis of this right, I would agree with the National Welfare Rights Organization in affirming its existence. It can and has been argued that it is no coincidence that the average amount paid to recipients of AFDC is significantly less than the average amount paid under the OAA category. The proportion of blacks in our society receiving Aid to Families with Dependent Children is considerably higher than the proportion of blacks receiving Old Age Assistance. Thus, the existence of our social security categories enables and encourages legislatures to discriminate against blacks in appropriating monies for our welfare programs. Again, legislation defining these categories functions in a racially discriminatory manner. For example, federal legislation defines the term "dependent child" in such a way as to exclude any child in a family with both parents present but impoverished because of underemployment of the parents (42 USCS section 606(a)). This exclusion, which affects a much higher proportion of black families than white families, has been upheld by the courts in *Cheley* v. *Burson* (324 F. Supp. 678) but branded an "inexplicable anomaly" of our welfare system. It is probably more than an anomaly; it is racial discrimination.

This moral criticism of our categorical welfare system could be developed in greater detail and at much greater length, but its nature is clear. The existence of a number of distinct welfare categories is used by our society to discriminate against blacks in allocating welfare resources among these distinct classes of citizens, and the categories themselves are legally defined in ways that exclude disproportionate numbers of black citizens with an ethical right to welfare benefits. To

my mind, there is strong, although not compelling, evidence of *de
facto* racial discrimination of these sorts, discrimination that does
indeed violate the ethical right to freedom from racial discrimination
in welfare of many of our black citizens. I willingly conclude that our
welfare system ought to be reformed to eliminate all vestiges of this
racial discrimination. It remains to be proven, however, that we
ought to entirely abandon our categorical system rather than to
redefine its categories and adjust the levels of welfare benefits to
achieve equity.

4) We ought to abandon our categorical welfare system because it
violates the ethical right to privacy in welfare treatment of many of
our citizens. Assuming the existence of a secondary welfare right to
privacy, one can argue that our categorical welfare system frequently
violates this ethical right in two ways. First, investigation by the
welfare agency in order to assure itself that some individual claimant
really does fall within one of the legally recognized categories, and is
therefore eligible for aid, often requires prying into very personal
affairs of the individual claimant or other members of the family. For
example, investigations necessary to show that some alleged dependent child really is "deprived of parental support . . . by reason of
. . . physical or mental incapacity of a parent" would necessarily
invade the privacy of the family. A more notorious example is the
"midnight searches" used to determine the presence of a "man-in-
the-house." Second, the welfare categories coerce individuals into
making private decisions against their wills in order to render themselves or others eligible for welfare benefits. Thus, the mother of a
very young child might be forced to enter a WIN program rather than
remain home and care for her child, or a husband unable adequately
to support his family might be compelled to abandon his family in
order to make it eligible for Aid to Families with Dependent Children.

Although not every alleged invasion of privacy is a real violation of
the individual's right to privacy, I have no doubt that our public
welfare system often has violated the individual's ethical right to
privacy concerning welfare treatment. I very much doubt, however,
that this is because we have a categorical welfare system. Any public
welfare system administered under law must have legally specified
conditions of eligibility for welfare benefits. The equitable application
of such eligibility conditions will require some sort of investigation by
the welfare agency. There is no reason to believe that a categorical
system as such requires any more or any different investigation than a
general system of welfare. That all depends upon the nature of the
eligibility conditions themselves. Again, every welfare system will
provide benefits to some and not to others. The opportunity to render
oneself or those for whom one cares eligible for benefits will be
present in every possible system, categorical or noncategorical. None
of this should suggest that the individual's ethical right to privacy in

matters concerning welfare is irrelevant to the reform of our welfare system. As far as humanly possible, we should eliminate all conditions of eligibility that call for invasive investigations or that would coerce individuals in making primarily personal decisions about their lives. But this does not imply that we ought to abandon, rather than modify, our categorical system of social security.

We have examined four arguments grounded on ethical welfare rights to show that we ought to abandon our categorical welfare system. This system excludes many individuals with an ethical right to welfare benefits, violates the right to equitable welfare treatment of those in the less favored categories, discriminates against blacks in our society, and violates the right to welfare privacy of many citizens. I am convinced that our social security system does in fact violate these ethical welfare rights in the ways alleged. But I see no reason to believe that this is necessarily true of an ideal categorical welfare system. In principle, we could reform our system rather than abandon it. In practice, however, this may not be politically feasible. Some classes of citizens can mobilize more political pressure than others. Financial exigencies exert a continuing and virtually irresistible temptation to reduce, or at least hold down, the amounts appropriated for welfare programs. Our society is infected with racial, sexual, and other sorts of discrimination. Given these contingent facts about our society, we probably ought to abandon our categorical welfare system and enact a general system of welfare in its place.

Eligibility on Need Alone

In order to receive welfare benefits under United States law, most poor families must establish eligibility for AFDC. In addition to need, eligibility conditions include membership in a family with a dependent child, as legally defined, and various nonneed factors, such as the willingness of the mother to participate in a Work Incentive Program and her cooperation with authorities in enforcing the father's legal duty of supporting their child. We have already noted that the federal definition of a "dependent child" excludes parental-intact families whose combined earnings still leave them well below the poverty level. Each of the nonneed conditions of eligibility excludes some citizens in dire economic need. Believing that such exclusions are unjust, the Committee for Economic Development has recommended "a federally supported program to provide a national minimum income with eligibility determined solely on the basis of need, whether need results from inadequate earnings or inability to work" (*Improving the Public Welfare System*, p. 36). Let us focus our attention on one aspect of this recommendation, that eligibility for welfare benefits ought to be based on need alone. How might an appeal to ethical welfare rights bear upon this proposed welfare reform?

1) A very plausible argument for the proposed reform can be sketched as follows: Being in need confers upon the needy individual an ethical right to welfare benefits. Since the needy individual has an ethical right to welfare, he or she ought to have a legal right to comparable welfare benefits. This is possible only if eligibility for welfare benefits is legally conditioned on need alone. We have examined the inference from a moral right to welfare to the obligation to create a legal right to welfare in Chapter Three. Here let us examine the assumption that need confers upon the individual an ethical right to some welfare benefit.

Why might one imagine that being in need confers upon the needy individual any ethical right to welfare? Well, if primary welfare rights were grounded in basic human needs, this would be so. In examining the grounds of ethical rights to welfare in the previous chapter, however, I reluctantly came to the conclusion that they cannot be grounded in needs per se. The logical link between needing something and having a right to it is far from self-evident. The most plausible ways of trying to explain some logical connection are by appealing to the great utility of fulfilling important needs, the unfairness of fulfilling the mere wants of some while the basic needs of others remain unfulfilled, and the harm that an individual suffers if his or her basic needs are not fulfilled. Since none of these seems adequate to ground the individual's ethical power of claiming fulfillment from his or her state, none of them is a logically sufficient ground for any ethical claim-right to welfare benefits.

Perhaps, however, being in need is the condition under which the individual's ethical claim to social security or to a fair share imposes a duty to provide welfare benefits upon the state, rather than the ground of that claim. But what might one mean by "need" on this view? The Committee for Economic Development seems to use the federally defined poverty level as its operational definition of need, for it equates the number of needy individuals with the number of individuals living below that figure. This simple conception of need is clearly inadequate. Some individuals doubtless live below the poverty line simply because they prefer living off private charity or public welfare to working for a living. But these individuals have no ethical claim to welfare benefits, either from a right to social security (since they do not lack the means of sustaining life "because of circumstances beyond their control") or from any right to a fair share (since they have been impoverished by their own choice rather than by the social institutions of economic distribution). We would not expect any ethical right to welfare benefits to be conditional upon so simple a conception of need, however, for the very concept of a welfare benefit explained in Chapter One presupposes a more complex definition of need. To be in need in the relevant sense, the individual must both lack something necessary for his or her human well-being and be unable to attain this something by his or her own unaided efforts. If we employ this double-barreled concept of need, it may well be true that being in need is a sufficient condition under which the individual's ethical rights to social security and a fair share do impose upon the state a duty to provide welfare benefits to the individual. On this interpretation, the slogan that individuals ought to be eligible for welfare on the basis of need alone is a close approximation to the truth.

The exact truth can be spelled out precisely only with a more complex, even a somewhat cumbersome, formulation. Ethical welfare rights are conferred upon an individual by his or her status and typically have a conditional claim as their core. For example, the civic right to social security is possessed by the right-holder as a citizen, in his or her capacity as a member of a politically and economically organized society. Moreover, it imposes a duty upon the state to provide a substitute livelihood only on the condition that the individual lacks the means of sustaining life because of circumstances beyond his or her control. Similarly, the individual possesses the right to a fair share as a citizen, and it imposes upon the state a duty to relieve the individual's poverty only if this economic deprivation results from the arbitrary operations of the social institutions that shape economic distribution in that society. Presumably, then, the legally specified conditions for eligibility for public welfare ought to reflect these two aspects of the individual's ethical rights to welfare. Not need alone, but being a member of the society, together with either lacking a livelihood because of circumstances beyond one's control or being unjustly impoverished, confers an ethical right to public welfare.

There is another plausible argument for the proposed reform that also calls for some attention. 2) All eligibility conditions other than need infringe some ethical welfare right of some individuals. Our society ought not to infringe any ethical welfare rights of any individuals. Therefore, our system of public welfare ought to require nothing other than need to render the individual eligible. How cogent is this argument for the proposed welfare reform?

The argument assumes that any eligibility condition other than need will inevitably violate some ethical welfare right of some individuals. Must this be true? Any other requirement for eligibility might violate a welfare right of an individual in either of two very different ways—by rendering ineligible an individual with a primary welfare right to some specific benefit or by requiring or encouraging welfare practices that violate one or more secondary welfare rights. The notorious man-in-the-house rule did both. The mere presence of a man in the house was taken to be sufficient for denying Aid to Families with Dependent Children even when that man was not in fact supporting the unemployed mother or her dependent children. Also, the "midnight searches" used to detect the presence of a man in the house invaded the privacy of the family and thereby violated the ethical right to privacy concerning welfare of the family members. Now I can imagine no reason to suppose that each and every eligibility condition other than need must violate any secondary welfare right. This will depend upon the specific nature of any such condition, the investigations necessary to apply it, and the exact way it modifies the actions of state officials in the welfare agencies. On the other hand, it would seem that, logically, any requirement other than need would either be empty, because every needy individual would satisfy it anyway, or objectionable, because it would deny welfare benefits to some needy individual. Let us remember, however, that it is not need *per se* that confers ethical rights to welfare. If, and this is a big "if," there are no human rights to welfare and the most fundamental primary welfare rights are civic rights, then citizenship as an eligibility condition would not violate the ethical right to welfare of any individual at all. The proper conclusion would seem to be that any condition of eligibility other than citizenship, in the very broad sense of being a member of the society, or the conditions under which the various ethical rights to welfare impose a state duty to provide benefits, such as lacking the means to sustain life because of circumstances beyond one's control or being unjustly impoverished, must necessarily be pointless because redundant or morally objectionable in that they infringe some ethical right to welfare of some individuals excluded by it.

There will often be, then, requirements other than those reflecting the status and conditions of our primary welfare rights that will infringe these rights of some individuals by rendering them ineligible for welfare benefits. Is it true, as the second premise assumes, that the state ought never to infringe any welfare right of any individuals? After all, there might be some moral justification for such state action sufficient to override the ethical rights of some individuals. In exploring this possibility, let us consider two eligibility conditions.

In our federal-state welfare program, welfare benefits are provided by the several states with the financial support and under the regulation of the federal government. Most, if not all states, require residence within the state as a condition for eligibility. This requirement is not simply citizenship, or membership in the society, under a different name, for the United States is not really a collection of fifty distinct societies, although its federal constitution confuses the issue. Probably some citizens of the United States are denied welfare benefits to which they have an ethical right by this residency requirement. This will be true of individuals who become destitute outside the borders of the state in which they reside and who lack the means to return to their home state and of some who are wanderers or nomads with a fixed residence at all. What justification might one offer for the residence requirement?

Some maintain that the state has a limited responsibility for public welfare. Specifically, each state is morally responsible for providing welfare benefits to its own residents only. But why should this be so? Presumably the state ought to provide police protection for the life and property of residents and visitors alike. Argument by analogy suggests a distinction. Each family is morally responsible for offering what protection it can to members and guests alike, but one family has no obligation at all to take in and care for needy children of other parents. Similarly, one state has no moral obligation to care for the economic needs of any resident of any other state. To my mind, the analogy between family and state is defective in several ways. But for the sake of argument, I will grant that no state *as* a single state in our federal system is responsible for the residents of other states. But ours is a federal-state welfare system, and the federal government at least has a moral obligation to ensure that no citizen of the United States is excluded from our public welfare programs without good and sufficient reason.

Among the moral responsibilities of the federal government is ensuring that both welfare benefits and the burdens of taxation are distributed among the residents of the several states equitably. The residence requirement might be justified as a means of spreading the burden of welfare programs evenly by having each state care for its own needy without any additional burden of caring for needy non-residents. Unfortunately, there is no reason to suppose that requiring residency is an effective means to this end because there is no reason to imagine that poverty or taxable income is distributed evenly across the land. Moreover, the welfare programs of the individual states are supported, in part, with federal funds. A better way to achieve equity between the states is by means of increased federal funding, adjusted to the special circumstances of each state.

Many would argue that a residence requirement is necessary to prevent welfare fraud. If nonresidents are eligible for welfare benefits, many individuals will apply for welfare from more than a single state. Investigation of claimants from out-of-state residents will be ineffective and unreliable. Hence, only a residency condition can prevent greedy individuals from collecting public welfare to which they have no moral right. I very much doubt that a residency requirement is necessary to control multiple welfare claims. In this age of data banks, computers, and rapid communications, it would be easy enough to compare on a nationwide basis the names and addresses of all applicants for public welfare. To be sure, this would be effective only if each state were to check the identity of each applicant carefully, but this is also required to prevent multiple claims from within the state. Moreover, the several states could work out cooperative programs of investigation so that the credentials of any out-of-state applicant could be investigated by the welfare agency of his or her home state, and the results reported to the state from which benefits were claimed.

But suppose that requiring residence would eliminate ten fraudulent welfare claims at the same time it excludes only one right-based claim. Would it then be morally permissible? In cases of criminal justice, moral philosophers often hold that it is not permissible to reduce the protection of due process in order to convict ten guilty individuals if the price will be the conviction of one innocent individual. One wonders whether the moral presumption against violating the welfare rights of a single individual might not be just as strong. One can appreciate the urgency of providing welfare to *each* individual with an ethical right to it; his or her welfare, even very life, depends upon receiving welfare benefits. It is less obvious why it is morally imperative to prevent welfare fraud. Saving the taxpayers' money in order to reduce the amount of their economic sacrifice, although highly desirable, does not seem of sufficient moral importance to justify violating moral rights of the individual. Nor do I place much stock in the view that the state has a moral obligation to enforce morality and, hence, to prevent those inclined to make fraudulent claims from wrong action. If, however, the funds available to finance welfare programs really are limited, so that permitting some individuals with no ethical right to welfare fraudulently to obtain it will necessitate the denial of welfare to those with a right to it, the situation is very different. Under that condition, and we must not be too lenient in assuming its presence, the protection of the welfare rights of legitimate claimants would justify a residence requirement provided—what is not true—it were necessary to prevent welfare fraud.

The fact that only limited resources are available to fund the welfare program of any state suggests another justification for a residency requirement. If nonresidents are eligible for welfare benefits, then those states with relatively high benefit levels will be flooded with applications from the residents of the low-benefit states. The magnitude of this threat to the financial integrity of the welfare programs in states like Rhode Island and Alaska is seen from the fact that, in 1979, their levels of AFDC benefits per individual were $139.26 and $130.62 per month, respectively, while the average benefit in Texas was a mere $35.90 and in Mississippi a lamentable $28.98. Were residents of Texas and Mississippi eligible for public welfare from the state of Rhode Island, poor little Rhode Island would be poor indeed. Its only course of action would be to reduce its levels of Aid to Families with Dependent Children far below the levels to which its own residents have an ethical right. Surely, it is morally preferable to infringe the ethical rights of a few nonresidents than to impair the ethical welfare rights of all its citizens.

But this way of formulating the alternatives is grossly misleading; this is not the choice at all. At stake are not simply the rights to welfare of those few individuals who would be completely denied welfare benefits by the residency requirements of the several states;

the grossly unequal levels of AFDC benefits between the states presently infringe the rights to welfare of many in those states with welfare benefits far below that to which their residents have an ethical right and also their right to equitable welfare treatment. Given limited resources, at least equity in our welfare system could be greatly increased by permitting out-of-state claims to welfare until states like Rhode Island and Alaska were forced to reduce their benefit levels considerably and states like Texas and Mississippi could raise their benefit levels by allocating their meager welfare resources to the residents who have not claimed welfare from other states. In this way, permitting the free operation of the welfare marketplace would promote equitable welfare treatment throughout the United States. If, in point of fact, the resources each state could allocate to its welfare programs were limited to something like the amount presently appropriated, then this course of action probably would be morally justified. There is, however, a morally preferable way to promote greater equity in our country. Our federal-state welfare system is funded primarily from federal appropriations. The proportion of federal funding and its allocation among the several states can surely be adjusted in such a way as vastly to reduce existing inequities in benefit levels. When this is done, the threat to the fiscal integrity of public welfare in states like Rhodes Island and Alaska will be ended, and this justification for a residency requirement outdated.

Still, a residence condition for eligibility might be justified as a means of promoting efficient administration of any state welfare agency. It will be much harder to plan budgets, request appropriations, and allocate welfare funds if out-of-state claims are valid for the number of such claimants will be relatively unpredictable. Again, handling claims for welfare benefits will be more inefficient because the necessary investigations will be more difficult, costly, and unreliable when the claimants live in other parts of the country. Above all, delivering welfare benefits, especially family services, such as counseling or vocational training, will be virtually impossible to out-of-state claimants. Readers who take rights seriously may object to sacrificing individual moral rights for mere efficiency, apparently only a social goal. But state resources used in the administration of a welfare program are typically diverted from meeting the rights-based claims of individual recipients. If welfare appropriations can be increased to cover inefficient operations without sacrificing some other moral obligation of the state, well and good. If not, then the ethical rights of individual recipients of welfare to the level required by their ethical rights to welfare might well justify a residence requirement as a means to efficient administration.

One last justification might be that a residence requirement is justified as a necessary means of maintaining political support for the state welfare program. At first glance, this seems more like an appeal to mere expediency than a moral justification, an argument grounded more in the self-interest of a politician concerned only with his or her future than in specifically moral considerations. No doubt, it often is just that when used in political debate. But it can be much more; it can be an appeal to the primary welfare rights of the residents of the state. Whatever an enlightened conscience might demand, it is surely true that large numbers of taxpayers resent having to make personal sacrifices to support welfare programs and would be even more resentful if they believed that their tax dollars were being used to provide welfare benefits to out-of-state applicants. Hence, the lack of residency as a condition of eligibility would make it more difficult to enact adequate appropriations for welfare programs. The inevitable result of lower appropriations would be either completely denying benefits to some residents with an ethical right to them or the reduction in the benefit level for all recipients below the level to which they have an ethical right. In this way, the justification of a residence requirement by an appeal to the need for political support is indirectly an appeal to welfare rights. Given the hard facts of power politics, it is probably true that the welfare rights of the many residents outweigh or override the welfare rights of a few nonresidents.

Although not all of the usual arguments for a residence requirement are sound, several of them are. In particular, the appeals to efficiency of administration, and to the need for political support constitute a moral justification for a residency condition even though this condition will cause the welfare agencies to infringe the welfare rights of some individuals. This is so because these arguments are more than appeals to social utility or to personal interest; they are based upon a respect for the welfare rights of the residents of each state.

Our conclusion must be that welfare rights do not in the end require the welfare reform proposed by the Committee for Economic Development. It is not true that need alone confers a fundamental ethical claim-right to welfare. What does confer an ethical claim to some welfare benefit upon the individual is his or her status as a citizen together with his or her satisfying the conditions in the conditional cores of rights, such as the civic right to social security or to a fair share. Nor is it true that every condition of eligibility other than need is morally unjustified because it would violate the welfare rights of some individuals. Some other conditions, such as citizenship, would not violate any such right because our most fundamental welfare rights are civic, rather than human, rights. Others might infringe some welfare right of some individuals, but the state might have a sufficient justification for overriding these rights. What is true is that the legal qualifications for welfare benefits ought to be the same as the status and conditions of our ethical rights to welfare unless there is some special moral justification for some additional condition of eligibility.

Raise Benefit Levels

A third welfare reform, perennially advocated but somehow unattainable, is that state welfare agencies ought to increase AFDC payments to a level that would provide a more adequate standard of living for welfare recipients. Present benefit levels are calculated by a two-stage process. First each state determines its standard of need, the amount it judges an individual resident would need to meet his or her basic economic needs. Second, the state decides what proportion of this standard it can afford to provide with its available welfare funds. Thus, judged purely by the state's own standards, its welfare benefits are usually below, and often drastically below, the amounts needed to enable welfare claimants to live adequately.

Another measure of the adequacy of benefit levels in our Aid to Families with Dependent Children program is the poverty level as defined by the federal government. This is the amount of income a family must have in order to live just at the line between poverty and not being poor. In 1979, the poverty level for a family of four, a typical size for a family receiving AFDC, was set at $153.54 per months for each member of the family. In the same year, the average amount per individual paid in AFDC benefits was only $92.88 per month. These statistics cannot be taken at face value. The federal definition of poverty is not beyond criticism, and, in addition to welfare payments, most families on welfare receive other benefits such as food stamps and family services. Nevertheless, I doubt that any knowledgable observer would deny that AFDC benefits leave vast numbers of individuals far below the poverty line. There can be no doubt that present benefit levels are too low. But they may be judged inadequate by a number of different standards. They may be inhumane, far below the amount of public assistance charity would demand. Or they might be economically inadequate, too low to prime the pump and stimulate the economy to expand to full employment once more. They might be inadequate to satisfy the constituents of state legislators. I will limit my attention to a single standard—ethical welfare rights. Does an appeal to the welfare rights of the citizen imply that present levels of AFDC payments are too low?

The benefit level required by our ethical rights to welfare depends, of course, upon the precise content of these rights. The civic right to social security, at least as I have defined it, calls for a minimal standard of living. It imposes upon the state the duty of providing the individual lacking a livelihood only those goods and services absolutely necessary to sustain life. It may be imagined that existing benefit levels are at least adequate to this standard, but such may not always be the case. To be sure, famines are not present in our fair country. But some recipients of welfare probably do die, directly or indirectly, from malnutrition. Others probably die from illnesses caused or aggravated by inadequate food or shelter. Each winter, individuals on welfare die from cold-related causes because they lack the income to purchase warm clothing or to heat their rooms or apartments. Each summer, individuals, mostly elderly, die from heat-related causes that prove fatal only because of lack of income. A minimal livelihood is not simply enough to keep the individual alive today or for a few weeks; it is an income sufficient to enable the individual to live something like a normal lifespan and to prevent death from economically caused threats.

The civic right to a fair share requires a higher level of benefits. On my unjust impoverishment conception, it imposes upon the state the duty to provide goods and services sufficient to raise the individual up out of poverty. This need not imply that amounts of aid must equal the poverty level, for the individual may have income from other sources. But it does imply that AFDC payments should be adequate to bring the total income of the recipient to that amount needed to enable the individual to live just barely above the poverty level. All evidence indicates that present benefit levels do not do so. Thus they infringe the ethical rights of all recipients who remain in poverty. If the citizen also has an ethical right to an adequate standard of living, it may be that benefit levels should be raised even higher. But since the case for this welfare right has yet to be made, I shall ignore it here. Appealing only to the rights to social security and a fair share, I believe that amounts of AFDC benefits should be drastically raised.

Some will object that, however well justified as a moral ideal, this reform is completely impracticable because economically impossible. The amounts of the AFDC payments in our federal-state system cannot be increased to the point where poverty is eliminated for welfare recipients because the state treasuries supplemented with the federal fisc do not contain such vast financial resources. This may be true, but it is irrelevant. More resources could be made available to state welfare agencies by increasing taxes on both the state and the federal levels. This may or may not be desirable, but surely it is possible. It is not literally true that our society cannot raise benefit levels up to the poverty level. It is possible that in some other societies, less affluent than ours, welfare benefits simply could not eliminate poverty among the recipients. But if this is ever the case, this would not imply that the civic right to a fair share must inevitably be violated by those states. Since the state cannot have any genuine moral obligation to do the impossible, under such dire conditions, the citizens have no ethical claim-right that requires this level of welfare payments. What we are considering, however, is a proposed reform of our system of welfare. This reform cannot be rejected on the ground that it is impossible.

Some economists argue that, although possible, this reform would have disastrous consequences. Raising the amounts of the AFDC payments to eliminate poverty would at the same time eliminate a very necessary and powerful incentive to get off welfare and engage in productive labor, the threat of poverty. Plus, in order to raise benefit levels dramatically, taxes would have to be increased greatly also. This would discourage labor among those who do work. Why try to work harder and better to earn a higher income if the result is merely that one must pay higher taxes? Any realistic and just system of taxation adequate to raise the huge revenues necessary to fund increased AFDC payments must be sharply progressive. This will make it almost impossible for any individuals to accumulate large fortunes, the primary source of capital improvement and venture capital. Economic stagnation and a falling standard of living for everyone is the only possible consequence. The proposed reform will also undermine certain character traits, such as independence, self-reliance, and moral responsibility, essential to personal welfare and any productive economy.

The arguments are familiar; they need little elaboration. IF these dire predictions were true, they would constitute a good reason to override the welfare rights of the individual. Some infringement of the rights to social security and a fair share would be justified as absolutely necessary in order to avoid a social and personal disaster. Fortunately, these effects of any adequate welfare program are greatly exaggerated. That this is so must be demonstrated by economic analysis rather than philosophical argument. Hence, I shall leave to professional economists the task of proving this fact.

Granted that we could implement the proposed reform without any disastrous consequences, there is no doubt that this would require much higher taxation. Many would argue that AFDC benefits ought not to be increased to the level required to raise welfare recipients out of poverty because to do so would be to impose excessive sacrifice upon the taxpayers in our society. The argument is that the necessary levels of taxation would be morally excessive: more than society has any moral right to exact and more than the citizens have any moral obligation to pay. I will leave to the economists the prediction of precisely what levels of taxation would be required in order to carry out the proposed reform. As a moral philosopher, I will ponder briefly the standard of excessive sacrifice. Surely at some point, taxation would impose excessive sacrifice upon the taxpayers. But by what criterion can one identify that point?

In another context, William Aiken has suggested that individuals have no moral obligation to share their economic resources with those less fortunate than themselves when to do so would reduce them to a position of equal or greater need than the right-holders. I would agree that taxation heavy enough to reduce the taxpayers to the poverty level would be excessive from a moral point of view, but I would add that it becomes morally excessive even before that point is reached. Charles Fried has an explanation of why this might be so. He is very much concerned to limit our moral obligations to share our limited resources because he holds that any adequate moral theory will account, no only for moral rights and moral obligations, but also for some area of human life in which the individual may use his or her resources freely in order to pursue personal goals and moral ideals. This insight strikes me as sound and important. Unfortunately, I am unable to provide any rational argument to support my presystematic intuition, nor do I find any real argument in *Right and Wrong*. Worse yet, Friend offers no criterion by which to determine how many spare resources ought to be left to the discretionary disposal of the individual. Therefore, he has not explained at what point taxation would become morally excessive.

Another approach to our problem is to appeal to the traditional distinction between obligatory acts and actions over and beyond the call of duty. Taxation is not excessive as long as the individual taxpayer has a moral obligation to share his or her affluence with the poor. But it might be morally excessive to impose a legal duty to perform supererogatory acts of supporting a public welfare system. Perhaps an act is beyond the call of duty when it asks so much of human nature that the normal or average human being would refuse to perform it. Perhaps, but I must confess that I remain puzzled by the distinction between the morally upright person who merely does his or her duty and the moral saint or hero. Accordingly, I can offer no criterion to determine at what point taxation does become morally excessive. At the same time, observing the very modest sacrifices most taxpayers make in the United States and contrasting our rates of taxation with those in many other countries suggest that our taxes could be drastically increased without imposing morally excessive demands upon us. Hence, although I recognize the theoretical cogency of this challenge to the proposed reform and recommend further analysis of the concept of an excessive sacrifice, I am prepared to reject this argument as inapplicable to our country under our present economic conditions. We live in an affluent land, and we could dramatically raise the levels of AFDC payments without becoming saints or heroes.

A more serious objection to the proposed reform arises from a consideration of the allocation of available state resources. Even granting a moral imperative to increase taxes far above the present levels, at some point taxation would become morally excessive. Thus, the amounts of economic resources that can be made available to our state and federal governments in a morally permissible manner are limited. Obviously, our governments are engaged in a wide variety of programs. Although some of these may be pursuing merely desirable goals, others are carrying out state duties. It might be that to allocate sufficient monies to our welfare programs to increase AFDC payments to the point where they genuinely eliminate poverty would necessitate withholding resources from other equally or more imperative programs from the moral point of view. Inadequate national defence or police protection would infringe upon the citizens' rights to protection by the state. Inadequate funding for public education would seem to violate the civic right to an education. Stingy support for our courts, so that dockets are overloaded and there are very few public defenders, infringes upon our rights to due process. Inadequate appropriations for jails, prisons, and the personnel to manage them violates, or at least fails to protect, the inmates' ethical rights to personal security, even life, and perhaps rehabilitation.

Given the necessity of allocating governmental resources among a number of competing programs, many of which answer to the ethical rights of the citizen, the justification of the proposed reform requires some sort of weighing of the civic rights to social security and a fair share against other ethical rights of the citizen. If, in fact, we must weigh infringements of one right against infringements of another right, I doubt that the appeal to rights is very helpful. We may hope for an easy way out of this difficulty, the possibility of raising sufficient funds to adequately support all morally imperative programs. Failing that, the only answer seems to be to go beyond our ethical rights to their ground. If moral rights are grounded in utility, one may then weigh one utility against another. If they are grounded in respect for persons, then one may consider which infringement is a greater affront to moral personality. Although I have assessed some of the proposed proximate grounds of our ethical welfare rights, I have yet to identify the ultimate ground of all moral rights. Therefore, I cannot provide any theoretically satisfactory reply to this objection to the proposed reform of our welfare system. On the other hand, I am not aware of anyone who has provided an adequate theoretical account of the grounds of our moral rights to support the objection. The result seems to be a stand-off. Since the objection can neither be sustained nor refuted, it must be ignored until the theory of rights has progressed further.

A final objection to this proposed reform appeals to what is called vertical equity. AFDC payments ought not to be raised to the point where they eliminate poverty among families with dependent children because this would be unfair to the working poor in our society. It would be unfair to raise the individuals in families that do nothing to support themselves above the poverty level while leaving individuals in families where the combined incomes are pitifully low through no fault of their own in dire poverty. I grant that this would be unfair. But this does not imply that we ought to hold down the level of welfare payments. Quite the contrary, a partial solution to this problem would be to modify the eligibility conditions for AFDC so that the working poor may also become recipients of welfare. This is one aspect of the reform considered in the previous section of this chapter. Were this reform carried out, the level of welfare benefits could and should be raised to the point where both working and nonworking poor would cease being poor. This would not, however, satisfy the usual criteria of vertical equity. The general public and many moral philosophers hold that it would be unfair to provide welfare payments to the unemployed that would raise them to the same level as the working poor, in this case the poverty level. In an equitable welfare system, the end result must leave the working poor with a higher income than the nonworking poor.

I agree. But once more it does not follow that the level of welfare payments ought to be held down below the poverty line; what follows is that the working poor ought to have incomes above that line. Why? Since public welfare is a supplementary assistance intended to bring the individual recipient up the level demanded by his or her right to a fair share, what could be unfair about a system under which both the working poor and the nonworking poor are raised just above the poverty line? It is not that the working poor have a greater right to welfare or a right to greater welfare. They have the very same primary welfare rights as any nonworking citizen in the society. But in addition the working poor have an ethical right to remuneration for their labor. If they wind up with the same income as the nonworking poor, then the welfare system is denying them any return for their productive activity. It is their dual claim to income that demands that their incomes be somewhat higher than those of the nonworking recipients of welfare. But this can easily be managed by raising the minimum levels of ADFC up to the poverty line and then allowing the working poor to retain some proportion of their earned income as well.

My conclusion is that we ought to increase the amounts our states pay in Aid to Families with Dependent Children, at least to the point where the recipients cease to live below the poverty level. This is demanded by the civic right to a fair share. Although there are several plausible objections to this reform, some of which raise theoretical problems I am unable to resolve, none of these objections can be adequately sustained. I support this reform heartily. Whether it is politically feasible remains to be seen. What can be seen is that we ought to do everything we can to realize it.

Eliminate State Inequalities

In our country, public welfare has been a responsibility of state and local governments. Relatively recently, the federal government has stepped in to provide financial assistance to the states and, increasingly, to impose regulations upon their welfare programs. The result has been considerable variations in the welfare programs of the several states. For example, each state is permitted to define its own standard of need and then to determine what proportion of that standard it will meet with its AFDC payments. Inequalities in the amounts paid are striking, even shocking. In 1979, the average amount paid to each recipient of Aid to Families with Dependent Children in Rhode Island was $139.26 per month; in Alaska, it was $130.62 per month; and in Washington, it was $128.56 per month. By contrast, the amounts in South Carolina, Texas, and Mississippi were $36.77, $35.90, and $28.98, respectively. Since all citizens of the United States have the same civic rights to social security and to a fair share, such grossly unequal AFDC payments clearly violate the right to equitable welfare treatment of the recipients of the much lower amounts. Therefore, we ought to eliminate all inequalities in welfare benefits among the several states. Here is a straightforward argument from the existence of specific ethical rights to welfare to a morally imperative reform of our welfare system.

One way to respond to this argument is to appeal to federalism. The United States government cannot be accused of inequitable welfare treatment because it does not provide higher welfare benefits to some of its citizens than it provides to others similarly situated. It does not make any AFDC payments at all. We do not have a national system of public welfare, but fifty state welfare systems. Nor, provided it pays equal welfare benefits to its own residents, can any state be accused of inequitable welfare treatment. No doubt it treats nonresidents worse than residents in its welfare program, for its conditions of eligibility exclude nonresidents entirely. But this is no violation of the nonresident's right to equitable welfare treatment, for nonresident and resident are not similarly situation with respect to such treatment; they do not share the same ethical claim to welfare against the state. Thus, our federal Constitution undermines any charge of inequitable welfare treatment aimed at either the federal or the state governments.

Now I am prepared to accept part of this rebuttal. The great inequality in the amounts of AFDC paid by two different states, for example Rhode Island's $139.26 and Mississippi's $28.98, do not prove that the state with lower benefits is violating its residents' right to equitable welfare treatment. This is not, of course, because the residents of Mississippi are not being treated worse than the residents of Rhode Island. It is because the residents of Mississippi are not similarly situated to the residents of Rhode Island with respect to the public welfare program of the state of Mississippi. Since only residents of a state have some moral claim to welfare from that state, the relevant comparison is that between the amounts received by the individual residents within the state. No argument to inequitable treatment can be based upon the civic rights to social security or to a fair share because these primary welfare rights hold, not against the several states, but against the government of our society as a whole.

I am not prepared to admit, however, that our federal Constitution or the federal-state cooperative nature of our welfare system counters the charge of inequitable welfare treatment when it is leveled against the United States government. Since all citizens of the United States are similarly situated with respect to its welfare treatment, in that they all have the same rights to welfare holding against it, the United States has a moral duty not to permit its welfare activities to treat the citizens residing in some states worse than the citizens residing in others. Granted, its activities do not include actually paying Aid to Families with Dependent Children to individual claimants. It does provide federal funding to support the various state public welfare programs, and it also regulates, through legislation and the code of federal regulations, the operations of those programs. It would be quite possible for the United States government to increase its support of AFDC sufficiently to equalize the amounts paid throughout the country by raising the benefits in the states presently less favored. Moreover, it could readily make its continuing financial support contingent upon the practice of each state to provide AFDC payments up to some specified national level. It may well be that existing state inequalities in AFDC benefits have resulted from our federal Constitution. Still, since the principle of federalism does not necessitate any such inequalities, it does not justify their continuation.

A very different way to respond to the argument for eliminating inequalities in AFDC payments between the states would be to reply that the right to equitable welfare treatment must be balanced against the right to equitable taxation. Suppose, to pick on Mississippi once more, that the state of Mississippi were to raise its level of AFDC payments from $28.98 per month to $139.26, the amount paid to the residents of Rhode Island. Obviously it would have to increase its taxes drastically in order to fund this much higher level of public welfare payments. Unfortunately, Mississippi is a relatively poor state. On the average, its individual residents and corporate bodies are much less wealthy than those in more prosperous states like Rhode Island. Were taxes to be markedly raised in the state of Mississippi, the burden placed upon its taxpayers would be disproportionate and thus inequitable. It follows that the right to equitable taxation of the residents of Mississippi limits the degree to which Mississippi ought to raise its level of welfare benefits.

I agree. A consideration of the rights of the taxpayers in the several states does limit the amounts which the less prosperous states ought to appropriate to fund their several welfare programs. But this is no argument that will speak against reforming our system by eliminating all state inequalities, for the burden of raising the levels of AFDC payments ought to fall upon the federal government, not upon the states. In fact, what this response shows is that there exists at present a double inequity in our welfare system—an inequity in the amounts of AFDC provided to citizens of the United States and an inequity in levels of taxation imposed upon citizens of the United States to support state welfare programs. Since the civic rights of United States citizens hold primarily against the federal government and since adjustments in federal taxation and in its financial support to the state welfare programs could eliminate such inequities, it has a moral obligation to do so.

But ought it to do so completely? Ought the reform of our welfare system be carried so far as to eliminate entirely state inequalities in AFDC payments? To be sure, unequal benefit levels between the states constitute prima facie evidence of inequitable welfare treatment. But there might be a justicizing difference to show that what appears to be inequitable treatment is really not inequitable at all. More specifically, differences in the costs of living in the several states might justicize the practice of permitting each state to calculate its own standard of need. After all, poverty is constituted, not by one's income measured in dollars and cents, but by the abnormally small amount of goods and services one can purchase with one's income or otherwise obtain. If it is true that a smaller amount of income is needed to raise one above the poverty level in Mississippi than in Rhode Island, then the state of Mississippi can provide smaller AFDC payments to its residents without treating them worse than Rhode Island treats its residents by paying larger amounts of Aid to Families with Dependent Children.

Very probably it is true that, on the average, the cost of living in Mississippi is considerably lower than the cost of living in Rhode Island, and similarly for many pairs of low-benefit and high-benefit states. And since the content of the core of the civic right to a fair share is an ethical claim of the individual who has been unjustly impoverished is to be provided with goods and services just sufficient to raise him or her above the poverty level, this cost of living differential is indeed a reason to justicize a corresponding difference in AFDC payments provided to individuals with the same ethical right to a fair share. This does not, of course, justify anything like the gross disparities presently existing in our welfare system. But it might be a good reason to modify our proposed reform to the claim that we ought to eliminate state inequalities in AFDC payments except as these reflect differences in the cost of living.

As soon as we begin to imagine how this proposed reform might be put into practice, we notice certain problems. Differences in the cost of living do not fall neatly along state lines. There are considerable differences in the cost of living within any single state. Typically, it costs much more to live in an urban environment than in a rural one; life in the suburbs is markedly more expensive than life in the core of a metropolitan area. Again, even when the average cost of living in one state is significantly higher than the average cost of living in another, it will usually be the case that there are some residents of the former who can live more cheaply than many residents of the latter state. Rights, we must remember, are distributive. Each individual citizen has his or her ethical right to a fair share. The corresponding moral duty imposed upon the state by each individual's civic right is that the state provide this individual right-holder, no other one, with sufficient goods and services to raise this individual above the poverty line. The average cost of living in a state, a monetary figure obtained by lumping together all the residents of the state, would seem to be irrelevant to the fulfillment of individual rights.

Let us try to put together the arguments, or insights, of the last two paragraphs. Differences in the cost of living justicize corresponding differences in the amounts of welfare paid to the individual. But since ethical rights to welfare are possessed by individual citizens, not by some mathematical average citizen, the directly relevant differences must be differences in what it would cost similarly situated individuals to purchase goods and services just sufficient to raise each of them above the poverty level. Therefore, from the moral point of view, the ideal welfare system would adjust welfare benefits to the circumstances of each individual welfare recipient.

Is this ideal practicable? In a very weak sense, yes. It would be possible to consider the circumstances of each individual recipient and to calculate for that individual the amount of income that would be needed to raise him or her above the poverty level. Any such calculation would, however, have to take into consideration reasonable changes in the life of the individual, such as moving to a cheaper apartment or buying groceries at a different store. Actually to calculate, and recalculate at reasonable intervals, the cost of living for each individual recipient of Aid to Families of Dependent Children would obviously be extremely expensive. A quantum leap in the cost of administering AFDC is almost certain to result in generally lower benefits, thereby infringing upon the recipients' rights in another, and morally more objectionable, manner. Moreover, any welfare system in which the amount of aid any claimant would receive were dependent upon an individual calculation of his or her individual cost of living would invite discrimination, miscalculation, and the abuse of discretion, probably resulting in very widespread inequities in welfare treatment.

It might be practicable to adopt a welfare system in which local areas or communities within each state calculate the local cost of living index and to use this, rather than some state-wide standard of need, to determine the amount of AFDC to pay to each individual. This would certainly be much less expensive than the more radical reform and subject to less abuse as well. I must admit that I am tempted by this proposed reform as a compromise between an impracticable moral ideal and our existing inequity. Whether this sort of system ought to be adopted, however, will depend upon two sorts of consideration. First, the cost of living patterns in this country will be crucial. Economic investigation is required to discover precisely how differences in cost of living are distributed. If they tend to fall along regional line, say New England in contrast to the Southeast, then cost of living adjustments ought to be made on a regional basis. If they fall more often or with greater precision along state lines, then standards of need for each state would be more equitable and not much more expensive in administrative costs. If there are marked differences in the cost of living within each state falling along some identifiable local lines, then these ought to be used to justicize unequal AFDC benefits provided this can be done without undue administrative expense and without inviting abuse by those who calculate local living costs. Second, as has been implicit in the last few sentences, one must consider what administrative procedures would be necessary in order to put any such proposed reform into practice. If greatly increased administrative expenses would be necessary, this might lead to the lowering of welfare benefits so that this infringement of the right to receive welfare would more than outweigh any projected gain in equitable welfare treatment. Also, the likelihood of error and abuse must be considered, for these would lead in a different way to violations of the right to equitable welfare treatment.

My conclusion, then, is that state inequalities in AFDC payments ought to be eliminated except to the extent that it is possible to devise a practicable and fair way to adjust payments to the individual right-holder to allow for some close approximation to his or her cost of living. The reasoning behind this conclusion applies far beyond this conclusion itself. State inequalities are of many sorts other than differences in the amounts of financial aid provided to welfare claimants. In addition to the uniform conditions of eligibility mandated by federal statutes and regulations, each state is permitted to impose certain conditions of its own provided only that these are not inconsistent with the Constitution or federal law. Such conditions of eligibility will exclude some class of individuals that would not be excluded in another state. The most obvious and important difference of this sort is the refusal of a state to participate in the Aid to Families with Dependent Children program for Unemployed Fathers. Almost half of the states have elected to have no such program. In this respect, the individual members of families with dependent children and unemployed fathers residing in these states are treated worse than family members similarly situated with respect to the United States but who reside in some state that has chosen to participate in the AFDC-UF program. All such state inequalities ought to be eliminated except in cases where some justicizing difference or other justifying reason can be found.

Extend to Unborn Children

During the past few years, many advocates of welfare rights have argued, often in the courts, that our Aid to Families with Dependent Children Program ought to be extended to provide payments to unborn children. This proposal has been adopted by some, but by no means all, states. The practical consequences of this welfare reform would be to render a needy pregnant woman eligible for AFDC payments even though she has not previously given birth to any children and to increase the size of the AFDC payment to a pregnant woman already eligible by virtue of needy dependent children already born. Although there are many grounds on which this reform could be defended, I shall consider only those that appeal to ethical welfare rights.

One argument for extending Aid to Families with Dependent Children to unborn children is straightforward enough, at least on the surface. The unborn child, that is to say the human fetus, is already a living human being and a member of the society. As a citizen, he or she has an ethical right to social security and to a fair share. Accordingly, if it lacks the means of subsistence because of circumstances beyond its control or has been arbitrarily impoverished, it has a moral right to be provided with welfare benefits such as AFDC payments. Moreover, to provide AFDC payments to born children but to deny them to the unborn child is to violate the unborn child's ethical right to equitable welfare treatment, for this is clearly to treat the unborn child worse than the born child even though they are similarly situated by virtue of being needy dependent children within the society.

An autonomy theory of rights such as mine would, however, deny that unborn children can have any ethical welfare rights. It is not merely that all such claims are groundless, but that they are meaningless. An ethical right is a complex structure of ethical liberties, claims, powers, and immunities. Now every ethical liberty is a liberty of performing some specific action. But it makes no sense to ascribe a liberty of action to a being, like the human fetus, that is entirely incapable of acting in the morally relevant sense. No doubt at some point the fetus begins to squirm and kick, but this is not voluntary action of the sort to which it makes sense to apply the notions of an ethical duty or a liberty. For similar reasons, it makes no sense to ascribe an ethical power to the unborn child, for an ethical power is the ability to perform some action that has ethical consequences. Nor can one meaningfully say that the human fetus has an ethical claim of any sort, for every ethical claim involves a power of claiming as well as a correlative duty. If my conception of a welfare right as articulated in the first chapter is accepted, then one cannot justify extending our Aid to Families with Dependent Children by appealing to the ethical welfare fights of the unborn child. It is conceptually impossible for the unborn child to have any welfare rights because the ascription of fundamental ethical elements essential to any right to the human fetus would be meaningless.

Some will imagine, indeed some have asserted, that my argument proves too much. On my theory, a legal right is a complex structure of legal liberties, claims, powers, and immunities. Since legal liberties, powers, and claims involve specific actions in precisely the same way that ethical ones do, my argument, if sound, would prove that the unborn child cannot have any legal rights either. But any student of our legal system knows that it does recognize several rights of the unborn, such as the unborn child's right to inherit and its right not to be wrongfully injured before birth. Far be it from me to deny this legal doctrine generally accepted by jurists and practicing lawyers alike. But I do suggest that it is a legal fiction. Taken literally or at face value, it is not so much false as meaningless for the reasons advanced in the previous paragraph. Properly interpreted, however, it is both meaningful and true. A clue as to how legal talk about the rights of the unborn should be understood lies in the fact that all such rights are conditional. The unborn child has a legal right to inherit its fair share of an estate *if*, but only if, the child is subsequently born alive; fetuses intentionally or spontaneously aborted and stillborn children can never inherit under United States law, nor can any other party inherit through them. Similarly, a fetus who is born with physical or mental defects caused by a wrongful prenatal injury can sue for damages, but the fetus so seriously injured that it never does get born cannot sue, nor can any proxy take legal action pursuant to its legal rights. Accordingly, all ascriptions of legal rights to the unborn are legal fictions that, correctly interpreted, ascribe retrospective rights to born children. By a retrospective right, in this context a claim-right, I mean a present right that implies a correlative past duty. Assuming for the moment that the notion of a present duty that implies a past correlative duty makes sense, one can and should interpret talk about the rights of the unborn as unperspicuous talk about the rights of the born.

This suggests that one might ground an argument for extending our AFDC program to the unborn on the ethical welfare rights the fetus will have if and when it does get born. Just as the newborn child's right to inherit its share of the previously deceased father's estate implies a duty of the executor to have set aside a fair portion of the estate in the past so that the child can now inherit its share, so the newborn child's civic right to a fair share implies a past duty of the state to have provided welfare benefits sufficient to care for the needs of the fetus to the mother while she was pregnant. In some such way, one might argue from the ethical welfare rights of the infant to an obligation to extend public welfare payments to unborn children and their mothers.

As it stands, however, this argument obviously will not work. I have denied that welfare rights can meaningfully be ascribed to unborn children on the grounds that the human fetus is incapable of acting in the morally relevant sense. Unfortunately, the infant or newborn child is equally incapable of the sort of voluntary action that it would make sense to call a duty or a liberty, either ethical or legal. Nor can an ethical or legal power be ascribed to a being entirely incapable of exercising it, like a human infant. Accordingly if one is to appeal to the rights of the born, one must appeal to the ethical welfare rights of the older child. Let us not pause to determine the precise age at which the growing child acquires its civic rights to social security and to a fair share. Let us try instead to explain how these welfare rights that the child will acquire at some unspecified time might impose a duty to have provided welfare payments while the child was still unborn and then an infant with no welfare rights at all.

The argument makes use of the notion of a retrospective right, a welfare right acquired by the child only when it has acquired the capacity to act rationally but that implies temporally prior duties to have provided welfare benefits for the fetus and the infant in the past. This notion of a retrospective right may seem as problematic, even as meaningless, as that of the rights of the unborn. Surely it makes no sense at all to say that a present right and a past duty can logically be correlatives, but what else could one mean by saying that a present right can imply a past duty? Precisely what, if anything, might be meant by talk of retrospective rights remains to be seen. But let us not be too quick to reject this notion as sheer nonsense. Knowing that I will be away all next week and that no rain is predicted for that period, I offer a neighbor the sum of ten dollars to water my lawn next Wednesday. Having accepted my offer, and my money, the neighbor now has a contract with me. Accordingly, I *now* have a right that implies a correlative duty of my neighbor to water my lawn in the *future*. So it does make sense to talk of a right at one time implying a duty at some other time.

Still, the notion of a retrospective right is more puzzling than that of a prospective right. The reason is that one element of any claim, be it legal or ethical, is a power of claiming. And although it seems sensible enough to assert that an act of claiming performance now can create an additional obligation to perform the correlative duty tomorrow, it is surely meaningless to talk of an act of claiming performance now bringing into existence any additional duty to have fulfilled some duty in the past. I agree. But in the paradigm cases of a claim-right, the possessor has a power to claim performance or remedy for nonperformance. And when it is too late for the right-holder to meaningfully claim past performance, it is not too late to claim remedy for past nonperformance. This is precisely what happens in the legal context when a newborn child, through its legal representative, goes to court and sues for compensation for personal injuries it now suffers as a result of some wrongful injury it received while it was still a fetus. Analogously, it would at least be meaningful to say that an older child suffering from the effects of past malnutrition now has the ethical power to claim a remedy from the state for its failure to perform its past duty of providing welfare benefits sufficient to have fed the child adequately. I do not yet assert that the older child does have any retrospective ethical welfare rights; I here allege only that it makes sense to ascribe such rights to the child.

Therefore, one could in principle argue from the welfare rights of the older child to the conclusion that our AFDC program ought to provide payments for the unborn child. But to construct any sound argument of this type one would have to explain just how present welfare rights logically imply past state duties to provide welfare. Two explanations spring to mind. One is that the content of the ethical claim at the core of the right is itself retrospective, that it is a claim to some past performance. Thus, the older child might acquire an ethical claim against the state to have been provided with his or her fair share continuously from the moment of conception onwards. Or the content of the core claim might span past, present, and future, say, an ethical claim to be provided with a fair share at any time in its life from conception to death at which it is arbitrarily excluded from the processes of economic distribution in the society. This is not, however, the way in which we have conceived of either the ethical right to social security or the civic right to a fair share. Accordingly, these rights as we have defined them cannot imply any past duties to provide AFDC payments in this manner. Of course, there may be other ethical welfare rights that are retrospective in their defining cores. But until these have been specified and established, we are in no position to construct any sound argument to justify the extension of Aid to Families with Dependent Children to the unborn by appealing to the rights the unborn will acquire at some later period in their lives.

There is, however, another way of explaining how a present right can imply a past duty. At some time after birth, a child may acquire a right to inherit its share of the deceased father's estate. This legal right imposes a legal duty upon the executor to have set aside a share of the estate for the child to inherit now. This is because the present right of the born child implies a correlative duty of the executor to convey a share of the estate to the child now and a necessary condition of fulfilling this present duty is the act of having reserved a share of the estate so that it will be available to convey at this time. But it is hard to see how this model could apply to the extension of AFDC payments to the unborn child. It might explain how the older child's ethical right to a fair share implies some duty of the state to reserve a share of the wealth in the society to provide to the child now, but it does not seem to imply any duty to have actually provided any of this share to the child at any earlier time.

My conclusion is that although in principle one could construct an argument for the proposed reform based upon the ethical welfare rights of the older child, we are not yet in a position to so argue and that the connection between later rights and earlier duties in this sort of situation is probably too slender and indirect to support the argument. The implications of this conclusion may turn out to be very awkward indeed, for by parity of reasoning one cannot justify the provision of Aid to Families with Dependent Children by an appeal to the rights of infants or young children either. But if one cannot appeal to the rights of the child, to whose rights can one appeal?

The remaining alternative is that one appeal to the rights of the parent, typically but not always the mother. But how on earth could one appeal to the rights of the mother in order to justify the extension of AFDC payments to the unborn child? I suggest that the pregnant woman has an ethical right to be provided with welfare aid sufficient to meet the needs of the unborn child because the mother has the duty of caring for it. In our society, the mother has the primary responsibility for taking care of her unborn child, and the parent or parents have the primary responsibility for taking care of their children. This is the form that the institution of the family takes in our society. Accordingly, the duty of the mother to provide for the basic needs of her unborn or born child confers upon her a right to be provided with the means necessary to carrying out this obligation. I do not wish to suggest that every duty implies a right to the means of fulfilling that duty. This is true under a limited set of circumstances, those that make it impossible for the duty-bearer to obtain such means through reasonable efforts of his or her own. Also, this implication holds only for institutional duties, and probably for only those institutional duties that are under the control of some other party.

I earn my living primarily by teaching philosophy at Washington University in St. Louis. One of my institutional duties is to hold regular office hours on campus at times convenient to my students;

Washington University demands this of its teachers. Now suppose that office space on our campus is in short supply and that I have no office, not even the use of an office for a couple of hours each week. I report this situation to my employer and explain that I will be unable to hold any office hours during which my students can obtain help with their work in my courses. Washington University responds by terminating my employment on the grounds that I have neglected my professional duties. Surely this is unfair. It is unjust for Washington University to impose a duty upon me while denying me the means of fulfilling that duty. Thus, my institutional duty to hold office hours and my fundamental right to just treatment imply a claim-right holding against Washington University to provide me with an office, at least for the few hours it expects me to make myself available on campus to meet my students.

A similar line of reasoning can be applied to the family. Our social institution of the family imposes upon the mother the duty of caring for her unborn child; this is a responsibility that goes with her social role. It is unfair for our society to demand that she perform this duty without making available to her the economic resources needed to care for her fetus, especially nourishment, rest, and medical care. The state as the corporate body of the society is the party against whom the mother's claim to be provided with goods and services holds. The state imposes the duty of caring for the fetus upon the mother because the state claims sovereignty and thus the power of regulating all social institutions and because the policies and practices of the state shape the development of those institutions, including the social institution of the family. Accordingly, the needy mother has an ethical right to welfare aid from the state, aid sufficient to enable her to care for the needs of the unborn child. On this ground, one could justify the extension of our AFDC Program to the unborn. Similar reasoning would, of course, justify the provision of Aid to Families with Dependent Children to infants and children too young to have yet acquired any welfare rights of their own.

This may seem to some readers to be an unnecessarily circuitous argument for extending AFDC payments to unborn children, an involved and implausible line of reasoning suggested to me by my excessively narrow conception of a right, a conception that forces me to deny rights to infants as well as the unborn. A full reply to this criticism would require a complete defence of my general theory of rights, a complicated endeavor best left to another occasion. But I might point out that historically our Aid to Families with Dependent Children has always been conceived in terms of the family, as this institution has functioned in our society and as an ideal social institution we ought to foster. AFDC grew out of an earlier Mothers' Aid program designed to enable mothers to care for their own children and as an alternative to taking needy children out of their homes and caring for them in public institutions, such as orphanages or children's homes. Since the program arose from the recognition that it was both unfair and impractical to expect impoverished mothers to fulfill their family responsibilities of caring for their children, it is hardly surprising that the continuation of the Aid to Families with Dependent Children program can be justified in the way I suggest. And if this sort of argument from the institutional duties of the parent to the ethical right to public welfare is sound in the case of the born, it is sound in the case of the unborn also.

Accordingly, I support the extension of our AFDC payments to cover the unborn child. But I do not do so by any appeal to the rights of the child himself or herself, either some right of the fetus or some right the child will acquire later in its life. I ground my argument on the ethical right of the mother to be provided with the means necessary to fulfill her institutional duty to care for the needs of her unborn child. This suggests a deviation from the proposed reform as commonly advocated. It may well be that it is less costly to care for the needs of the fetus than to care for the needs of the child after birth. It may be that the required medical care is less; certainly the need of clothing is less. Therefore, although AFDC ought to be extended to unborn children, the amount of the AFDC payments might well be less than that for the born child. Another way of approaching this issue is to point out that in calculating the poverty level for a given family, it must not be assumed that the amount of income needed to sustain a pregnant woman at the poverty line is equal to the amount needed to sustain a mother and her born child at this line.

Final Conclusion

We began with a general conception of a right as a system of normative elements that, if respected, confers autonomy concerning the exercise or enjoyment of some defining core upon its possessor in face of one or more second parties whose wills are or might be opposed. Accordingly, a primary welfare right is a right to some welfare benefit, to some form of assistance provided to an individual in need; a secondary welfare right is a right concerning, but not to, some welfare benefit. This conception of a welfare right is not incoherent, as some allege, nor does it require us to render the language of rights ambiguous between autonomy and welfare rights. Its application to the legal right to receive AFDC payments and the legal right to a fair welfare hearing reveals the full complexity of these rights and spells out their practical implications in detail. The further application of this legal model to our ethical rights to social security, to a fair share, and to equitable welfare treatment forces us to abandon the obscure labels and ambiguous catch phrases usual in the literature and to define the content of these rights in terms of specified ethical claims, liberties, powers, and immunities. Not only does this add greatly to the precision of our thinking about ethical welfare rights; it also makes explicit the moral obligations such rights impose on second parties.

We saw that creating and maintaining a specified legal welfare right can be justified by appealing to utility or justice or some ethical right. The grounds of ethical welfare rights are considerably harder to identify. We argued that our most fundamental welfare rights cannot be universal human rights holding against the world; at best they can be civic rights holding against one's state. There really are at least two civic rights to welfare: the right to social security grounded in a more general civic right to protection and the right to a fair share grounded in the right to remedy for wrongful harm.

Finally, we have seen that these and other welfare rights have definite implications of considerable importance for the reform of our current welfare system. This is not to suggest that welfare rights are the whole story. It is only to insist that a proper understanding of welfare rights plays a central role in the moral assessment of the public welfare practices of any society. Too often, political and moral debates over public welfare are unreasoning and dogmatic or idealistic and impractical. My aim has been to make possible a more reasoned and relevant discussion of those public welfare programs essential to the future of our society and the well-being of its less fortunate citizens.

Bibliography

American Declaration of the Rights and Duties of Man. In *Basic Documents on Human Rights,* edited by Ian Brownlie, pp. 389–95. Oxford: Clarendon Press, 1971.

Bedau, Hugo. "The Right to Life." *Monist* 52 (1968): 550–72.

Benn, Stanley. "Human Rights—For Whom and For What?" In *Human Rights,* edited by Eugene Kamenka and Alice Erh-Soon Tay, pp. 59–73. London: Edward Arnold, 1978.

Bentham, Jeremy. *Works of Jeremy Bentham.* Vol. 2. Edited by John Bowring, pp. 489–534. New York: Russell & Russell, 1962.

Beveridge, Sir William. *Social Insurance and Allied Services.* London: His Majesty's Stationery Office, 1942.

45 Code of Federal Regulations. Parts 200–499. Washington, D.C.: Office of the Federal Register, 1979.

Committee for Economic Development. *Improving the Public Welfare System.* New York: Committee for Economic Development, 1970.

Cranston, Maurice. "Human Rights, Real and Supposed." In *Political Theory and the Rights of Man,* edited by D. D. Raphael, pp. 43–53. Bloomington: Indiana University Press, 1967.

Dandridge v. *Williams.* 397 US 471. 1970.

Declaration of the Rights of the Child. In *Basic Documents on Human Rights,* edited by Ian Brownlie, pp. 188–90. Oxford: Clarendon Press, 1971.

Declaration of the Rights of Man and of the Citizen. In *Basic Documents on Human Rights,* edited by Ian Brownlie, pp. 8–10. Oxford: Clarendon Press, 1971.

Equality of Treatment (Social Security) Convention. In *Basic Documents on Human Rights,* edited by Ian Brownlie, pp. 305–12. Oxford: Clarendon Press, 1971.

Feinberg, Joel. *Social Justice.* Englewood Cliffs: Prentice-Hall, 1973.

———. *Rights, Justice and the Bounds of Liberty.* Princeton: Princeton University Press, 1980.

Frankena, William K. "The Concept of Social Justice." In *Social Justice,* edited by Richard B. Brandt. Englewood Cliffs: Prentice-Hall, 1962.

Fried, Charles. *Right and Wrong.* Cambridge: Harvard University Press, 1978.

Goldberg v. *Kelly,* 397 US 254. 1970.

Golding, M. P. "Towards a Theory of Human Rights." *Monist* 52 (1968): 521–49.

Hart, H. L. A. "Are There Any Natural Rights?" *Philosophical Review* 64 (1955): 175–91.

――――. "Bentham on Legal Rights." In *Oxford Essays in Jurisprudence*. Second Series. Edited by A. W. B. Simpson. Oxford: Clarendon Press, 1973.

Hohfeld, Wesley Newcomb. *Fundamental Legal Conceptions*. New Haven: Yale University Press, 1919.

Honoré, Tony. "Property, Title and Redistribution." In *Equality and Freedom: Past, Present and Future*, edited by Carl Wellman, pp. 107–15. Wiesbaden: Franz Steiner, 1977.

King v. *Smith*. 392 US 309. 1968.

Komisar, Lucy. *Down and Out in the USA*. New York: Franklin Watts, 1973.

Martin, Rex. "Human Rights and Civil Rights." *Philosophical Studies* 37 (1980): 391–403.

McCloskey, H. J. "Rights." *Philosophical Quarterly* 15 (1965): 115–27.

Murphy, Jeffrie G. "Rights and Borderline Cases." *Arizona Law Review* 19 (1978): 228–41.

National Welfare Rights Organization. *Bill of Welfare Rights*. Pamphlet issued in Washington D.C., 1970.

Nelson, William N. "Special Rights, General Rights, and Social Justice." *Philosophy & Public Affairs* 3 (1974): 410–30.

Nickel, James W. "Is There a Human Right to Employment?" *Philosophical Forum* 10 (1978–79): 149–69.

Nozick, Robert. *Anarchy, State and Utopia*. New York: Basic Books, 1974.

Peffer, Rodney. "A Defense of Rights to Well-Being." *Philosophy & Public Affairs* 8 (1978): 65–87.

Rawls, John. *A Theory of Justice*. Cambridge: Harvard University Press, 1971.

Reich, Charles A. "Individual Rights and Social Welfare." *Yale Law Journal* 74 (1965): 1245–57.

Rosado v. *Wyman*. 397 US 397. 1970.

Scheffler, Samuel. "Natural Rights, Equality, and the Minimal State." *Canadian Journal of Philosophy* 6 (1976): 59–76.

Shapiro v. *Thompson*. 394 US 618. 1969.

United Nations. *Universal Declaration of Human Rights*. In *Basic Documents on Human Rights*, edited by Ian Brownlie. Oxford: Clarendon Press, 1971.

42 *United States Code Service*. Sections 601–644. San Francisco: Bancroft-Whitney Co., 1973.

Wellman, Carl. "A New Conception of Human Rights." In *Human Rights*, edited by Eugene Kamenka and Alice Erh-Soon Tay. London: Edward Arnold, 1978.

Index